American Sign Language

A Teacher's Resource Text on Curriculum, Methods, and Evaluation

Dennis Cokely
Charlotte Baker-Shenk

Clerc Books
Gallaudet University Press
Washington, D.C.

Clerc Books
An imprint of Gallaudet University Press
Washington, DC 20002

Originally published 1980 by T. J. Publishers, Inc., Silver Spring, Maryland
Published 1991 by Gallaudet University Press. Third printing 1999
Printed in the United States of America

Cover design by Auras Design, Washington, D.C.
Drawings by Frank A. Paul
Photographs by Thomas Klagholz

Photograph of Charlotte Baker-Shenk taken by Viki Kemper.

ISBN 0-930323-85-8

CONTENTS

PREFACE

This text is part of a total, multi-media package designed for the teacher and student of American Sign Language (ASL). Included in this package are two texts for teachers and three texts for students:

American Sign Language: a teacher's resource text on grammar and culture

American Sign Language: a teacher's resource text on curriculum, methods, and evaluation

American Sign Language: a student text (Units 1-9)

American Sign Language: a student text (Units 10-18)

American Sign Language: a student text (Units 19-27)

Also included in this package is a set of five one-hour videotapes which are especially designed to accompany these texts.

As a package, the texts and videotapes provide the teacher with information about the structure of ASL and an interactive approach to teaching the language. They provide the student with carefully prepared ASL dialogues and drills as well as information about the structure of ASL and the Deaf community.

The videotapes are designed so that there is a one-hour tape for each text. The first tape illustrates all of the examples in the grammar and culture text. The second tape provides a 'live' demonstration of a number of the techniques described in the curriculum, methods, and evaluation text. Each of the final three tapes (one for each student text) not only illustrates the dialogues for a particular text but also provides several ASL stories, poems, and dramatic prose of varying lengths and difficulty for use in the classroom or language lab.

ACKNOWLEDGEMENTS

It is simply not possible to mention all those individuals whose support and encouragement have made this text possible. Likewise, it would be very difficult to list all those individuals whose own ideas and creativity have influenced this text. However, there are several people we wish to mention by name because of their invaluable assistance in preparing this text:

For their helpful and critical review of an early draft—Robbin Battison, M. J. Bienvenu, Larry Berke, Mel Carter Jr., Betty Colonomos, Larry Fleischer, Bob Johnson, Ella Mae Lentz, Marina McIntire, Carol Padden, Ken Rust, Bill Stokoe.

For permission to use and adapt the Sign Language bibliography—Larry Fleischer.

For permission to use the illustrations on pages 5 and 10—Ed Klima and Ursula Bellugi.

For assistance in preparing the index and glossary—Micky Cokely.

For their patience during long photo sessions and skill as models of ASL—two native Deaf signers, M. J. Bienvenu and Mel Carter Jr.

For his unique artistic skills, beautiful illustrations, and willingness to change countless lines on brow raises, puffed cheeks, and 'mm' mouths—Frank Allen Paul.

Finally, for typing, re-typing, and more re-typing of various drafts as well as for back rubs and unfailing good cheer during the past two years—Beverly Klayman.

FOREWORD

These teacher texts—*American Sign Language: a teacher's resource text on grammar and culture* and *American Sign Language: a teacher's resource text on curriculum, methods, and evaluation*—are an outgrowth of the evolution of Sign Language instruction. The history of Sign Language instruction in the U.S. has been closely linked with the history of deaf education. In fact, there is reason to believe that Laurent Clerc began conducting Sign classes at the Hartford School in 1817. However, for the next 150 years the field remained fairly small and received little attention. Then in recent years, it experienced a spiraling growth and a rapid increase in the number of classes and students. Yet up till now the field of Sign Language instruction has been severely hampered by a lack of resource texts, videotapes, and other materials designed for the teachers of Sign Language. Especially lacking have been clear descriptions of the grammar of American Sign Language and appropriate methods for teaching it.

As Sign Language teachers, the two of us look back upon those days when we first began. We remember clearly that we were teaching simple sign equivalents for common English words. We remember noticing that our students could sign quite neatly but could hardly understand anything we signed. We also remember telling our students again and again to use their faces and bodies more; but much to our chagrin, they continued to sign like statues with movable arms. From time to time, we told ourselves, "Gee, there must be a better way than this. But this is all I know how to do and, besides, everyone else is doing the same thing I'm doing. (Sigh)" There were also times when our students battered us with questions about why a sign was formed in a particular way, or used in one context and not in another. We felt frustrated because we often were not confident in the answers that we gave them. And yet the students kept asking us more and more difficult questions.

Exercises developed in the field of drama gave us hope for helping our students become more flexible in using their bodies and faces. However, our hopes were shattered when the good results we obtained with these exercises were not carried over to the way the students communicated with signs. The activities were helpful, but not enough. Once again, we asked ourselves what was wrong.

Then, amazing and puzzling information on complicated phonological, morphological, and syntactic principles in our visual-gestural language began to pour out of linguistic research labs, shocking us. What had been referred to as "bad English", "true deaf signs" and "shortcut language" was actually a highly capable, complex, and independent language! These discoveries and linguistic descriptions instilled a strange feeling in us and in many other Deaf people. It stirred anew a confidence in ourselves as a people with dignity, viewing ourselves not as incapable but as *capable* people with a language and a culture that we can share proudly with speakers of other languages, as well as with future generations of deaf children.

Excited as we were about this information and reconfirmation in ourselves, we still had to proceed with the teaching of our classes. We wanted to share the information with our students, but how? We wanted the latest for our classes; we wanted the best for and from our students. We sat on the bleachers and rooted for the researchers, little comprehending their linguistic, psychological, and neurological theories or terminology. And as we began to understand, more questions haunted us: "How do we teach these new findings? Are the students ready? Are we ready? What do we teach first?"

We had to start somewhere—so we began by giving complicated grammatical explanations, followed by a few exercises to give the students a feel for Sign Language and then went on to more principles. The students, assuming from past exposure that Sign Language was "simple" and "fun", were amazed at the complexity and wealth of this visual-gestural language. However, as knowledgable and respectful as they became about that language, they didn't become much better communicators. Instead, the students acted as quasi-linguists, attempting to analyze what we signed and what they signed—which created a slow and awkward communication process.

It soon became clear that our enthusiasm in accepting American Sign Language as a true language and our attempts to explain what we knew about its formal structure were not enough. Convinced that ASL is a language separate from English, it seemed logical to explore the methods that are used to teach foreign languages. There was a gold mine of established research, theories, and methods in the field of second/foreign language instruction. But we still needed more understandable descriptions of ASL. And we needed a way to successfully apply what we knew (and were learning) about second/foreign language instruction in order to help our students become competent communicators in ASL.

These problems highlighted the need for Sign Language teachers to exchange ideas and information with each other and to receive basic training in methods that could be used for teaching ASL. In late 1978, the Rehabilitation Services Administration contracted with the National Association of the Deaf's Communicative Skills Program to begin a National Consortium of Programs for the Training of Sign Language Instructors. Two primary goals for the Consortium were to create better communication and exchange of ideas among instructors and to develop a standard basic training curriculum for current and prospective instructors.

Concurrently, two of the foremost experts in the areas of Sign Language research, instruction, and evaluation began work on this comprehensive set of teacher resource texts, videotapes, and student texts. The authors then dedicated more than two hard years toward preparing these materials. These authors, both hearing individuals, have been extremely careful and conscientious in attempting to verify and confirm their linguistic description of ASL and their interactive approach for teaching it. A group of 15 Sign Language teachers and linguists—both Deaf and hearing—were asked to review and comment on the manuscripts for these texts. This unusual step is a tribute to the authors' sensitivity and desire to provide the best possible materials to date for Sign Language teachers. They have made a new beginning in the history of Sign Language instruction. They have paved the road so we, instructors, can travel with more ease and confidence.

The Communicative Skills Program of the National Association of the Deaf is most enthusiastic about the long-awaited arrival of these materials for the teaching of Sign Language, because they are written with Sign Language instructors in mind. As a set, the two teacher texts offer the most thorough and clear description of ASL currently available for Sign Language teachers as well as an effective method for teaching and evaluating ASL as a second/foreign language.

For the first time, Sign Language instructors have materials especially prepared for them which address the questions of what is ASL and how to teach it. "What is ASL?" is addressed in the teacher text on grammar and culture. Drawing upon available linguistic research and their own resources, the authors present a clear and detailed explanation of major grammatical features of ASL, accompanied by some of the finest and most accurate line drawings of signs we have seen. "How to teach ASL?" is addressed in the teacher text on methods, curriculum, and evaluation. Drawing upon theories and methods developed in the field of second/foreign language teaching as well as their own experience, the authors present an interactive approach to teaching and evaluating ASL, which is supported by numerous activities, techniques, and a well-thought-out, six-course curriculum. This interactive approach is based on an untraditional (in our field) but logical idea—the instructor should teach Sign without voice and without English equivalents, using only gestures and American Sign Language.

In our personal experience as Sign instructors searching for more successful ways to teach our classes, we have experimented with this untraditional approach. The results have been amazing. We could see the students *really* learning the language, and developing *real* confidence in their faces and bodies (often unconsciously). Every time we left the classroom, we felt delighted at the results. We were reaching our primary objective—producing *real* communicators.

As program developers and administrators concerned with the implementation of quality programs, we consider these texts and this approach as a significant step forward in the process of refining the instruction of ASL. We hope you will find this approach exciting and fruitful, too.

Through the National Consortium of Programs for the Training of Sign Language Instructors, we anticipate increased communication among Sign Language teachers and the development of quality teacher training programs. With the success of these programs and the widespread use of the comprehensive materials provided by the authors, Sign Language instructors will be better prepared to meet the challenge of instilling in their students a respect for the language and culture of Deaf people and an ability to successfully communicate with members of the Deaf community.

With great respect for signers who are the source of inspiration for Sign Language teaching and an appreciation for all those Sign Language teachers who have been a part of the evolution of Sign instruction, we recommend this set of teacher resource texts. We commend the authors for their vision, dedication, and love in bringing them to completion.

S. Melvin Carter, Jr.   Ella Mae Lentz

Director   Project Coordinator
Communicative Skills Program   National Consortium of Programs
National Association of the Deaf   for the Training of
                                             Sign Language Instructors
                                         National Association of the Deaf

INTRODUCTION

During the past decade there has been an increased interest in the language of the Deaf Community—American Sign Language (ASL). This interest has led to a remarkable number of Sign Language classes and programs nationwide. Although many of these classes have traditionally focused on teaching vocabulary alone, an increasing number are now attempting to teach ASL as a language—providing opportunities for students to learn the grammar as well as the vocabulary of ASL. And as linguistic research on ASL has begun to influence Sign Language teaching, several texts have been published. These texts present teachers with information and examples concerning *what* to teach in an ASL class. However, none of these texts address the question of *how* to teach ASL. Now, as the status of ASL as a language is gaining wider acceptance, it seems appropriate to begin to explore those techniques and methods which have been developed in the field of second language and foreign language teaching and to apply these methods to the question of how to teach ASL.

Very few Sign Language teachers have had any formal training in how to teach a second or foreign language. Thus, it is not surprising that the widely accepted methods of teaching second or foreign languages are not widely used in teaching ASL. Understandably, there has been more concern in the past decade about *what* to teach in an ASL class than *how* to teach an ASL class. With linguistic research constantly uncovering new facts about ASL, it has been difficult enough for the teacher to keep up with this new information. However, in the past few years, there have been strong indications that the teaching of Sign Language is indeed becoming a profession, and that Sign Language teachers are beginning to develop their skills and knowledge in the same way as is expected of spoken language teachers.

Since 1975, a national organization of Sign Language teachers—the Sign Instructors Guidance Network (S.I.G.N.)—has been attempting to upgrade the quality of Sign Language teaching. This organization has sponsored short-term training, evaluation, and certification of Sign Language teachers. Another new program— the National Consortium of Programs for the Training of Sign Language Instructors (NCPTSLI)—has also begun to provide more formal training. Through this consortium, teachers will receive specialized training in such areas as the structure of ASL, second language teaching methods, curriculum development, and the evaluation of Sign Language skills. In conjunction with the NCPTSLI, it is highly probable that some programs will begin to offer M.A. degrees in Teaching Sign Language.

All of these factors have influenced the development of this text. Linguistic research on the structure of ASL will continue and teachers of ASL will still have to keep up with the latest research findings. However, it seems that now is the appropriate time for teachers to begin to focus on how to most effectively teach what is already known about ASL. Most of the techniques described in this text are widely used in teaching spoken languages; some are not. All of them have been used in ASL classes by a number of people with a high level of success. Students who have been instructed in ASL through the use of these teaching techniques seem to be considerably more successful in acquiring ASL skills than those instructed through more traditional teaching approaches.

However, this text and the ideas and techniques described within it certainly do not provide any formula for instant success; nor are these methods presented as the *only* way to teach ASL—but they have been found to be effective in helping students acquire competence in the language. At this point it may be helpful to examine exactly what this text is and what it will and will not do for the teacher.

This text will not provide a ready-made set of "tried and true" lesson plans for teaching ASL. It will provide the basic theoretical framework for understanding and using certain second language teaching techniques.

This text will not provide a list of signs to teach in a specific class or course. It will provide an understanding of how to enhance vocabulary development in a meaningful, success-oriented fashion.

This text will not simply provide a list of teaching activities. It will provide a rationale for using a particular teaching approach and an understanding of how certain activities and techniques fit this approach.

This text will not make teaching ASL any easier. It will help to re-direct instructional time and energy so that these become more profitable for both the teacher and the student.

This text will not turn a person into a successful teacher of ASL overnight. It will provide a sense of direction and purpose for teaching ASL.

Finally, this text will not provide all the answers to the problems encountered in teaching ASL—in fact, it may provide no answers to certain problems. However, it will stimulate thinking and suggest a certain approach to teaching the language.

The basic methodology which is encouraged in this text can best be described as an "interactive approach" to language teaching. That is, the teacher is encouraged to create or use situations in which the students learn how to interact in ASL *by interacting in ASL*. The logic of this is obvious and is supported by many other types of learning situations—for example, children acquire their first language by interacting in their first language, people learn how to play tennis by playing tennis, and so on. The familiar saying "Experience is the best teacher" is an appropriate summary of this interactive approach. This approach is also "open-ended". That is, while there are a number of specific activities discussed in this text, the teacher who adopts this approach will surely generate many more different kinds of interactive activities.

Shifting the traditional focus of Sign Language teaching from "How many signs should be taught in this course?" to "What interactional opportunities should be provided in this course?" is not an easy task. However, if students are to attain communicative competence in ASL in the classroom, it is a shift which must occur.

Communicative competence is not determined by the size of a person's vocabulary, but rather by the ease and success with which a person interacts with others in a wide range of situations. This text offers a number of suggestions for helping teachers focus on success-oriented, interactive activities that are specifically designed to develop the communicative competence of their students.

In one sense, this text is not yet completed—the teacher will need to adapt and apply the ideas and suggestions in this text to his/her own classroom. The teacher will also need to constantly search for new activities which will provide students with a positive, meaningful learning environment. The teacher should not rely solely upon the ideas and activities discussed in this text, but rather use them as a starting point.

For some teachers, the interactive approach suggested in this text may produce skeptical or even negative feelings: "I can't do that!", "I won't do that!", "Imagine, a person my age doing that!", "That's ridiculous! It'll never work!", "The students will all laugh at me!" For other teachers it may evoke feelings of inadequacy or insecurity: "I don't know how to do that!", "Where do I start?", "What happens if . . . ?", "Suppose I make a mistake?", "I've been teaching my way for a long time, I can't change now!", "I'm afraid I might embarrass myself". For still others it may evoke feelings of agreement and acceptance: "Well sure, that makes sense", "Why didn't I think of that", "Yeah, that's right!", "Well, it's worth a try!", "Sounds like it might work". Whatever the reaction, this text will have served its purpose if it stimulates teachers to think about their own classes and their own instructional methodology.

To those who may be skeptical or negative or who may feel inadequate or inferior, we offer the following advice: look at yourselves as students—students of the art and skill of teaching a language. Learn by doing and improve with practice.

To those who may agree and accept, we offer the following encouragement: to teach is to learn and to learn is to grow—an exciting process!

To all who read this book, we offer the following thought: teaching a language brings with it not only the satisfaction of helping others learn a language, but also a responsibility to the community of people who use that language. This responsibility does not end with helping students to develop skills in ASL. Rather it extends to introducing the students to a different culture, a different set of values, and a different way of looking at the world. Thus, the teacher of ASL must be sensitive to and respect the cultural values of the Deaf community and the unique ways in which these values are expressed and realized. It is this sensitivity and respect which should motivate teachers of ASL to constantly upgrade their skills and knowledge. We hope that this text will contribute to that process.

May 1, 1980   D.C.
Washington, D.C.   C.B.

Chapter I

"Language" and the Sign Language Teacher

Beginning with a description of the major characteristics of spoken and signed languages, this chapter attempts to define the types of knowledge and attitude necessary for a successful teacher of American Sign Language. Following the general discussion of "Language", the chapter focuses on American Sign Language and its users—the Deaf community—and highlights the crucial nature of the teacher's own attitude toward ASL and the Deaf community.

A. What is a Language?

In this section, we are going to examine some of the most important characteristics of the phenomenon called "Language". These major characteristics occur in every known ('living') language of the world. Put together, they give us the following definition of "Language":

> A language is a system of relatively arbitrary symbols and grammatical signals that change across time and that members of a community share and use for several purposes: to interact with each other, to communicate their ideas, emotions, and intentions, and to transmit their culture from generation to generation.

To understand this definition and how it applies to both spoken and signed languages, we will examine each of its components, one-by-one.

(a) A language has *symbols and grammatical signals*.

All languages have words or signs that stand for or represent something else. These words or signs are *symbols*. For example, the English word 'cat' is a symbol for a particular kind of furry, four-legged animal. In the same way, the ASL sign illustrated below is a symbol for that animal.

CAT

English symbol

(Drawing of a)
"furry four-legged animal"

(Drawing of) ASL symbol

1

All languages have *grammatical signals,* that is, ways of showing how the symbols are related to each other. For example, in the sentence 'John looked at Peter', which noun is the subject and which noun is the object? A speaker of English knows that John is the subject (i.e. John did the 'looking') and that Peter is the object (i.e. Peter was 'looked at') because in English, the subject noun normally occurs first in the sentence. *Word order* is an important grammatical signal in English that indicates the grammatical role (e.g. subject, object) of the symbols in English sentences. It is also important in Mandarin Chinese, Thai, and Vietnamese.

Many other languages like Russian, Swahili, Finnish, Latin, and Greek do not rely as much on word order to show the relationship between symbols. Instead, these languages rely more on a different type of grammatical signal called an *inflection.* Most of the time, inflections involve adding an affix to a word. That affix might mean 'subject' or 'object'. For example, in Latin (see example below), one can say either (a), (b), or (c), and all three sentences mean basically the same thing—i.e. 'John was looking at Peter'. Speakers of Latin know which noun is the subject because of the affix '-es'. ('Ioannes' means 'John' + 'subject'.) The affix '-um' indicates that Peter is the object in the sentence.

(1)   a. Ioann<u>es</u> aspiciebat Petr<u>um</u>.
      b. Ioann<u>es</u> Petr<u>um</u> aspiciebat.
      c. Petr<u>um</u> Ioann<u>es</u> aspiciebat.

Similarly, in Russian, the order of the symbols can vary since inflections are frequently used to signal grammatical relationships. The three Russian sentences below also basically mean 'John was looking at Peter'. The addition of the affix '-a' indicates that Peter is the object in both sentences.[1]

(2)   a. Ivan smotrel na Petr<u>a</u>.
      b. Ivan na Petr<u>a</u> smotrel.
      c. Na Petr<u>a</u> smotrel Ivan.

In this regard, ASL is more like Latin and Russian. ASL tends to change the form of the signs themselves to show grammatical relationships, rather than to rely on word/sign order to show those relationships. For example, the sentence 'John looks at Peter' could be signed in either of the two ways transcribed on the next page.[2]

---

[1]The Russian word 'na' is a prepositional case marker which also indicates that what follows it (i.e. Petra) is an object.

[2]In the transcription of ASL sentences, words in capital letters stand for signs. When the letters in a word are separated by hyphens, it means the word is fingerspelled. When words are separated by hyphens, it means the ASL sign requires more than one English word to translate it; those hyphenated words represent one ASL sign. The letters '*rt*' stand for 'right'; '*lf*' for 'left'. So in example (3a), the name 'John' is fingerspelled on the right side, then the verb moves from the right (John's location) to the left, and the name 'Peter' is fingerspelled on the left side. In example (3b), the line with the small '*t*' above the fingerspelled name 'Peter' indicates that the non-manual signal for 'topicalization' occurs while that name is fingerspelled. The comma after the fingerspelled name 'Peter' represents a pause.

(3) a. J-O-H-N-*rt* *john*-LOOK-AT-*lf* P-E-T-E-R-*lf*
$$\overline{\qquad\qquad t\qquad\qquad}$$

b. P-E-T-E-R-*lf,* J-O-H-N-*rt* *john*-LOOK-AT-*peter*

In these examples, the verb ____ -LOOK-AT- ____ moves from right to left and indicates that John is the subject and that Peter is the object. Whereas the inflections in the Latin and Russian examples were attached to certain nouns, the inflection that shows who is the subject and who is the object in the ASL sentence occurs on the verb ____ -LOOK-AT- ____ . This inflection involves changing the direction of the verb so that it moves from the spatial location of the subject (i.e. on the right) to the spatial location of the object (i.e. on the left).

However, like many other languages with such inflections, not all orderings of the symbols are possible in ASL. For example, one cannot sign (4).[3]

(4) **rt*-LOOK-AT-*lf* J-O-H-N-*rt* P-E-T-E-R-*lf*

Most languages use both word/sign order and inflections as grammatical signals. However, in general, languages tend to use one kind of signal more than the other. So, for example, English and Chinese are more dependent on word order to show how symbols are related, and ASL and Russian are more dependent on inflections to show how symbols are related.

(b) **A language has symbols and grammatical signals that *members of a community share*.**

A language doesn't work if its users mean different things when they use a symbol. For example, if you (the reader) use the imaginary word 'kerdit' to mean 'a place where people sleep', and someone else uses the word 'kerdit' to mean 'a place where people swim', then you and that person would not understand each other if you talked about 'kerdits'. Similarly, if someone thought that the *second* noun in an English sentence was the subject, then that person would not understand you correctly when you said 'John looked at Peter'. Members of a language community must agree about the meanings of symbols and how to use them in order for communication to take place through that language.

(c) **A language is a *system* of symbols and grammatical signals that members of a community share.**

All languages are composed of a limited number of units that are related or connected to each other in specific ways. For example, spoken languages use sound units as their basic building blocks. Each spoken language uses a particular set of these building blocks (i.e. sounds) and combines them in specific ways to form words. The words are then combined in specific ways to form sentences. Sentences, then, can be combined in specific ways to form speeches, stories, poems, conversations, and so on.

---

[3]A double asterisk indicates that something does not follow the rules of the language. The double asterisk preceding example (4) means that sentence in ungrammatical (i.e. it does not follow the rules of the language).

Similarly, the basic building blocks of a signed language are its handshapes, its palm orientations, its movements, and the locations where these occur. By combining a specific handshape, palm orientation, and movement in a particular location, one makes a sign. Combinations of signs form sentences, and combinations of these sentences can form speeches, stories, poems, conversations, and so on.

As such, languages are "hierarchical"—they are many-layered *systems*. At each layer, there are rules for determining what units can occur. As stated earlier, each language has its own particular set of building blocks. For example, English has the 'th' sounds [Θ] as in 'thirty' and [ð] as in 'them'.[4] English does not have a uvular trill [R], as in the French way of saying 'Paris', or the high, front vowel [ü], as in the French word for 'you' (familiar, singular)—[tü]. On the other hand, French doesn't have the [Θ] or [ð] sounds that are used in English.

Similarly, ASL has the handshape ⟨🤛⟩ which does not occur in French Sign Language. However, Taiwan Sign Language has handshapes which do not occur in ASL. For example, the handshapes illustrated below are used in the Taiwan signs for 'brother' and 'sister', respectively.

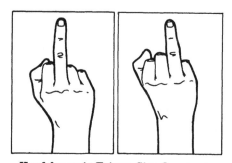

Handshapes in Taiwan Sign Language

The handshape with extended middle (third) finger also occurs in British Sign Language in such signs as those meaning 'holiday' and 'to trick/fool'.[5]

At each layer, there are also rules determining how these units can be combined with each other. These are called "co-occurrence rules". For example, English uses the sounds [s] and [t], as in 'sew' and 'toe'. These two sounds can occur next to each

---

[4]Brackets are used in linguistics to denote actual sounds (which are often written differently from the way they are written in words). For example, the sounds in the English word 'cat' are written as [kæt]

[5]One could argue that the handshape with extended middle finger *does* occur in ASL in certain socially restricted signs. However, it is likely that this handshape derives from the pejorative gesture used by hearing and deaf members of the American population. All uses of this handshape in ASL have a related, pejorative meaning, whereas most of the regular handshapes in ASL freely occur in a wide variety of signs with non-related meanings. (It is interesting to note that this handshape does not commonly have a pejorative meaning among Britons, and thus, it is used more freely in British Sign Language.)

other in words like 'stop', 'nest', and 'cats'. However, if they occur together as the first sounds in a word, the [t] cannot be the first sound. No regular English words begin with the sequence [ts], for example **tsin. Similarly, the sequence '-ng', transcribed as [ŋ], occurs at the end of many English words (e.g. song, rang, string), but cannot occur at the beginning of an English word—**ng____ . However, Bantu (a family of languages spoken in southern and central Africa) has words that begin with [ts]; Luiseño (a Uto-Aztecan language spoken in Nigeria) has words that begin with [ŋ]. Thus, each spoken language has a set of rules for determining *which* sounds can occur together and *where* they can co-occur in a word.

Similarly, ASL has rules determining which handshapes, movements, locations, and palm orientations can co-occur. For example, ASL (like Chinese Sign Language) has the handshape 🤟 that occurs in ASL signs like **CAT, IMPORTANT,** and **FRANCE.** ASL also has movements and locations which involve contacting the body. However, if signs with the above handshape contact a part of the body, that contact must be at the point where the thumb and index finger join (e.g. **CAT, INDIAN, TEA, VOTE, SENTENCE, INTERPRET, COUNT**) or on the side of the thumb and index finger (e.g. **BUTTON, HOLE, FLUNK**). In ASL, the three upright fingers in this handshape do not contact the body.[6] However, many signs with this handshape in Chinese Sign Language (CSL) operate in the opposite way.[7] In CSL, the contact is made with the three upright fingers and *not* the thumb and index finger. This contact is seen in the following signs from Chinese Sign Language:

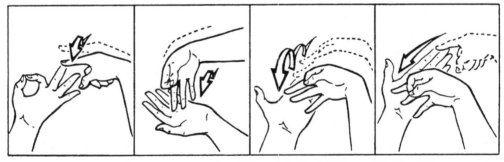

(Borrowed with permission from Klima & Bellugi 1979, pg. 157, Fig. 6.7)

Thus, ASL and CSL have different rules for that handshape when it contacts the body.

---

[6]An exception to this rule is the sign **FAIR** (used by some signers) where contact is made on the side of the middle finger.

[7]Klima & Bellugi 1979.

FAIR

Other types of co-occurrence rules in ASL concern the use of two-handed signs. Linguistic research[8] has described two of these rules in some detail. One rule, called the rule of *Symmetry,* says that if both hands move, then they will have the same handshape and type of movement. This rule is illustrated in the signs VISIT, FOOTBALL, DARK, PROCEED, EXCITED, MAYBE, TRY, CHAIN, HOPE, WALK, BOOK, etc. The second rule, called the rule of *Dominance,* says that if each hand has a *different* handshape, then only one hand (the 'dominant' or 'active' hand)[9] will move. This rule is illustrated in the signs ENOUGH, THAT, AMONG, SODA-POP, FIRST (in a series), WORD, CANDLE, WEAK, GROW, FLATTER, etc. A second part of the Dominance rule says that the non-dominant hand will have one of the seven most 'unmarked'[10] handshapes (illustrated below).

Unmarked Handshapes

So far, we have shown that there are rules in spoken languages which determine what sounds can occur and how they can be combined with each other. And we have shown that there are rules in signed languages which determine what handshapes, palm orientations, movements, and locations can occur and how they can be combined in a sign (with special rules for their combination in two-handed signs).

At the next layer, there are rules for determining how words or signs can be combined to form sentences (called 'syntactic rules'). For example, 'Thelma has seen the man' is a grammatically correct sentence of English. The construction of that sentence follows the rules for forming sentences in English. The sentence '**Thelma has the man seen' does *not* follow the rules for combining words in English. However, that is exactly how the same sentence would be formed in German (which has different rules for the ordering of words in sentences).

---

[8]cf. Battison 1978.

[9]The 'dominant' hand in a right-handed signer is his/her right hand. The 'non-dominant' hand would then be the left hand.

[10]In linguistics, 'unmarked' is an adjective used to describe language units which are easier to produce and are more frequently used. In the study of ASL, 'marked' handshapes like those illustrated below are observed to be: (1) more difficult to produce, (2) learned later by deaf babies with deaf parents (Boyes-Braem 1973, McIntire 1974), and (3) occur less frequently in ASL as well as in other signed languages (Woodward 1978).

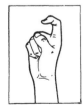   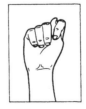 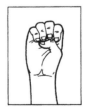 

Marked Handshapes

(5) Thelma hat den Mann gesehen.

'Thelma has the man seen' (English transliteration)

Looking at how signs are combined to form sentences in ASL, we see that sentence (6) is grammatically correct, and means 'Yesterday, after I finished my homework, I left'. However, re-arrangement of these same signs can yield ungrammatical sentences in ASL (i.e. sentences which do not follow the rules of the language), as seen in (7) and (8).[11]

(6) _____ *brow raise*
YESTERDAY HOME WORK FINISH, ME GO

(7) _____ *brow raise*
**YESTERDAY HOME WORK GO, ME FINISH

(8) _____ *brow raise*
**HOME WORK YESTERDAY ME, FINISH GO

Thus we see that languages (spoken or signed) are composed of a limited set of units which are combined with other units according to specific rules. As such, languages are "systems".

(d) **A language is a system of *relatively arbitrary* symbols and grammatical signals that members of a community share.**

The terms "arbitrary" and "iconic" are adjectives used to describe the relationship between the *form* of a symbol and the *meaning* of that symbol. If there is no resemblance between the form of a symbol and the thing it stands for (i.e. its meaning), then the relationship between the symbol and meaning is purely *arbitrary*. That is, there is no particular reason why that particular symbol is used to stand for that thing. For example, the English symbol 'pencil' does not look like or sound like the rectangular writing instrument that the word represents. The relationship between the word 'pencil' and the meaning 'thin, wooden writing instrument' is *arbitrary*. However, a drawing of a pencil (e.g. ⊂════════▷) *does* resemble the thing it represents. Therefore, the relationship between a drawing of a pencil and an actual pencil is *iconic*.

In addition, there are *degrees* of "arbitrariness" and "iconicity". Whenever a symbol is less than an exact physical replica of the thing it represents, the symbol is less iconic and more arbitrary. Thus, symbols can be iconic in some ways and arbitrary in other ways. For example, which of the symbols on the next page most closely resembles the thing it stands for? In other words, which drawing is more iconic?

---

[11]The symbol '⌒' in the gloss **HOME WORK** means that this sign is a compound sign.

Clearly, drawing C is more *iconic* because it resembles an actual female more than do A and B. However, drawings A and B are also iconic because the circle resembles a 'head', and the other lines resemble, in proportion, the body, legs, and arms of a person. Speaking from the opposite perspective, we can say that A is clearly more *arbitrary* than C. Drawing A gives a minimal amount of visual information necessary for iconically representing a person whereas drawing C more closely resembles the thing it stands for.

We can represent these differences through the use of an arbitrariness-iconicity *continuum*, as seen below:

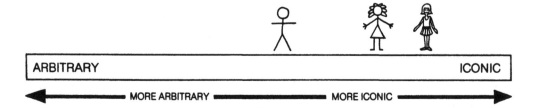

All of the drawings are located more to the right of the continuum because all of them resemble the thing they represent and are, therefore, iconic.

What kind of drawing would be located on the left side of the continuum? Suppose that a group of people decided to use ⋈ as a symbol for a girl. Does ⋈ resemble a girl? No, not at all. Therefore, the symbol ⋈ would be located on the far left side of the continuum.

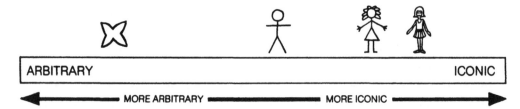

Returning to the definition of a language, stated above, we said that a language is a system of *relatively arbitrary* symbols and grammatical signals. Why is this arbitrariness important? If the symbols and/or signals of a language were completely iconic, then that language could only talk about (encode) a limited number of things. For example, if the symbols of our language were very iconic drawings, then we could only 'talk' about things that we could draw, like 🌲 , and 🌼 , and 📖 . We couldn't talk about abstract things like 'love' and 'beauty' and 'faith'. (What does 'love' look like?) However, if our symbols could be more arbitrary, then we could use ⊂⊃ for 'love', and ◇ for 'beauty', and (·) for 'faith'. Then, if we wanted to talk about something, but didn't have a symbol for it, we could either invent a new symbol or modify one we already had—for example, ⊂⊃ could mean 'not love'. Using this combination of some relatively iconic (and relatively arbitrary) symbols, we could say ◇ ⚲ ⊂⊃ 📖 📖 (i.e. 'The beautiful girl does not love books.').

No languages that we know about are totally arbitrary. That is, all languages seem to have some symbols and/or signals which are iconic in some way. For example, the English words 'sneeze, snort, snoot, snout, sniff, snot, snarl, sneer, snicker, snob, snorkle, snub, and snuff' are somewhat iconic in that the nasalized sound in the sequence [sn] resembles the nose-related meaning of these words. Onomatopoeia (e.g. 'meow', 'bow-wow', 'moo') is also a clear instance of iconicity in spoken languages because the sounds in these symbols try to imitate the sounds made by the things they represent.

In addition, one well-known linguist[12] has reported that in at least 38 spoken languages, words with high front vowels (like the vowel sounds in 'bee' and 'tin') tend to refer to small things. Similarly, words with low vowels (like the vowel sounds in 'might' and 'father') tend to refer to larger things. Think about the words 'teeny' and 'tiny' (which is smaller?), or the nonsense words 'plib' and 'plab' (which is larger?). One explanation for this relationship between certain vowel sounds and the meanings 'largeness' and 'smallness' is that the tongue position for producing these vowels is quite different. One position (e.g. during the vowel in 'plib') results in a very small opening in the mouth cavity; the other (e.g. during the vowel in 'plab') results in a larger opening. Here the result of producing those sounds seems to resemble the meanings of the words in which these sounds occur. These are all examples of iconicity in a spoken language, which is often called "sound symbolism".

Iconicity in a signed language refers to a *visual* resemblance between signs and the things they stand for. Many signs in ASL visually resemble their meaning; some do not. In all signs, there is a degree of arbitrariness. This is because there are always many possible ways to represent something in a signed language—just as there were several possible drawings to represent a 'girl' in the earlier discussion. For example, the sign TREE in Chinese Sign Language is symbolized by moving the signer's thumbs and crooked index fingers upward along an imaginary trunk; TREE in Danish Sign Language is made by 'shaping the boughs' with the palms and then moving downward along the trunk; TREE in American Sign Language uses the upright arm and spread fingers of the signing (dominant) hand as the 'tree' which rests on the 'ground' provided by the non-dominant hand and arm.[13]

---

[12]Bolinger 1975.

[13]Illustrations below borrowed with permission from Klima & Bellugi (1979), pg. 21, Fig. 1.8.

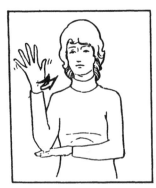

Chinese Sign Language   Danish Sign Language   American Sign Language

If the signs in a signed language were very iconic, then their meanings would be transparent and even people who have not studied that language would be able to understand it—just as a person could see the drawings of **B** and **C** on page 8 and know what they were symbols for. However, experiments with people who do not know ASL have shown that most signs in ASL are <u>not</u> iconic enough to be understood without being told their meanings.[14] On the other hand, if you tell someone the meaning of a sign, then that person can often see an iconic relationship between the form of the sign and its meaning. However, that relationship usually is not transparent enough for him/her to guess the meaning without being told. (Thus, signs are clearly different from "mime" or "pantomime" since mime and pantomime can be understood without prior explanation.)

Linguistic studies of ASL[15] have also shown that signs tend to become more arbitrary as time goes by. For example, the old ASL sign **HOME** was a compound of the signs **EAT** and **BED**. Now the sign is often made by touching the cheek (i.e. the location of the sign **BED**) twice with the handshape used in the sign **EAT**. Thus, the sign has changed and has become more arbitrary and less iconic. (Several more examples will be discussed in the next section on 'language change'.)

EAT BED   HOME

In conclusion, we see that the symbols and signals of a language must be arbitrary enough to be able to encode anything the user wants to talk about (and to allow for

---

[14]Hoemann 1975, Klima & Bellugi 1979.
[15]Woodward & Erting 1974, Frishberg 1975.

efficient use of the language), but can also be somewhat iconic. Thus, we say that language symbols and signals are *relatively arbitrary*.

(e) **A language is a system of relatively arbitrary symbols and grammatical signals that *change across time* and that members of the community share.**

Languages are as alive and changing as the people who use them. In the 1950's and 1960's came the 'beatniks' and the 'hippies' and their jargon 'hip', 'cool', 'neat', 'uptight', and 'groovy' (much of it borrowed from the 'rapping' and 'jiving' of the Black community). Teenagers started 'turning on' and 'digging it'. Then people became more 'mellow' and 'laid back' with the seventies, deciding to 'go with the flow' and 'keep on truckin'. Slang is one part of a language that changes especially rapidly.

Another type of vocabulary change reflects the growth and technological advances of a society. A hundred years ago, we didn't have words like 'television', 'videotape', 'microphone', and 'jet lag', or 'acrylon', 'dacron', and 'polyester', or 'astronaut', 'lunar module', and 'space capsule'. Languages change to meet the changing needs of their users.

The ability of a language to coin or create new words like 'groovy' and 'dacron' and to combine old words or word parts in new ways like 'space capsule' and 'tele-vision' is one kind of language "productivity". Without this ability, a language could not grow and change with the expanding needs of the people who use that language.

Although languages frequently grow by using their own internal resources for expressing new meanings, sometimes languages "borrow" words or signs from other languages rather than invent their own words or signs. English, for example, has borrowed extensively from many languages: for example, 'boutique', 'detente', and 'discotheque' from French, 'igloo' from Eskimo, 'patio' from Spanish, 'cookie' from Dutch, 'moccasin' from an American Indian language, 'klutz' and 'chutzpah' from Yiddish, and 'algebra' from Arabic.

American Sign Language has several major ways of creating new signs.[16] One way is by "compounding"—a process also used in English, but not in all spoken languages. A compound is created by combining two words or two signs so that they become like one word or one sign with its own meaning—like the compounds 'cupboard' and 'blueprint' in English. Notice that you can put plates (not just cups) in a cupboard, and a blueprint doesn't have to be blue. Examples of ASL compounds are EAT͡NOON (meaning 'lunch') and GIRL͡SERVE (meaning 'waitress'). An example of a new compound created by ASL signers is RECTANGULAR͡'ZAP' for 'microwave oven', which is illustrated on the next page.

---

[16]Bellugi 1977, Klima & Bellugi 1979.

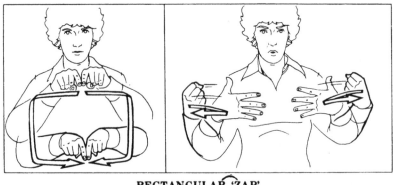

RECTANGULAR 'ZAP'
'microwave oven'

Another way of expressing new meanings in ASL involves changing the movement of an existing sign. For example, slightly changing the movement of the sign **QUIET** can change the meaning to 'acquiesce' or 'to give in to an argument'. (This derived sign can be made with one or both hands.)

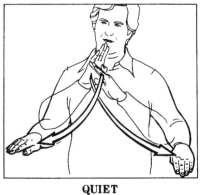
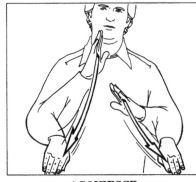

QUIET   ACQUIESCE

Similarly, nouns can be created by changing the movement associated with related verb signs. In this way, the movement that occurs during the sign **COMPARE** can be changed to express the meaning 'comparison', and the movement of **GO-BY-SKIS** can be changed to express the meaning 'skis'. Another familiar example is the verb **SIT** and its related noun **CHAIR**.

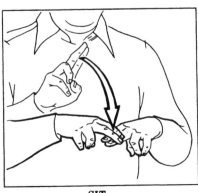
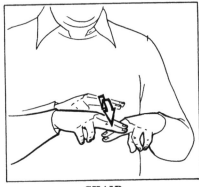

SIT   CHAIR

These are just some of the natural processes that ASL uses to express new meanings and create new signs. Linguists who are responsible for most of this research on productivity in ASL have observed that only a small fraction of the vocabulary of ASL is "borrowed" from other languages like English.[17]

Besides changes in vocabulary, changes in the grammar of a language also occur. As an example, let's look at "Old English"—a form of the English language used during the approximate period 600–1100 AD. Old English was less dependent on word order; it had many more inflections than are now present in Modern English. For example, the form of an English noun used to be different depending on its grammatical role in the sentence. Like the example from Latin described earlier, if the English noun was the subject, it had a special ending attached to it. If it was the direct object, it had a different ending attached to it. If it was the indirect object, it had another ending attached to it. Now only nouns in the possessive case like 'John's' and 'the cat's' are inflected. For many older signers of ASL, adjectives are signed after nouns, as in **BALL RED**. Now, however, many younger signers sign the adjective before the noun (i.e. **RED BALL**).

Another way that spoken languages change concerns how words are pronounced. For example, the first sound in the French word 'cherie' (meaning 'darling') is like the 'sh' sound in the English word 'ship'. However, in the 14th century, the same French word was pronounced with a 'ch' sound, as in the English word 'cheese'. Thus, during the period of 600 years, the French 'ch' sound was replaced by a 'sh' sound.[18] Similarly, the Old English way of pronouncing the word 'foot' was with a 'long o' [ō] so that the vowel sounded like the vowel in the word 'boat'. Thus, we see that the pronunciation of vowels and consonants in spoken languages changes across time.

Some of these changes in the pronunciation, vocabulary, and grammar of English can be seen in the following excerpts from the Lord's Prayer as they were written during four periods in the history of the English Language.[19]

1. Eornostlīce gebīddaþ eow þus Fæder ūre þū be eart on heofonum, sie bin nama gehālgod,
2. Tōcume þīn rīce. Gewurþe þīn willa on eor þan swā swā on heofonum.
3. Ūrne daeghwæmlīcan hlāf syle ūs tōdæg.
4. And forgyf ūs ūre gyltas swā swā we forgyfaþ ūrum gyltendum.
5. And ne gelæd þū ūs on costnunge ac ālys us of yfele.

Old English (ca. 1000)

1. Forsothe thus ȝe shulen preyen, Oure fadir that art in heuenes, halwid be thi name;
2. Thy kyngdom cumme to; be thi wille don as in heuen and in erthe;
3. ȝif to vs this day oure breed ouer other substaunce;

---

[17]Most of this research has been done by Dr. Ursula Bellugi and her associates at the Salk Institute in San Diego, California.

[18]Lockwood 1969.

[19]Excerpts from Clark *et al* 1977, pgs. 181–182.

4. And forȝeue to vs oure dettis, as we forȝeue to oure dettours;
5. And leede vs nat in to temptacioun, but delyuere vs fro yuel. Amen.

Middle English (Wycliffe, 1389)

1. After thys maner there fore praye ye, O oure father which arte in heven, halowed be thy name;
2. Let thy kingdom come; thy wyll be fulfilled as well in erth as hit ys in heven;
3. Geve vs this daye oure dayly breade;
4. And forgeve vs oure treaspases, even as we forgeve them which trespas vs;
5. Leede vs not into temptacion, but delyvre vs ffrom yvell. Amen.

Early Modern English (Tyndale, 1526)

1. Pray then like this:
   Our Father who art in heaven,
   Hallowed be thy name.
2. They kingdom come,
   Thy will be done,
      On Earth as it is in heaven.
3. Give us this day our daily bread;
4. And forgive us our debts,
      As we also have forgiven our debtors;
5. And lead us not into temptation,
      But deliver us from evil.

Modern English (1952)

During the past 150 years, ASL has also undergone major changes in the way that signs are made.[20] For example, many older signs which in the past were made by contacting the elbow are now made on the hand (e.g. **HELP, SUPPORT**). Some signs that were made at the waist are now made higher up the body (e.g. **YOUNG, FUTURE**). These are all examples of changes in the location parameter. Some handshapes have also changed. For example, **LAST** used to be made by striking the little finger of the non-dominant hand with the index finger of the moving hand. Now both handshapes tend to be the same (i.e. little fingers extended). Similarly, the handshapes in signs like **DEPEND, SHORT, INSTITUTE,** and **WHISKEY** have changed so that both hands have the same handshape. Many signs that used to be made with both hands on the face or head (e.g. **CAT, COW, HORSE, RABBIT, CHINESE**) are now often made with only one hand.[21] This change is also beginning to occur in French Sign Language.

Thus we see that the vocabulary, grammar, and 'pronunciation' of spoken and signed languages *change across time,* and that the vocabulary of these languages tends to change most rapidly.

---

[20]Woodward & Erting 1974, Frishberg 1975.
[21]Frishberg 1975, Woodward & De Santis 1977.

(f) **A language is a system of relatively arbitrary symbols and grammatical signals that change across time and that members of a community share and *use* for several purposes: to interact with each other, to communicate their ideas, emotions, and intentions, and to transmit their culture from generation to generation.**

As "social animals", human beings tend to live in groups, or communities, and to seek out opportunities to interact and communicate with other human beings. To facilitate such communication, every human community has a language which has arisen and evolved to meet the needs of its users. Members of each community use their language to express themselves and to understand the expressions of other members. Adults use this language to teach their children about the world, in general, and about the culture of their own community.

B. The Sign Language Teacher

A basic understanding of these major characteristics of "Language" is very important for the teacher of any language. A language teacher must realize that s/he is engaged in teaching not only the symbols and grammatical signals that members of a community share but also, and perhaps more importantly, how the community uses its language to communicate ideas and to transmit its culture.

For a teacher of American Sign Language, this means teaching students how the Deaf community uses ASL to transmit ideas, emotions, intentions, and cultural values. This statement has several important implications for the teacher of ASL: first, it assumes that the teacher possesses sufficient competence in and understanding of ASL to be able to teach it; second, it assumes that the teacher has an understanding of the cultural values of the Deaf community and how its members use ASL; third, it assumes that the teacher is aware of language teaching methodology which will help students develop both skills in ASL and an understanding of Deaf culture in order to interact in ASL with members of the Deaf community.

The companion teacher text, *American Sign Language: a teacher's resource text on grammar and culture,* is intended to assist teachers of ASL in developing and/or solidifying their understanding of ASL. The following section and a similar section in the companion text offers a discussion of the Deaf community which may assist teachers in developing an awareness of and a sensitivity toward the Deaf community. Finally, the remaining chapters in this text offer the teacher an interactive approach to language teaching. It is hoped that, with these resources and aids, the teacher of ASL will be enabled to teach ASL as a *language,* and in fact, as the unique means of communication of a unique cultural group—the Deaf community.

C. What is the Deaf Community?

Attempting to define the Deaf community is not an easy task. Within the past ten years, several widely-varying definitions have been proposed. However, it appears that these definitions can be categorized into either of two general types: (1) the "clinical" or "pathological" view which takes the behaviors and values of the hearing majority as the "standard" or "norm" and then focuses on how deaf people deviate from that norm, and (2) the "cultural" view which focuses on the language, experiences, and values of a particular group of people who happen to be deaf.

The first view (the "pathological" view) has been traditionally held by the majority of hearing persons who interact on a professional basis with deaf people. In a sense, this is the "outsider's" view—a view which focuses on how deaf people are different from hearing people and which generally perceives these differences negatively. The second view (the "cultural" view) has been discussed and described only very recently, seemingly as a result of the recent recognition of ASL as a separate language (not a deviant code for English). This recognition has encouraged a new examination of the Deaf community and its language in and of itself (an examination from the "inside").

Thus, we might categorize some of these specific definitions of the Deaf community as follows:

(1) Clinical-Pathological
   (a) an audiologically definable group of persons whose hearing loss is sufficient to interfere with but does not preclude the normal reception of speech (Schein 1968)
   (b) a group of hearing-impaired persons who have learning and psychological problems due to their hearing loss and communication difficulties (Levine 1956, Davis & Silverman 1960, Myklebust 1960, Rainer *et al* 1963, Altschuler 1964, Rainer & Altschuler 1966)
   (c) a minority group composed of hearing-impaired persons who are treated in certain negative ways by the hearing majority (Vernon & Makowsky 1969)

(2) Cultural
   (d) a group of persons who share a common means of communication (signs) which provides the basis for group cohesion and identity (Schlesinger & Meadow 1972)
   (e) a group of persons who share a common language (ASL) and a common culture (Woodward & Markowicz 1975, Padden & Markowicz 1976, Markowicz & Woodward 1978)

The attitude of those who hold the first view is generally that there is something wrong with deaf people and that, as much as possible, society should help them become as "normal" as possible. The attitude of those who hold the second view is that the Deaf community should be accepted and respected as a separate cultural group with its own values and language. Certainly this latter view is justified by linguistic and sociological research findings. However, these findings make defining the Deaf community a complex task. For example, the Deaf community is not like an ethnic or religious community where it is generally clear whether or not a person is a member—e.g. of the Black community, Jewish community, etc. That is, there does not seem to be a single distinguishing characteristic or trait that all members of the Deaf community share. Rather, there is a complex set of factors which must be considered when trying to understand who are the members of the Deaf community.

One factor which does seem very basic in understanding who is a member of the Deaf community is called *attitudinal deafness*. This occurs when a person identifies him/herself as a member of the Deaf community (which means supporting the values of that community), and other members accept this person as part of the community. Research has found that this factor is more important than the actual degree of hearing loss *(audiometric deafness)* —which does not actually seem to be very important in determining how a person relates to the Deaf community.[22] Using the criterion of "attitudinal deafness" to understand who are the members of the Deaf community has several important implications. First of all, it means that:

(a) not all hearing-impaired individuals are members of the Deaf community. Some individuals choose to function—or attempt to function—within the hearing community and do not become involved in matters affecting the Deaf community.

Secondly, although the vast majority of members of the Deaf community do, in fact, have a hearing loss,

(b) it may be possible for hearing individuals to be accepted as members if they display the appropriate "attitudinal deafness".[23]

Thirdly, since attitudes can be expressed in many different ways and to differing degrees,

(c) there may be several potential avenues through which a person may gain acceptance by the Deaf community.

(d) there may be different levels of acceptance into the Deaf community depending upon a person's skills and experience as well as attitudes.

The model presented on the next page is an attempt to describe the complex nature of the Deaf community and to illustrate various membership stages within the community. It is a tentative analysis based on available research and the descriptions of many members of the Deaf community. This diagram shows four potential avenues to membership into the community. Likely, there are more avenues than the four described and illustrated here. However, the model should serve to illustrate the complex interaction of factors which are important for understanding who are the members of the community—in addition to the basic criterion of attitude.

The four avenues to membership described here are: audiological, political, linguistic, and social.

(a) *Audiological:* refers to actual loss of hearing ability; as such, this avenue to membership is not available, by definition, to hearing people. It seems apparent that those individuals with a hearing loss are accepted by and identify with the community at a much deeper level ("the core") and much more

[22]Padden & Markowicz 1976.
[23]Meadow 1972, Furth 1973, Woodward & Markowicz 1975.

quickly than a hearing person with similar skills, experience, and attitudes.

(b) *Political:* refers to the potential ability to exert influence on matters which directly affect the Deaf community on a local, state, or national level. For example, a person might hold an office in a state NAD chapter. Of course, the types of decisions and proposals which s/he makes will also influence how well other members of the community accept that person.

(c) *Linguistic:* refers to the ability to understand and use American Sign Language. The level of fluency seems to be related to the level of acceptance into the community. Since the values and goals of the community are transmitted by its language, it is not surprising that fluency in ASL is very important.

(d) *Social:* refers to the ability to satisfactorily participate in social functions of the Deaf community. This means being invited to such functions, feeling at ease while attending, and having friends who are themselves members of the Deaf community. This ability may presuppose other factors, such as linguistic skills in ASL.

The complex way in which these avenues to membership may interact is illustrated in the following diagram:

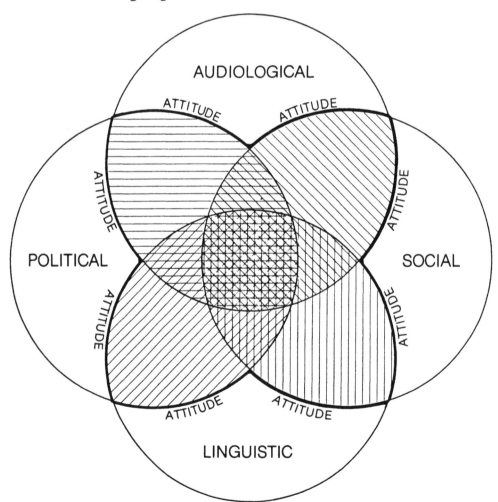

It should be apparent from this diagram that a person's attitude toward the Deaf community is of utmost importance in being accepted into the community. Identifying with and being accepted by the Deaf community is not simply a matter of linguistic skill in ASL or degree of hearing loss. Rather, it is a somewhat complex process in which certain skills (social, linguistic, political) and realities (hearing loss) are weighed in relation to the individual's attitude toward the community. The avenues of access depicted here are, from our point of view, channels through which an individual's attitudes and the community's attitudes meet and are either compatible or incompatible. If they are compatible, and if the individual identifies with the community, then s/he may be accepted as a member of the community.

The most heavily shaded area in the center of the diagram represents the "core Deaf community": those individuals who have a hearing loss and who share a common language, common values and experiences, and a common way of interacting with each other, with non-core members of the Deaf community, and with the Hearing community. The other shaded areas represent the wider Deaf community. With this diagram, we see that each member of the community is "attitudinally deaf" and can be identified with at least two of the four factors described above—i.e. linguistic and social, audiological and social, or audiological and political. Thus, according to this model, it is possible for a person to have a hearing loss and not be a member of the Deaf community (AUDIOLOGICAL), or for a person to be appointed to some political position in the government which influences the Deaf community and not be a member of the community (POLITICAL). It is also possible for a person to possess some degree of competence in ASL and not be a member of the Deaf community (LINGUISTIC). Finally, it is possible for a person to attend or support social functions of the community and not be a member of the Deaf community (SOCIAL).

It is also clear from this model that hearing people are not considered "core members" of the Deaf community since they do not have a hearing loss. It should also be clear that because of this fact, the avenues of access for hearing people are more limited (i.e. restricted to only three of the four avenues). In fact, the area which depicts a convergence of the political, linguistic, and social factors illustrates the highest level of acceptance into the Deaf community that a hearing person can attain. Likewise, the area which depicts a convergence of political, audiological and social factors illustrates the highest level of acceptance in the Deaf community which a hearing-impaired, non-ASL user can attain. In actual practice, the avenues of access for hearing people are even more limited than the diagram suggests since it is very difficult for a hearing person to have real political influence *within* the Deaf community. This means that generally the avenues of acceptance for hearing people are the linguistic and the social avenues.

Finally, it should be pointed out that, within certain limits, over time people may move from possessing or using one combination of factors to another. This means that individuals within the Deaf community relate to each other and are accepted by the community in a dynamic, not a static, fashion. A person's role within the community may change depending upon the development of or change in certain linguistic, political, and social skills. Of these skills, the most important seem to be social and linguistic. However, as was stated earlier, "attitudinal deafness" stands as the foundation for all such considerations and entails an understanding, acceptance, and identification with the culture of Deaf people.

Thus, the teacher's role is not only one of providing students with a certain level of linguistic skill and information. The teacher also has a strong influence on the type of attitude which the students will acquire. And research on second language learning has shown that a student's attitude toward a language and its users significantly affects that student's ability to learn the language. Hence it is vital for the teacher to examine his/her own attitudes toward the Deaf community and its language since the teacher's attitudes will probably be passed on to the students. A positive, accepting attitude toward the Deaf community as a cultural group with its own language is a prerequisite for a truly successful teacher of ASL. This is quite different than the previously described "clinical" view of the Deaf community which looks at Deaf people as "handicapped" or "disabled" because they can't hear. (Consider for a moment a hypothetical "clinical" view of hearing people by the Deaf community: hearing people are handicapped or disabled because they can't use ASL effectively!). The point again is that the teacher's own attitudes are as important for student success as his/her skills in ASL.

Assuming that the teacher has given some thought to his/her attitudes and that s/he possesses the necessary competence in ASL, the question remains—how to most effectively encourage students to develop linguistic skills and knowledge as well as an appropriate understanding of the Deaf community? The remainder of this text addresses that question.

References

Altschuler, K. Personality Traits and Depressive Symptoms in the Deaf. In J. Wortis (Ed.) *Recent Advances in Biological Psychiatry,* Vol. VI, New York: Plenum Press, 1964.

Battison, R. *Lexical Borrowing in American Sign Language.* Silver Spring, Md.: Linstok Press, 1978.

Bellugi, U. Formal Devices for Creating New Signs in ASL. Paper presented at the National Symposium on Sign Language Research and Teaching, Chicago, May 1977.

Bolinger, D. *Aspects of Language* (Second edition). New York: Harcourt, Brace, Jovanovich, Inc., 1975.

Boyes-Braem, P. A Study of the Acquisition of Dez in American Sign Language. Working paper, Salk Institute, San Diego, California, 1973.

Clark, V., P. Eschholz, & A. Rosa (Eds.) *Language: introductory readings* (Second edition). New York: St. Martin's Press, 1977.

Davis, H. & S. Silverman. *Hearing and Deafness* (Revised edition). New York: Holt, Rinehart and Winston, Inc., 1960.

Frishberg, N. Arbitrariness and Iconicity: Historical Change in American Sign Language. *Language 51;* 3, 696–719, 1975.

Furth, H. *Deafness and Learning: A Psychosocial Approach*. Belmont, California: Wadsworth Publishing Co., Inc., 1973.

Hoemann, H. The Transparency of Meaning of Sign Language Gestures. *Sign Language Studies 7*, 151–161, 1975.

Klima, E. & U. Bellugi. *The Signs of Language*. Cambridge, Mass.: Harvard University Press, 1979.

Levine, E. *Youth in a Soundless World: a Search for Personality*. Washington Square, New York: New York University Press, 1956.

Lockwood, W. B. *Indo-European Philology*. London: Hutchinson & Co., 1969.

Markowicz, H. & J. Woodward. Language and the Maintenance of Ethnic Boundaries in the Deaf Community. *Communication and Cognition II*, 1, 29–38, 1978.

McIntire, M. A Modified Model for the Description of Language Acquisition in a Deaf Child. M.A. Thesis, California State University at Northridge, 1974.

Meadow, K. Sociolinguistics, Sign Language and the Deaf Sub-Culture. In T. O'Rourke (Ed.) *Psycholinguistics and Total Communication: The State of the Art*. Silver Spring, Maryland: American Annals of the Deaf, 1–10, 1972.

Myklebust, H. *The Psychology of Deafness: Sensory Deprivation, Learning and Adjustment*. New York: Grune and Stratton, 1960.

Padden, C. & H. Markowicz. Cultural Conflicts Between Hearing and Deaf Communities. In *Proceedings of the Seventh World Congress of the World Federation of the Deaf*. Silver Spring, Maryland: National Association of the Deaf, 1976.

Rainer, J., K. Altschuler, & F. Kallman (Eds.) *Family and Mental Health Health Problems in a Deaf Population*. New York State Psychiatric Institute, Columbia University Press, 1963.

Rainer, J. & K. Altschuler. *Comprehensive Mental Health Services for the Deaf*. New York State Psychiatric Institute, Columbia University, 1966.

Schein, J. *The Deaf Community: Studies in the Social Psychology of Deafness*. Washington, D.C.: Gallaudet College Press, 1968.

Schlesinger, H. & K. Meadow. *Sound and Sign: Childhood Deafness and Mental Health*. Berkeley, California: University of California Press, 1972.

Vernon, M. & B. Makowsky. Deafness and Minority Group Dynamics. *The Deaf American 21*, 11, 3–6, 1969.

Woodward, J. & C. Erting. Synchronic Variation and Historical Change in American Sign Language. Paper presented at the Summer meeting of the Linguistics Society of America, Amherst, 1974.

Woodward, J. & H. Markowicz. Some Handy New Ideas on Pidgins and Creole Languages. Paper presented at the International Conference on Pidgin and Creole Languages, Honolulu, January, 1975.

Woodward, J. & S. De Santis. Two to One It Happens: Dynamic Phonology in Two Sign Languages. *Sign Language Studies 17*, 329–346, 1977.

Woodward, J. Sign Marking: "Stage" Four Handshapes. Paper presented at the Summer meeting of the Linguistic Society of America, July, 1978.

Chapter II
Teaching ASL as a Second Language

There is little doubt that the types of materials which have been available to teachers of ASL have had a definite influence upon the types of teaching methods or approaches used. When you consider that the majority of books available today are simply lists of English words with attached pictures or drawings of signs, it is not hard to see why most Sign classes are basically vocabulary classes. In addition, most Sign Language teachers are not teachers by training and very few Sign Language teachers have had any formal training in second language or foreign language[1] teaching techniques (or, for that matter, in the grammar of the language they are supposed to be teaching, ASL). This chapter will provide a discussion of some of the basic theories behind second language learning and teaching (since for the majority of students, ASL will be approached as a second or foreign language) and subsequent chapters will provide some practical suggestions for the teacher in applying second language techniques to the teaching of ASL.

There are certain basic principles involved in teaching a second language which should have direct bearing on the method(s) that a teacher will use. These principles are:

1) The ultimate aim of teaching a language is to develop the student's ability to communicate creatively and purposefully in that language. The goal, then, is communicative competence in the target language (TL).[2]

2) The most crucial factor in learning any Target Language (and any Native Language for that matter) is that the students have adequate exposure to the TL. Thus it is important that the teacher not dwell on teaching *facts about* the language but rather that the teacher provide as much *exposure to* the language as possible.

3) The student must have the desire and the opportunity to communicate in the TL. This means that classroom activities must be provided which require the students to use the TL and which are interesting to the students.

---

[1]The term *second language* is used when referring to a language which has a community of users with whom the student can or must have direct, frequent contact. The term *foreign language* is used when referring to a language which has a community of users with whom the student does not or cannot have direct, frequent contact. In a city with a large Deaf population, ASL might be considered a second language for hearing students and English might be a second language for some members of the Deaf community. In a small town with no Deaf population, ASL might be considered a foreign language.

[2]Normally the students' Native Language is referred to as NL or L_1; the language which is being taught is the Target Language, TL or L_2.

4) The use of dialogues, drills, and communication activities and games are essential for meaningful exposure to the TL. However, too much imitation or repetition may cause boredom on the part of the students. Imitation and repetition by themselves are not communication.

5) Language learning, especially among adults, is, in part, a conscious process and not just the imitation of teacher-produced utterances. This means that the students should have a clear idea of what they are doing and signing. What the students understand they will retain longer. Thus what is needed is a limited amount of explanation followed by meaningful opportunities to practice.

6) In any language course, the materials and activities should focus on natural use of the TL. This means that what the students are learning in the classroom should reflect the way fluent users actually speak/sign the TL.

7) Errors will occur in the learning process and, in fact, are an important part of the learning process. As students begin to converse spontaneously, they will make mistakes. The teacher must be careful not to over-correct and thereby overly frustrate the students. Since even native speakers and signers of a language make errors, the teacher should not expect an unnatural level of perfection from the students.

1) *The ultimate aim of teaching a language is that the students develop communicative competence.*

With some languages, there are four levels of communicative competence which the students must attain—listening, speaking, reading and writing. With other languages that do not have written forms, the focus must be on face-to-face, conversational competence. ASL is such a language. Thus, any teaching methods or strategies must be evaluated on the basis of how well they prepare a student to participate in a conversation in ASL. Any method or strategy which does not contribute in a positive way toward the attainment of this goal is a misuse of valuable instructional time.

A language, of course, does not exist in a vacuum. It is heavily influenced by the social and cultural values of the community of people who use that language. Thus, it is very important for the students in any language learning situation to become aware of the attitudes and values of the community of users. Consequently, in teaching ASL, it is necessary to provide the students with information about the Deaf community. This can be accomplished in a number of ways: a specific time in each class for discussion of some facet of the Deaf community, handouts, guest lecturers, incorporating the information into regular activities, assigned readings, etc. The point is that the students need to gain an understanding and appreciation of the Deaf community and culture before they can attain true competence in ASL.

2) *The most crucial factor in learning any TL (and any NL, for that matter) is that the students have adequate exposure to the TL.*

If we stop and think about how children learn their Native Language, we realize that they have many months and sometimes years of hearing or seeing the language before they are expected to speak or sign in the NL. This means their receptive skills (i.e. their understanding) are developed before their expressive skills (i.e. their production). In learning a TL, a similar process seems appropriate: receptive before expressive. This is just common sense—if a student has limited exposure to a particular lexical (vocabulary) item in the TL or a particular syntactic (grammatical) structure, s/he cannot be expected to use it appropriately.

One very serious problem with many Sign Language classes is the amount of spoken English which is used. Many teachers think that it is necessary to use spoken English so that hearing students will understand. Let us carefully consider the implications of this way of thinking. First, any time the teacher is speaking English, s/he cannot be exposing the students to ASL. Since most classes meet only 2-5 hours per week, the loss of any exposure time is crucial. Second, if the students are 'spoon-fed' English equivalents all the time, they never learn how to determine the meaning of a sign or phrase from context in ASL. Third, by providing English equivalents all the time, the teacher may be misleading the students into thinking that a sign in ASL can be used in the same way as an English word. Fourth, the tendency to sign while speaking English in the classroom can only cause confusion in the minds of the students and lead to the mistaken notion that ASL and English can be produced simultaneously. Fifth, by providing English equivalents, the teacher does not take advantage of a primary source of motivation in language learning—the motivation to understand.

The point is that constant use of the students' NL has some very grave consequences. If this practice is maintained, the student never makes the 'leap' into comprehension of the target language or the target culture. This means that the teacher should seriously consider *not* using any spoken English in the classroom and conducting the class entirely in the TL—in this case, ASL. (See Chapters V–VII for specific ideas and methods for doing this.) Such exclusive use of the TL is known as the Direct Method. Use of the Direct Method or Direct Method techniques places the student in a more natural language learning situation. This means that s/he must develop appropriate receptive skills and must struggle for comprehension before being asked to express him/herself.

One of the strongest motivations to learn is the desire and the need to understand the meaning of something. Once a meaning has been given to the student, s/he has no motivation to keep probing. However, when students have to work at grasping the meaning of a sign, a phrase, or a sentence (via explanations by the teacher in the TL), their initial frustration and tension is soon replaced with the satisfaction of having conquered the situation by having successfully figured out the meaning. Such frustrations and tensions are, to some extent, quite healthy and can be used very effectively by the teacher. There is also the fact that students *retain longer* those things which they have to work at to understand as opposed to those things which are given to them. Even if TL explanations are long and difficult, they have the distinct advantage of being in the TL, thereby increasing exposure time to the TL. Thus, in order to make maximal use of limited classroom time with the students, the teacher should use the TL as much as possible and encourage the students to build receptive skills in the TL as soon as possible.

3) *Students must have the desire and the opportunity to communicate in the TL.*

In most cases it is fairly safe to assume that students have, at least, a minimal level of desire to learn ASL. After all, they did register for the course and show up for the first class! However, if this minimal level of desire does not increase, the student will never successfully learn the language. It is the teacher's responsibility to transform what may be simple curiosity into an appropriate desire to communicate in ASL. Certainly such a change cannot occur if the student is placed in a very passive role with the teacher lecturing in the student's NL. This change also cannot occur if the students are never challenged to function in the TL (ASL). This means that from the beginning, the teacher must provide structured opportunities for the students to successfully interact via the TL in a meaningful way.

The two key factors here are *success* and *meaningful interaction.* It is important that in the early stages of any course the teacher conduct structured activities and exercises which will provide the students with feelings of success and accomplishment. This does not mean making things easy just so the students will feel successful. Rather, it means that the teacher must select activities and approaches which will challenge the students and force them to struggle with a specific task. The mark of a successful teacher is an ability to sense when the student's creative struggling is becoming counter-productive—i.e. the successful teacher can sense when to assist a student in a particular task and when to let the student struggle a while longer.

In addition to feeling successful, the students must also sense that their success has some bearing on meaningful interaction in the TL. This means that the teacher must select structured activities and exercises which provide ample opportunities for the students to *communicate* in the TL. Thus, the teacher should avoid over-use of simple imitation activities and instead focus on dialogues, communication games, and interactive activities since these will provide opportunities for exposure to and use of the TL in more meaningful ways.

4) *Dialogues, drills and communication activities and games are essential for meaningful exposure to the TL.*

While Chapters V, VI, and VII will provide more detailed discussion of these activities and approaches, it is important to realize that the various activities used in an ASL class (or in any language class) must provide the students with an understanding of the process of interacting in the TL. This means that the student will have to engage in a certain amount of guided repetition and practice which has obvious relevance and applicability beyond the classroom.[3] Thorough practice and repetition are extremely helpful and very often necessary in the artificial confines of

---

[3]For example, it is not especially relevant for a beginning student to spend valuable class time learning signs for animals since these signs are seldom used outside the classroom.

the classroom. But, while there are several techniques for varying practice and repetition tasks, the teacher must take care that such tasks do not lead to boredom or to a serious misuse of students' time. Whenever practice and repetition tasks become simple mechanical exercises without meaning, they stop contributing to the overall purpose of any language class—acquisition of meaningful communicative competence. Repetition itself will not promote effective language learning. However, effective use can be made of limited repetition and practice of meaningful statements which are context-related and which the students know will have practical use outside the classroom.

If dialogues, drills and other communication games and activities are carefully developed, they will provide the student with exposure to and repetition of features of the TL which will facilitate communication with members of the TL culture.

5) *Language learning, especially among adults, is a conscious process and not just the imitation of the teacher's utterances.*

Rote memory or imitation without some level of understanding and explanation is simply not an effective teaching strategy to use with adults. Because adults in Sign classes have already mastered at least one language (their NL), they are usually aware that languages have rules and specific patterns which must be followed. Therefore, when learning a new language, adults will begin the conscious process of searching for the rules and patterns of the TL. If no concrete explanation of the rules is provided, there is the danger that the students will formulate inaccurate rules for themselves. If this occurs, then they will have to go through a period of unlearning in order to assimilate the appropriate rules.

It is important, therefore, for the teacher to provide clear, concise explanations of the rules and predictable patterns of the TL in order to assist the adult learner in assimilating the appropriate rules of the TL. It is also desirable that these explanations be given to the student in a printed format rather than a verbal one. There are some reasons for this: first, the use of print means that the teacher can use class time for practice in the TL and not for lectures in the students' NL; second, the handouts can be retained by the students for future reference; third, written explanations tend to be clearer and more concise than short lectures by the teacher.

The point here is simply to provide the adult learner with ample explanations of exercises, activities, cultural factors, and syntactic features in printed form until the student can deal with such explanations through use of the TL. The use of a print format will enable the teacher to make best use of the limited classroom time for exposure to and interaction in the TL.

6) *In any language course, the materials and activities should focus on natural use of the TL.*

In the selection of target vocabulary, the teacher should be guided by a key question: 'What signs will be most frequently encountered by the students?'—not 'What is the next set of vocabulary items in the book?'. Only through using the criterion of "functional yield"[4] in the TL can the teacher be reasonably sure that what the students acquire in the classroom will be of direct benefit outside the classroom. Since classroom time is limited, the criterion of functional yield is extremely important in guiding the teacher to make the most effective use of this time.

The notion of natural use of the target language also applies to the production of certain lexical items. Thus, while we know that certain signs have changed historically, we also know that the production of certain signs changes in context—that is, in conversation, certain signs are made differently than they are drawn in sign books. For example, illustrations of the sign KNOW almost always show the fingertips contacting the temple or forehead. In actual conversation, however, it is much more frequently made with contact at or below the cheekbone. (See *Grammar and Culture* text, Chapter VI, for a more detailed discussion of such conversational changes.)

Failure to focus on natural use of the TL vocabulary and syntax may lead to the students using the TL in a much more formal or archaic manner than members of the Deaf community normally use the TL. This may cause problems of understanding and expression when the students attempt to interact with members of the Deaf community because the language forms the students have learned will be different than the forms that fluent signers normally use in conversation. Instead, the students are prepared to receive and express only a highly formal, stilted, and rarely used variety of the TL.

Thus, the materials and activities used should focus on those vocabulary items and language forms which represent actual usage by members of the Deaf community. Such vocabulary items and language forms should include greetings, expressions of surprise, disappointment, agreement, disagreement, question and answer forms, etc. The students are then spending classroom time acquiring features of the TL which can be immediately used in communicating outside the classroom.

7) *Errors will occur in the learning process and, in fact, are an important part of the learning process.*

The teacher must expect that students will produce errors in the language learning process. However, the teacher must give careful thought to the types of errors which the students are producing and why they are producing these errors. Through an analysis of the types of errors and reasons for such errors, the teacher is in an excellent position to determine whether or not the students are indeed making

---

[4]The concept of "functional yield" is often used in second language teaching as a means of deciding what to include in a specific lesson or course. Lexical items or syntactic features of high functional yield in a language occur very often in the language and/or are very important to the overall effective use of the language. For example, in English, the vocabulary items 'is', 'are', 'was', etc. have high functional yield because they occur frequently and are important to the language. However, the vocabulary items 'velvet', 'satin', 'burlap', etc. have low functional yield because they are not frequently used, nor are they crucial to the language.

progress and where there are potential difficulties which might require more intensive work.

The errors which students are likely to make can be analyzed in many different ways. For simplicity's sake, it will be best to view such errors as either lexical or syntactic. Lexical errors can be caused either by a student's inability to perceive or inability to physically produce a given vocabulary item correctly. This may be due to a lack of receptive and/or expressive readiness (discussed in Chapter IV) which the teacher can easily identify. Lexical errors can also be caused by a lack of understanding of the appropriate range of meanings of lexical items. This is much more complex and may be due to either the teacher's method, or the student's search for the limits of acceptability in the TL.

Consider, for example, the situation of a teacher who constantly provides English glosses or equivalents for signs in ASL. The teacher may demonstrate a sign and then say "This is the sign RUN". Because the teacher has given an English gloss for the sign, it is very easy for the student to assume that the sign which the teacher has glossed as RUN has the same range of meanings and the same use as the English word 'run'. Despite statements by the teacher that the sign is only used to mean people running, the fact that the word 'run' in the student's NL has a broader range of meanings (which have been reinforced for years and years) leads the student to assume that the sign has the same range of meanings. Thus, the student will produce the sign in inappropriate contexts because the teacher, by relying upon English glosses, has unknowingly caused confusion about the meaning of the sign more appropriately glossed as GO-FAST-BY-FOOT.

Student errors may also occur on the syntactic level. These errors can occur either because the student does not understand a particular grammatical feature of the TL or because the student thinks s/he understands that feature but is overextending the use of that feature. Additionally, such syntactic errors may be due to certain production factors which exist on the lexical level as well.

Syntactic errors of overgeneralization may be a necessary stage of development which the student must go through in acquiring mastery of certain syntactic features. For example, a student may demonstrate that s/he knows a particular syntactic feature of the TL and can use it appropriately in teacher-directed activities. However, in non-directed conversation-type activities, the student may use the feature inappropriately. This could indicate that the student is trying to test the limits of appropriate usage of that particular feature. Thus, a student who has learned that it is possible to negate certain signs by use of an outward, twisting movement (e.g. NOT-KNOW, NOT-WANT) may think that it is possible to negate all signs this way. S/he may then try to use this movement in order to sign **NOT-LOVE, **NOT-THINK, etc. This is very much like a child who will overgeneralize a particular linguistic feature that s/he has acquired in order to test the limits of acceptability (e.g. hearing children will overgeneralize the use of '-ed' to verbs like **runned, **singed, **writed, etc.). This type of error can be a positive indication that the student is beginning to gain command of a grammatical rule, and is finding out how to use it appropriately in the TL.

In discussing errors, perhaps the most important factor to consider is how the teacher attempts to correct errors. Since it is virtually certain that all students will make errors of one type or another at some point, this issue is significant and will come up often during a particular course. The teacher should remember two very important factors in attempting to correct errors. First, even native users of a language make errors. Therefore, the teacher should not expect a level of unnatural, error-free performance of second language learners that does not exist even among native users of the TL. Second, it is not beneficial to spend a great deal of time in a single class session trying to correct one error or error-type. Constant correction will only embarrass and frustrate a student and may be a misuse of other students' time. It is far better, if the teacher has noticed a particular error, to spread out the correction process over a longer period of time—perhaps several classes—and to accept a slightly more improved performance each time instead of expecting perfection in one intensive session. Thus, for example, if a student has a problem in the production of a specific sign, the teacher might select an activity which includes that sign, or ask the class or a group of students to imitate (two or three times) a sentence containing that sign. With each imitation the teacher might highlight the particular sign, thus drawing the student's attention to it. The student's production should slightly improve each time as s/he better understands how the sign is made. The teacher should reinforce the student's performance each time even though it is not perfect and then move on to another activity. The following week a different activity involving that same sign might be conducted so that the student again can focus on that sign. This process may continue for perhaps three or four weeks but each time the student's performance improves. In this way, the teacher has used a variety of activities and contexts which have benefited other members of the class, the student has not been embarrassed or frustrated, and both teacher and student have not wasted a large amount of time solely to correct that error.

This approach to correction requires that the teacher accept successively better approximations from the students. Approximations are the various attempts that a student makes in the process of attaining a particular level of performance. Thus, the teacher must be sensitive to the fact that reinforcing appropriate use of TL features will be more effective if spread out over time than if concentrated in a single class.

The successful teacher, therefore, must begin to consciously analyze the types and causes of student errors and recognize that effective TL learning is a process in which students constantly attain closer and closer native-like performance.

In summary, teachers need to consider all of the above basic principles quite carefully since they will have a direct bearing on the curriculum, on the teaching method and, ultimately, on the success of the students. These principles form the basis of a philosophy which represents a useful synthesis of current thinking about language teaching. Without an adequate philosophy of language instruction, it is unlikely that the teacher can provide consistent instructional opportunities for the students. In short, the teacher must give a great deal of thought to what it means to teach a language.

Chapter III
Guidelines for Teaching ASL

The following guidelines are proposed as general principles for anyone teaching ASL. Of course, in some cases there will be minor adjustments due to particular program objectives or program designs. Before discussing each of these guidelines in detail, it is necessary to point out one overriding condition which cannot be altered if one is serious about teaching ASL—*The teacher must possess native or near native competency in ASL.* The reason for this should be very obvious—the teacher first and foremost must function as a model of ASL for the students. If the teacher's skills in ASL are not highly developed and highly natural, then the students are presented with a false model of ASL. No book or set of materials can compensate for a teacher's lack of ASL skills. Nor is it very likely that a teacher (or any individual, for that matter) can acquire such ASL skills without continuing interaction with the Deaf community. This means that courses alone cannot provide the level of ASL skill necessary for a teacher to spontaneously and adequately model ASL.

Additionally, there must be a clear distinction between four different groups of individuals: those who know something *about* ASL, those who know *how to use* ASL, those who can *teach* ASL, and those who can *interpret* using ASL. The fact that a person knows something about the structure or history of ASL does not mean that that person can teach others the skill of using ASL. Certainly such a person may be qualified to teach others about ASL. But there is a vast difference between a course *about* a particular language and a course designed to impart proficiency in the *use* of that language. Likewise, a person who uses ASL is not, by that fact alone, qualified to teach ASL. Such a person also needs appropriate teaching skills and training in order to effectively and efficiently teach ASL to those who wish to learn it. Finally, there is also a vast difference between the ability to use ASL for interpreting purposes and the ability to teach ASL. In a highly specialized way, an ASL interpreter is in the same category as a user of ASL. However, the ability to interpret and use ASL and the ability to teach are very different skills.

A teacher of ASL must unquestionably possess a high level of skill in ASL. However, this alone is not sufficient to be a successful teacher. In addition to ASL skills, the ASL teacher also needs to have good teaching skills—e.g. a sensitivity to the needs of students, an awareness of how languages are taught and learned, the ability to plan and evaluate. Finally, a teacher of ASL must have appropriate training, background, and awareness of linguistic research on ASL, cultural aspects of the Deaf community, etc.

With these distinctions clearly in mind (i.e. an ASL teacher is not just a user of ASL and is not just someone who knows something about ASL), the following specific guidelines are suggested for teachers of ASL.

1) *The teacher should not use voice at all in the classroom.*

While some people may have difficulty accepting this particular guideline, there are two very good reasons for it:

a. It will foster the development of receptive skills in the students since they must actively attend to the teacher. If the teacher uses his/her voice, the students need not actively attend since they will be able to rely on their hearing. This will decrease the quantity and quality of receptive input.

b. It will avoid possible confusion of ASL and English. If the teacher signs and speaks English ("Simultaneous Communication"), then certain problems may arise for the student who may see many familiar signs used in a different structure than ASL. Also, the teacher will not be modeling the structure of ASL since one cannot sign ASL and speak English at the same time. (This guideline is further discussed in Chapter V.)

2) *Students should not be permitted to use voice at all in the classroom.*

While this may seem harsh at first, the reason for it is quite simple — it forces the student to become more expressive with his/her body. In short, this fosters the development of expressive skills in students. If they are permitted to use voice, there is no motivation to use their bodies — "Why bother, I can always talk". This also assists the students in becoming more visually aware and sensitive to their peers in terms of attention-getting behaviors, visual accessibility, etc.

3) *Students are permitted (in the beginning stages) to write questions or comments on the blackboard or through the use of an overhead projector.*

This provides a comfortable communication outlet for some of the more inhibited students. However, this should only be permitted for a limited number of class meetings (3-5) in order to ease the students into beginning to use ASL more readily.

4) *All information (course forms, explanatory materials, background information, assignments, etc.) should be presented to the students in writing through the use of blackboards, overhead projectors, xeroxed handouts, etc.*

This should continue until the students develop sufficient receptive skills in ASL to be able to deal with such information strictly in ASL. (Of course, there will always be information that the teacher wants to provide which will be best passed on via handouts). The primary reason for presenting all information in written form rather than through the use of "Simultaneous Communication" is to ensure that there is a clear distinction in the student's mind between English and ASL. This means that all of the teacher's non-written communication with the students occurs in ASL. It also means that more class time can be spent actually using ASL instead of talking about ASL.

5) *Except for the above (3 & 4), all in-class teacher communication will be conducted in ASL.*

In cases of misunderstanding or lack of understanding on the part of the students, the teacher should first re-phrase or paraphrase in ASL. If this fails, s/he can then use mime or gestures to explain. If that fails, then s/he can make use of objects or people in the environment or use drawings or pictures. In other words, the teacher should avoid the use of writing, if possible, except for any prepared materials to be handed out. This approach helps to increase the visual sensitivity of the students as well as creatively challenge them.

6) *The teacher should not demand that the students express themselves in ASL until they have had ample, meaningful receptive exposure to the language.*

Initially, this means delaying required student production of ASL for a period of time (perhaps 3-5 classes) in order to give the students an opportunity to feel comfortable processing visual information. This does not mean that the students cannot develop the readiness skills for expressive signing during this time. Certainly the use of expressive readiness tasks (Chapter IV) and a certain amount of meaningful vocabulary imitation (Chapter V) can occur during this period. However, as a general rule, and especially with the meaningful vocabulary imitation tasks, the teacher should provide ample receptive exposure before requiring any expressive tasks from the students. This gives the students a period of time to focus on the development of one skill—understanding—before being asked to develop another—expression. Certainly the students are permitted to try to express themselves in ASL if they wish, but are not required to do so until the teacher feels it is appropriate.

7) *All vocabulary should be taught in meaningful contexts through the use of interactional techniques, dialogues, narratives, stories, etc.*

The teacher should not routinely present signs out of context (i.e. in isolation), have the class imitate, and then move to the next sign. Such an approach does not help the student understand and retain vocabulary nor does it allow signs to occur naturally. The main point is that vocabulary is not learned in isolation, but rather it is learned through context and through meaningful use in conversation.

8) *The use of popular folklore or "stories" to explain the origins or reasons for the formation of particular signs should be avoided.*

While it is true that such "stories" are generally interesting to students, and while they may be helpful as memory aides in some cases, the fact is that knowing about a sign or set of signs does not necessarily help a student use the sign correctly and appropriately. Also, for a large number of signs, there are several stories which are used to explain their origins. Obviously not all of these stories can be correct, but no one knows which explanations are, in fact, true and which have been created after the sign evolved and was widely used. Given this, the teacher must refrain from calling such stories "origins" or "etymologies"; otherwise, the teacher puts him/herself in the rather embarrassing position of claiming or assuming to know more than the facts will support. If the teacher wishes to provide the students with *possible* explanations of certain signs, then these can be distributed in writing or briefly explained in class using ASL. However, the teacher should avoid spending too much class time on such explanations.

9) *The teacher should bring in a variety of Deaf individuals who use ASL to function as team teachers and/or additional models for the class.*

It is important that the students be exposed to a wide variety of Deaf ASL users. If the teacher is a hearing person, it is absolutely essential that Deaf individuals be brought into the classroom. Even if the teacher is Deaf, it is important that the students have as wide a range of models as possible, otherwise the students become adept at communicating with the teacher but have little or no experience communicating with other members of the Deaf community.[1]

10) *When a Deaf individual is brought in to class, the teacher should meet with him/her before the class to explain in detail what will happen in the class, what the individual is expected to do, any 'ground rules' that the teacher has established for the class, how much control the individual will have in the class, etc.*

It is not sufficient for the teacher to say "Well, just come to class and sign ASL with the students". This lack of careful preparation will make the experience less valuable for the students than if the teacher has carefully planned and explained to the Deaf individual his/her role, function, and activities.

11) *Fingerspelling and the manual alphabet should not be taught until after the students have completed at least one semester-length course in ASL.*

The only exceptions would be certain fingerspelled loan words which are used like signs (e.g. #JOB for 'job', #BACK for 'go back', etc.).[2] The reasons for this are as

---

[1]When the teacher arranges to bring a Deaf person into the class, that person should be paid at an equitable rate. The reason for this is twofold: first, while Deaf people have been willing to 'volunteer' their time and energy in the past, there is a point at which certain individuals are taken advantage of or are exploited; secondly, since teaching is a profession, teachers must act as professionals. This means that teachers must pay for services rendered by those who are not teachers. After all, if a teacher is paid to teach a class and invites someone in to work with the class, it is only fair that the other person be paid. A general rule of thumb might be that if a person works with the students for a full class period, s/he should be paid half of what the teacher earned for that class period. While that may not be much, it is a token honorarium and it does establish a sense of professionalism for the teacher and the consultant.

[2]See *Grammar and Culture* text, Chapter V.

follows: first, fingerspelling demands fine visual perception and fine motor skills; signing does not. To expect a student to begin with a very difficult task is unfair and unwise. Second, the eyes and body need a period of adjustment before being able to handle fingerspelling effectively and efficiently. Third, teaching students to fingerspell early may discourage growth of their sign vocabulary base. Fourth, fingerspelling is simply a code for English and the students need to detach themselves from English and focus on ASL. Fifth, even if a student becomes fluent in fingerspelling, that in itself is no guarantee that s/he will be able to communicate with and be accepted by members of the Deaf community.

12) *As frequently as possible, the teacher should videotape the expressive signing of each student.*

The primary reason for this is to provide the student with constructive feedback from the teacher as well as the opportunity for self-analysis and self-evaluation by the student. The opportunity for students to "see themselves as others see them" is an especially valuable one which should be utilized by the teacher. Another important reason for videotaping the students is to make them more aware of and more comfortable with their own body and bodily movements. This can be quite helpful in developing more native-like competency with ASL. Still another advantage to frequent videotaping is its usefulness in providing the teacher with opportunities to gauge instructional effectiveness.

13) *The teacher should obtain permission from appropriate personnel for the class to engage in any planned interactions with the Deaf community.*

The appropriate personnel referred to would be the president of the local Deaf club, the chairperson of a given activity, etc. The reason for this particular guideline is simply that social functions of the Deaf community should be times of relaxation and enjoyment for the members of the Deaf community. If these functions become 'classrooms' or times of laborious interaction with students, then the relaxation and enjoyment are greatly reduced. Also, any uninvited or unapproved interactions may be viewed as an invasion of privacy. In short, interactions with the Deaf community should be ethically and professionally arranged for and carried out in order to maintain the good will of the Deaf community.

14) *The teacher should carefully evaluate any proposed text or combination of texts or other materials and determine their appropriateness for achieving course objectives.*

While it is true that some students prefer to have a textbook for a specific course (since they feel it gives them a sense of security—or teachers feel that way), it is not as important to provide a textbook as it is to provide meaningful materials. Since a single textbook is rarely sufficient for any course, the teacher must carefully examine any proposed text to determine its strengths and weaknesses and, most importantly, to identify areas that will have to be filled in from other sources. Once the teacher has identified a text which seems to fit most of the course objectives, s/he must then secure supplemental materials to satisfy the other course objectives. The essential point is that the teacher must be very critical in selecting a text or in assigning a text. The teacher should not select a text simply because it is the most popular, or because the author is well-known, but rather because that text fits course objectives better than any other text.

15) *The teacher should avoid having the students participate in the interpretation or transliteration of audiotaped materials.*

The reason for this is simply that while such activities are appropriate for training interpreters, they are totally inappropriate for developing proficiency in ASL. As an example, one would not ask a student to listen to a story, paragraph, or song in English and simultaneously interpret it into Russian as a means of developing the student's Russian ability. The skills of *communicating* in a language and *interpreting* in that language are quite different, as are the activities used to develop those skills. Thus the teacher should avoid activities designed to train interpreters and, instead, use activities which are designed to enhance and foster communicative competence.

16) *The teacher should be aware of the limitations and barriers to effective signing posed by the classroom environment—desks, tables, etc.*

The teacher should attempt to provide as comfortable an environment as possible and should alter the environment periodically. The comfort factor is especially important since an uncomfortable environment can create mental as well as physical barriers and blocks to learning. Also, many students take Sign classes during the evening hours when minor discomforts may be exaggerated after working or studying all day. The teacher should alter the environment frequently. Since very little of the students' future communication in ASL is likely to occur in a classroom, the teacher should try to create a wide range of environments for the students. The teacher can change the environment either by periodically holding class in another room or locale or by altering the classroom itself (move chairs, change seating arrangements, use different lighting, etc.).

17) *The optimum class size is approximately 10-12 students per teacher.*

Although this is difficult to achieve in some programs, it is essential if each student is to be given adequate individual attention and encouragement. The larger the class size, the less individual attention each person receives. Unless the teacher and students have ready access to a language lab (with a sufficient amount of prepared, scaled videotapes) it is doubtful that sufficient classroom time can be given to accommodate a larger number of students. Of course this limit of 10-12 students per class is applicable only to skill development courses. If one is talking about a more content-oriented course (e.g. Structure of ASL, Linguistic Analysis of ASL) where students are responsible for information but not signing skills, then there is no pre-set limit to the number of students. However, in a skill development course the number of students must be large enough to provide variety and interaction but small enough to allow the teacher to monitor individual progress and growth.

18) *Classes should meet a minimum of four (4) hours per week.*

Six (6) hours a week (two hours per class, three classes per week) is actually a more beneficial schedule which will facilitate learning and allow sufficient reinforcement. However, this arrangement may be inappropriate for some programs. Thus, four (4) hours a week (two hours per class, two classes per week) is seen as a reasonable minimum for the development of ASL skills. A two-hour class period is desirable since it probably allows 1½ hours of actual instructional, developmental activities (after breaks, late starting times, etc.). The class should meet twice a week to permit spaced reinforcement and practice. If the class meets for four (4) hours in a single period, then factors such as fatigue, lack of sufficiently spaced practice, boredom, etc., become problems. It is desirable to pace and space the periods of TL exposure so as to avoid these problems.[3]

These guidelines are intended to maximize teacher effectiveness and to ensure that the student is given every possible chance to successfully acquire ASL skills. While certain adaptations may be needed in some programs, it is felt that these guidelines are essential to student success and, consequently, to overall program success. Certainly there are areas which are not included in these guidelines (e.g. teachers' background and training in applied linguistics, teachers' lesson planning skills, teachers' classroom management skills); however, the purpose of these guidelines is to focus on certain classroom behaviors and not on teacher training per se.

These guidelines or similar guidelines within a specific program (especially those that pertain to methodology) are crucial for the success of any program. Only with an agreed-upon set of guidelines can a supervisor or program coordinator be sure that the students receive consistent instruction that is still compatible with individual teaching styles. This is especially important in programs where students have different teachers for different courses. The teachers' styles will usually be

---

[3]There is a model of instruction called Total Immersion which places the student in an intensive instructional setting on a daily basis for up to ten hours a day. Total Immersion programs range in length from a few days to several weeks. The aim of such programs is to create a situation for the students similar to what they would face if they moved to another country. Consequently, all instruction takes place in the TL (often with several instructors rotating every 30-45 minutes) using the Direct Method (Chapter V). Since the students may go through a period of 'culture shock', the instructors must be sensitive to this fact and plan their activities accordingly.

Since a Total Immersion program of several weeks is impractical for most Sign Language programs, what is suggested here is a somewhat modified version in which the students are immersed in the TL for a few hours a week.

different, but if there is no agreement on basic approaches, the students will suffer because of program inconsistency. If students are to gain fluency in ASL, there must be a consistent approach used in all of their classes. A student cannot be exposed to one approach for one course and a completely different approach in the next course and be expected to gain native-like competency. The student cannot build upon the skills s/he already has when the approaches conflict and demand different types of performance.

The purpose of any set of guidelines is to ensure consistent and fair performance on the part of those who are affected by the guidelines. Students in ASL classes have a right to expect that teachers in the program are being consistent in their instructional approach. Such consistency is not at all guaranteed simply by having teachers use the same materials or the same textbook. Instead such consistency depends upon the attitudes of the teachers and their approach to instruction. Consequently, these basic guidelines are an attempt to point out those attitudes and behaviors which are considered crucial for the overall success of any program.

Chapter IV
Readiness Activities: Training the Eyes and the Body

In teaching ASL, it is important to remember that ASL is a language produced by the body for the eyes. While this may seem rather obvious at first, there are several important implications of this statement which should not be overlooked. For example, the vast majority of students in ASL classes are hearing adults who have rarely used their bodies or their eyes in the way that ASL requires. As such, it is important to present some activities which will help to 'loosen up' the students and encourage them to develop the visual and motor skills needed for ASL.

Before examining specific activities or games, it will be helpful to consider some of the basic visual and gestural skills which are necessary for effective communication in ASL. This will help teachers determine the proper value and use of various games and activities.

A. Eyes and Ears: Similarities and Differences

First of all, we know that visual messages are transmitted to the brain via the optic nerve. In this way, the eyes are like the ears—that is, barring any physiological or neurological problems, the individual has no conscious or voluntary control over whether or not a particular stimulus reaches the brain. There is, however, some level of conscious filtering that does occur. Hearing people 'hear' a variety of sounds at any given moment but 'listen' or 'attend' only to those sounds that they wish to focus on. Consider all the noises at a party—several different conversations occurring simultaneously, glasses banging on tables, ice cubes clicking, records playing, cars passing by outside, etc. However, hearing people will ignore most of these sounds—even though they will *hear* them—and will attend to the voice of the person(s) with whom they are talking.

The eyes also function in a similar fashion—that is, the optic nerve transmits thousands of bits of information to the brain at any given moment—sizes, shapes, colors, movements, distances, etc. Even when a person focuses his/her vision on a particular stimulus, there are still hundreds of pieces of visual information conveyed to the brain via peripheral vision. So in the sense that there are many simultaneously occurring stimuli which must be 'screened' in the brain, the eyes and the ears are alike.

There is, however, one way in which the eyes and ears are quite different. With the eyes there is a greater amount of conscious control which can be exercised. For example, people can consciously tune out visual stimuli by closing their eyes or by looking away. Hearing people cannot do this with their ears. Basically, this means that people can choose what they wish to look at and therefore, to some extent, can control what visual information reaches the brain.

Deaf people take advantage of this conscious control of the eyes (See Chapter VI on Conversation Regulators), and indeed, ASL, as a visual-gestural language, requires efficient use of the eyes. This fact is crucial for those who wish to learn American Sign Language and for those who are teaching it.

Hearing students need be taught where to look in order to receive optimum visual input from a signer. Generally, the focal point of visual attention is the face, with the hands and arms perceived more with one's peripheral vision. This is difficult for most beginning signers to understand since their natural impulse is to focus on the largest moving stimuli (i.e. the hands). However, focusing on a signer's hands would mean that facial expressions and eye and head movements must be perceived with one's peripheral vision. This is contrary to the needs of the language since a significant portion of the meaning of signed sentences is conveyed by the accompanying facial activity, and since such facial activity is generally harder to perceive (because it is smaller) than the manual portion and thus, requires more direct visual attention. As such, students need to learn to look at the signer's face.

B. Visual Discrimination

Up to this point the discussion has centered on establishing the conditions necessary to permit the optimum amount of ASL input to reach the brain. There are, however, some other considerations which must be raised at this time. Any bit of information (stimulus) which reaches the brain must first be analyzed for its meaning and relevance in an extremely short period of time, and not necessarily at a conscious level. In order to attach a specific meaning to a given stimulus, a person must be able to distinguish that stimulus from other stimuli which may be very similar. Sometimes small differences can result in a total change in meaning. For example, the pair of English words 'pin' and 'bin' are different only in the first sound. But those first sounds—'p' and 'b'—are very similar to each other. A speaker of English must be able to discriminate (recognize the difference between) these sounds in order to attach the appropriate meaning to each word.

Similarly, in ASL, it is necessary to develop *visual* discrimination skills. This is very important for hearing people who are not accustomed to using their eyes in the way ASL requires. Consider the four parameters of signs—handshape, location, movement, and palm orientation. It is important for students to be able to discriminate similar handshapes, locations, movements, and palm orientations since slight differences can result in a change in meaning. Consider the following signs which differ in only one parameter:

1) handshape: (a) **GREEN----PURPLE----YELLOW**
                 (b) **CHINA----ONION**
                 (c) **WHITE----LIKE**

2) location: (a) **FATHER----MOTHER**
                (b) **APPLE----ONION**
                (c) **SUMMER----UGLY----DRY**

3) movement: (a) **SCHOOL----PAPER**
                (b) **TOMORROW----GIRL**
                (c) **HAPPY----ENJOY**

4) orientation: (a) **NAME----CHAIR**
                (b) **TRAIN----BRIEF/SOON**
                (c) **WANT----FREEZE**

Because the difference in only one parameter can result in a change in meaning, it is crucial that students develop the visual discrimination skills necessary to perceive such changes. Hearing people do this unconsciously with spoken English and Deaf people do this unconsciously with ASL. Hearing people, however, have to be taught that visual discrimination is as important for understanding ASL as auditory discrimination is for understanding English.

C. Visual Memory

Another area that requires some attention is that of visual memory. Since most hearing people are not as visually oriented, it is understandable that they will have some difficulty remembering vocabulary items and sentences in ASL. However, the ability to remember linguistic units is crucial in the early stages of learning a language in order to allow for imitation, dialogue and drill exercises, story repetition, etc. The student of ASL faces two types of memory tasks—(1) memory concerning *how* a given sign or facial expression is made, and (2) in some situations, memory concerning *what* the specific ordering of signs is. In the early stages of learning, it is likely that these memory tasks will operate at a fairly conscious level—that is, the student will consciously think about what handshape, movement, etc., is needed for a particular sign, or what sign came first and what sign came second, etc. The ultimate goal, of course, is that the student is able to obtain a high level of unconscious control of these types of memory so that s/he can focus on *what* is to be communicated rather than *how* it is to be produced.

D. Rationale for Readiness Activities

In addition to the visual readiness skills discussed above, it is important to remember that ASL requires the use of the face, hands, and body in ways which are strange and uncomfortable for many hearing people. Just as many hearing people tend to be non-visually oriented, many also tend to be gesturally inhibited. This means that many students will feel and look awkward when attempting to sign. Thus it is necessary to provide some activities which will help 'loosen up' the students. There are several advantages to such readiness activities: first, they help make students less inhibited; second, they help students understand that they can communicate without speech; third, they help students gain an awareness and control of the space around them; and fourth, they can give the students a feeling of success and accomplishment. Almost *all* students will need training in both visual and body readiness areas. Some students may require more training than others, but all students should be provided with early opportunities to prepare their eyes and their bodies for communicating effectively in ASL.

It is indeed difficult to separate eye training and body training. It can be argued that almost any activity designed to 'loosen up' students' bodies is, in fact, training their eyes. While this is true, this type of global approach may not be helpful to students with very specific difficulties. Consider the following example:

A teacher asks a student to imitate a specific sentence in ASL. If the response is correct, we can assume that the visual and other physical factors necessary to acquire and use ASL are intact. However, if the response is incorrect, there may be several possible reasons:

1) The student may not be 'seeing' the signs correctly. This means that there may be a visual discrimination problem which may be similar to the types of visual problems that some children have (e.g. the word *saw* is misread or is perceived as the word *was*). If this is the case, then the teacher will need to provide special assistance to that student since the student must 'see' the signs correctly in order to understand and imitate them correctly.

2) The student may have motor difficulties which prevent him/her from correctly imitating or producing signs. In this case, the student may 'see' the signs correctly but not yet have the motor skills necessary for appropriate production.

3) The student may 'see' the signs correctly and may have the skills needed for production but may not be able to perform the necessary 'transposals' for imitation. Thus, if both teacher and student are right-handed and are facing each other, the sign GIRL, for example, will be produced by the teacher on his/her right cheek. The student perceives this sign on the left side and in order to sign GIRL must then 'transpose' this sign to his/her own right side. (There is a tendency for right-handed students who have not mastered this 'transposal' process to imitate signs with their left hands).

4) The student may 'see' the signs correctly and have the necessary production skills but may not have the visual memory to remember which signs s/he is supposed to produce nor how they are to be produced.

5) The student may 'see' the signs correctly but may feel inhibited in using his/her body as freely and openly as required by signing. Such a negative affect will not only influence production but may also influence the student's ability to correctly perceive signs.

In order to overcome these difficulties and to begin the process of preparing the students' eyes and bodies for ASL, the teacher may find some of the following activities helpful. Some of these activities have been developed by Gilbert Eastman of the Gallaudet College Drama Department and Jane Norman and are used by Eastman in a summer course which focuses on the visual-gestural basis of ASL. In addition, Norman has described some of these activities in a booklet published by the N.A.D. for the Sign Instructors Guidance Network (S.I.G.N.). The activities with asterisks (*) indicate activities developed by Eastman and Norman.

E. Activities for Eye Training

1. *EYE TAG

RATIONALE: to help students develop visual focusing skills
                        to help students develop peripheral vision skills

PROCEDURE:
—teacher arranges the class in a circle (preferably standing)
—one person is chosen to be 'it' (by the teacher or some other means)
—the person who is 'it' quickly looks at the other students one-by-one until s/he decides to 'tag' someone by either blinking or winking
—the person who was 'tagged' then is 'it' for the next round
—the game should proceed very rapidly after the students get accustomed to the game

VARIATION:
—students choose pieces of paper to determine who is 'it'
—as each person is 'tagged', s/he must leave the circle
—the game ends when the person who is 'it' has been discovered or when everyone has been 'tagged'

2. VISUAL DISCRIMINATION

RATIONALE: to help students develop visual discrimination skills for signs
                        to help students realize that small differences in sign parameters are important
                        to help students begin to develop their visual memory for signs

PROCEDURE:
—teacher presents two signs (actual or invented nonsense signs) with a brief interval between the two signs
—teacher then calls upon a student who must respond with a headnod ('yes') if the two signs are the same, or with a headshake ('no') if the two are different
—signs which are different should be different in only one parameter to help the student focus on fine differences in signs

> —pairs of signs should be mixed so that there is a random sequencing of signs which are the same and signs which are different
> —teacher should call on students in random fashion after each pair has been presented

VARIATION:

> —teacher may choose to have the students respond with the signs **SAME** and **DIFFERENT** or **YES** and **NO** instead of a headnod and a headshake
> —teacher may choose to have the class respond as a group instead of only calling on one student after each pair

SAMPLE ITEMS:

GIRL	AUNT
MOTHER	FATHER
ME	YOU
NAME	CHAIR
IN	OUT
TRAIN	SHORT
DEPEND	CAN'T
YELLOW	GREEN
THINK	REASON
BROTHER	SISTER
FAMILY	GROUP
YESTERDAY	TOMORROW
COW	DEER
WANT	NOT-WANT

NOTE: It does not matter whether or not the students understand the meanings of the signs used in this exercise. In fact, it is preferable if they do *not* know the signs. The purpose is not to teach vocabulary but simply to help the students become visually attuned to certain similarities and differences which will be crucial in later vocabulary learning. If the students know the meanings or have had some prior exposure to signing, then it may be necessary for the teacher to invent some nonsense signs or to use signs taken from the Sign Language of another country.

3. VISUAL MEMORY:

RATIONALE: to help students develop visual memory skills
to help students refine visual discrimination skills

PROCEDURE:

> —the teacher presents a set of signs (either actual or invented signs) which range from two to six signs in length

—teacher then waits a brief period of time (and this time can be increased as the students become more adept) and then presents the same set or a slightly different set of signs
—teacher calls on one student at random to respond
—the manner of response is the same as for the discrimination task—headnod if the same and headshake if different

SAMPLE ITEMS:

Set #1	Set #2
a) BOY HOUSE PAPER	BOY PAPER HOUSE
b) MONEY TREE HAT DRINK	MONEY TREE HAT FACE
c) DRAMA WORK MOTHER	DRAMA WORK FATHER
d) SIGN LION KNOW FAT TALK	SIGN FAT LION KNOW TALK
e) CRY EAT LIE AUNT GERMAN TO	CRY SPELL EAT LIE AUNT TO

NOTE: As in the discrimination task, it is preferable if the students do not know the meanings of the signs. This will help to force the students to focus on the form of the signs used. As can be seen from the sample items, it is possible to simply alter the sequence (e.g. #a) which will produce a set that does not match or to change a sign (e.g. #b) which also produces a non-matching set.

The above tasks or activities essentially require no expressive behavior on the part of the students other than a 'yes-no' or a winking/blinking response. Thus, they very clearly focus on visual readiness level skills. The following activities begin by focusing on individual expressive participation, then group response, and then group participation. As such they continue to develop visual readiness skills and begin to develop the level of bodily awareness and comfort necessary for expressive signing.

F. Activities for Body Awareness

1. *FACIAL STRINGS

RATIONALE: to help students become aware of the capabilities and limitations of their face
to develop visual skills through imitation
to begin to develop comfort in using a range of facial expressions

PROCEDURE:
—teacher arranges the class in a circle
—teacher takes two imaginary needles with thread
—the class imitates
—the teacher 'ties' one thread to the right corner of his/her mouth and one to the left

—the class imitates
—the teacher pulls on one string and his/her mouth reacts appropriately
—the class imitates
—activity continues with eyes, chin, cheeks, etc.
—the teacher picks a student at random to be leader

2. *PICTURE 'DRAWING' EXERCISE

RATIONALE: to help students become aware of spatial relations
to help students develop visual memory skills
to help students begin to feel free with their bodies

PROCEDURE:
—teacher shows the class a picture (preferably a cartoon-like drawing, e.g. a flower with face/eyes/mouth)
—teacher has a series of separate drawings each building up to the final picture (e.g. the first picture only has grass, the second has grass and the flower stem, the third has grass, stem, and 'head' of the flower, etc.)
—teacher calls on one student at random and shows him/her the first picture in the series (e.g. just grass)
—the student must gesture or act out that picture
—teacher calls on a second student, shows the second picture
—the student must gesture or act out the second picture using the first student's description to build on
—process continues until the picture is completely described.

VARIATION:
—teacher does not show the full picture to the class
—the class must draw what they see described
—at the end, the class drawings can be compared with the actual picture as an index of students' visual readiness skills

3. *PROPER POSITIONS

RATIONALE: to help students become aware of spatial relations
to help students become free with their bodies
to continue developing visual awareness skills

PROCEDURE:
—teacher has several pictures containing approximately four objects in a definite spatial relation to each other (e.g. the roof of a house with a window, chimney, and the sun)
—teacher has a list of drawings of the objects in each picture—e.g.

—teacher calls on one student and gives him/her a picture list of objects (Do not show final, full picture)
—student must use gestures to 'draw' the objects in the air (in the relationships they have in reality)—e.g.
—teacher shows class and student the full picture
—teacher can vary the order of objects on the list

VARIATION:

—class can draw the picture that is described
—more than one student can be involved in describing a particular picture

4. *CHANGE-THE-STICK

RATIONALE: to help develop visual sensitivity in the students
to help develop a sense of group cohesion
to help students feel less inhibited
to help provide an opportunity for students to be visually creative

PROCEDURE:

—teacher arranges the class in a circle
—teacher holds an imaginary 'stick'
—teacher does something with the 'stick' so that it changes to a new object (e.g. a baseball bat, a golf club, fishing pole)
—teacher passes the 'stick' to a student at random
—student changes the 'stick' to another object and passes it on to another student
—activity continues until everyone has had a chance or until there are no more ideas

5. *MIRROR GAME

RATIONALE: to help develop visual awareness skills
to help students become comfortable with moving their bodies
to help develop visual focusing skills

PROCEDURE:

—students are arranged in pairs facing each other
—one person in the pair is the leader
—s/he makes nonsense movements of the face and/or hand(s) and arm(s)
—the other person must imitate (or 'mirror')
—the person who is mirroring should focus on his/her partner's eyes, *not* hands or arms
—continue for a few minutes and then change roles

6. *PASS-IT-ON

    RATIONALE: to help develop visual memory
                        to help students become comfortable with their bodies
                        to build group cohesion

    PROCEDURE:

—class is arranged in a line, all facing the same direction
—teacher goes to the last student in line (student A)
—teacher gives a gestural message to student A
—student A taps the next student (B) on the shoulder
—student B turns and A repeats the gestural message
—B taps C, repeats the message
—game continues until the message reaches the first student in line
—that student repeats the message, teacher repeats the original message and compares

    VARIATION:

—two teams can be formed
—the last student in each line is given the message at the same time
—teams race to see which team finishes first with the most accuracy

G. Additional Activities

In addition to the above games and activities, there are two commercially-made games which are helpful for eye training and body training. These games are:

1) *Body Talk* —published by Communications Research Machines, Inc., 1970, Del Mar, California.
   (This game is one in which students select a card with a specific emotion on it and then must show that emotion through facial expression; other students try to guess the emotion.)

2) *Simon* —by Milton Bradley, Co., Springfield, MA 01105.
   (This game helps to develop visual memory for light sequences or patterns. However, there are also auditory cues (buzzers and tones) which should be disconnected to ensure that hearing students really rely on their visual memory and not their auditory memory. The game can be played with one or more players.)

Additional games and activities can be found in the following three books:

1) *Play It By Sign* —Suzie Kirchner, 1974, published by Joyce Media, Inc., P.O. Box 458, Northridge, California 91324.

The following games from this book may be especially helpful in developing awareness/readiness skills (other games may be useful as students become more skilled):

Role Playing

Spot-The-Leader

2) *Signs For All Seasons* — Suzie Kirchner, 1977, Joyce Media, Inc.

The following games from this book may be especially helpful in developing awareness/readiness skills (other games may be useful as students become more skilled):

Animal Antics

The Invisible Game

The Magic Wand

Make A Face

Mime Time

Mirror Game

Picture Game

Rhythms

What's Cookin'

3) *Games and Activities for Sign Language Classes* — Mary Anne Royster, 1974, National Association of the Deaf, 814 Thayer Avenue, Silver Spring, MD 20910.

The following games from this book may be especially helpful in developing awareness/readiness skills (other games may be useful as students become more skilled):

Facial Charades

Description

Nonverbal Communication

The following publishers also provide catalogs of foreign language games. These catalogs may be obtained by writing directly to the publisher:

Gessler Publishing Company, Inc.
220 East 23rd Street
New York, NY 10010

Goldsmith's Audiovisuals
(Playette Corporation)
301 East Shore Road
Great Neck, NY 11023

The Kiosk
19223 De Havilland Drive
Sarratoga, CA 95070

National Textbook Company
8259 Niles Center Road
Skokie, IL 60076

In summary, teachers need to be aware of the fact that hearing students must go through a period of preparing their eyes to receive ASL and preparing their bodies to express ASL. The length of such activities will, of course, vary with the skills and quickness of the students. However, at a minimum, a preparation period of 3-4 classes seems reasonable. The teacher may also wish to continue using some of the activities at the beginning of each class. This will help to 'loosen up' the students for each class.

In addition to the advantages described above, this period of readiness will also enable the teacher to get a clear picture of the limitations and abilities of each student. Although each of the activities discussed above are conducted in a relatively brief period of time, they can reveal much about each student's needs. This, in turn, will help the teacher provide the best possible ASL instruction for the students.

Chapter V

Teaching ASL Without the Use of Spoken English: Structured Activities

A. Introduction

The next three chapters are devoted to a discussion and explanation of various techniques and communication games and activities which the teacher can use without having to rely on spoken English (or the students' NL). However, before discussing these in detail, it is useful to examine more carefully the concept of Direct Method teaching—that is, the use of the TL only, without reliance on the students' NL.

The Direct Method of language instruction has been popular during this century largely because of the efforts of Maximillian David Berlitz (1852-1921). Berlitz insisted upon using the TL from the very beginning of instruction in order to avoid interference from the students' NL. However, Berlitz was not the first person to propose this approach. It is possible to find full or partial support for the Direct Method (or "Natural Method") among such authors as Erasmus (1466?-1546), Martin Luther (1483-1546), Michel De Montaigne (1533-1592), Johann A. Comenius (1592-1670), Geraud de Cordemoy (1624-1684), John Locke (1632-1704), Immanuel Kant (1724-1801), Johann Von Herder (1744-1803), Johann Pestalozzi (1746-1827), Johann Fichte (1762-1814) and others. The point here, of course, is to illustrate that the idea of using the TL to teach and model the TL is not new.

The basic premise of this approach to language teaching is simply that a language is best learned in realistic settings where there is a real need to learn the language or a comparable need that is artificially produced by the teacher. The techniques and ideas presented here attempt to provide the teacher with a variety of ways for creating a need for the students to interact directly within the TL.

The reasons for not using the students' NL while studying the TL are given by Berlitz himself. Berlitz, an internationally recognized language teacher who developed the teaching procedures utilized in the Berlitz Language Schools, states:

> From the very first lesson, the student hears only the language he is studying (the TL). The reasons for this mode of introducing the new tongue are as follows:
>
> 1. In all translation methods, most of the time is taken up by explanations in the students' mother tongue, while but few words during the lesson are spoken in the language to be learned. It is evident that such a procedure is contrary to common sense.

2. He who is seeking to acquire a foreign language by means of translation, neither gets hold of its spirit nor does he become accustomed to think in it; on the contrary, he has a tendency to base all he says on what he would say in his mother tongue and he cannot prevent his vernacular from assimilating the foreign idiom, thereby rendering the latter unintelligible or, at least, incorrect.

3. A knowledge of a foreign tongue acquired by means of translation is necessarily defective and incomplete; for there is by no means for every word of the one language, the exact equivalent in the other. Every language has its peculiarities, its idiomatic expressions and turns, which cannot possibly be rendered by translation. Furthermore, the ideas conveyed by an expression in one language, are frequently not the same as those conveyed by the same words in an other.[1]

Generally, in the beginning of a course taught using the Direct Method, students are immediately exposed to complete meaningful sentences which often form part of a simple question-answer dialogue. Initial vocabulary learning centers around objects and actions within the classroom itself. When these are understood and used fairly easily by the students, the learning shifts to common situations, settings and experiences of everyday life. Very often the lesson centers around the use of pictures to portray certain actions or cultural patterns. If the meaning of certain lexical items cannot be made clear through explanations in the TL or the use of objects or pictures, the teacher will resort to gestures or mime. But the teacher never supplies an equivalent or a translation in the students' NL.

In recent years, a modified form of the Direct Method has become quite widely used. This modified form of the Direct Method encourages limited explanation of certain grammatical features of the TL by the teacher, using the students' NL. These explanations are generally very brief and are generally given orally since the student can easily distinguish his/her NL from the TL. In addition, more specific practice and form is given to lessons through the use of carefully constructed dialogues and drills which are meaningful and have somewhat immediate application outside the classroom.

If we apply the above description to an ASL class, it is easy to see that the only potential source of difficulty or confusion which will arise is in the use of the students' NL for explanation. If the teacher were to speak only while giving such explanations, then the difference between ASL and English would be kept clear for the student. It is when the teacher signs and speaks at the same time that there are serious problems. One reason given by teachers for signing and speaking while giving such information is that the students can acquire more vocabulary items. However, as has been pointed out, the range of meanings for a sign in ASL and an English gloss for that sign are very often quite different. In addition to distorting the meaning of certain ASL signs, the teacher is also modeling and exposing the students to non-ASL grammatical patterns. Thus, even though the teacher may mean well, s/he is unconsciously creating obstacles for the students and undermin-

---

[1]Berlitz, M. D. *Berlitz Method for Teaching Modern Languages,* New York: M. D. Berlitz, 1907.

ing the very goal of the course—communicative competence in ASL. It is for these reasons that it is strongly suggested that any and all signing done by the teacher be in ASL and that background information and explanations be given to the students in printed form via handouts, blackboard, overhead projector, etc.

B. Vocabulary and Syntax-Building Activities

The following activities are intended only as examples of the types of activities which a teacher may conduct solely through use of the TL (ASL). There are, obviously, many more types of activities which can be conducted in the TL and only the teacher's creativity and ingenuity will limit the possibilities.

1. Object/Picture Vocabulary Development

The purpose of this activity is to enable the students to develop vocabulary and to respond to certain commands only through use of the TL. This activity provides for direct learning of the targeted vocabulary without reliance on English glosses. The students are initially exposed to the vocabulary, are encouraged and expected to imitate, and then are expected to respond to various questions and/or commands. All of this takes place only in the TL.

a) *Preparation* —The teacher has identified a set of vocabulary items to be taught (the 'target items') and has collected an object or a picture for each item. For example, the target items might be BOOK, PAPER, PENCIL, CAR, etc. The teacher also has targeted three colors—RED, BROWN, BLACK. The teacher then collects three books (red, brown and black), three pieces of colored paper (red, brown and black), three toy cars (red, brown and black), etc.

b) *Initial Presentation* —The teacher brings all of the objects to class. At the appropriate time, the colored objects (e.g. book, car, paper, car, pencil, book, pencil, paper) are placed in a random fashion on a table/desk or a chalkboard ledge. The teacher now goes through the following process:

   1) Point to the first object and make the appropriate sign (e.g. BOOK), perhaps repeating the pointing and the sign two or three times.
   2) Through the use of gestures and a slight movement toward the class, the students may be encouraged to imitate the sign BOOK.
   3) Move to the next object (e.g. CAR) and repeat steps 1 and 2.
   4) Move to the third object (e.g. PAPER) and repeat steps 1 and 2.
   5) Return to the first object—BOOK—and point to the object. Then with a questioning facial expression and gestures, encourage the class to produce the sign—BOOK.
   6) When the class has produced the sign BOOK (or when the teacher has given the sign again), move to the second object or the third object and repeat step 5.
   7) After the teacher has gone through all of the objects, s/he then points to several of the objects at random and, through gestures and facial expres-

sion, has the class produce the appropriate signs. The teacher may wish to call on students one at a time or let them respond as a group.

8) When the class responds easily to step 7, the teacher then regroups the objects—the three books together, the three cars, the three pencils, etc., or all objects that are red, all that are brown, and all that are black.

9) The teacher then points to one book and signs BOOK RED, repeating the statement two or three times and encouraging the class to imitate.

10) The teacher repeats step 9 with each book (BOOK BROWN, BOOK BLACK) or with each object of the same color (BOOK RED, CAR RED, PAPER RED, etc.).

11) The teacher then points to an object and through gestures and facial expression has the class (or individuals) produce the appropriate statement.

12) The teacher repeats steps 9, 10, and 11 for each group of objects.

13) The teacher then may repeat step 7—pointing to any object at random and expecting the class (or individuals) to respond with the appropriate statement—e.g. BOOK RED, CAR BLACK, PAPER BROWN, etc.

14) The teacher may then hold or point to a particular object (e.g. the red car) and ask a question—BOOK BLACK INDEX—and then answer NO (with negative facial expression and headshake). Then the teacher points to another object (e.g. the black pencil) and repeats the question—BOOK BLACK INDEX—and the answer—NO. This continues until the teacher points to the black book and then, of course, the answer is YES (with positive facial expression and head nod).

15) This question-answer process continues with the teacher encouraging the class to respond appropriately to the simple YES-NO questions.

c) *Interactive Presentation*—Once the class has correctly mastered the initial presentation, the teacher produces a series of commands or questions designed to reinforce and provide further exposure to the target items. In addition, new items can easily be introduced using this process. The teacher now goes through the following procedure:

1) The teacher points to a particular student (or uses his/her name sign[2]) and motions for that student to come to the front of the room.

2) The teacher signs BOOK RED, me-GIVE-TO-you and then hands the student the red book. The teacher repeats this action several times with several different object.

3) The teacher then signs to the student BOOK RED, you-GIVE-TO-me and if the student does not respond, uses gestures to help the student. This is

---

[2]Name signs can easily be established without use of the students' spoken NL. Once the teacher knows the students' names by having the students write them or even before the names are known, the teacher may 'assign' name signs based on physical characteristics of the students. The process for doing this is essentially the same as was outlined above—except that the students are used instead of objects. In the beginning phases of learning ASL, there is no reason why a student needs a name sign which is initialized.

repeated with the teacher requesting several different objects several times until the student responds quickly.

4) The teacher should call upon several students one at a time to participate in this exercise.

5) When a sufficient number of students have participated, the teacher may call two students to the front of the room.

6) The teacher will then sign to one of the students **PAPER RED, you-GIVE-TO-him/her.** After the first student has given the paper to the second student, the teacher signs to the second student **CAR BLACK, you-GIVE-TO-him/her** or **CAR BLACK, you-GIVE-TO-me.**[3] The teacher continues to give commands to the pair of students (mixing the commands appropriately) until the students respond readily.

7) Through gestures and facial expression, the teacher then encourages one of the students to give the commands. This can be done by the teacher pointing to one of the students and then standing next to the other student, arms folded, waiting for the command.

8) Once the student has given a few commands, the teacher should pick a third student to participate, and the teacher should observe the activity.

9) The teacher can then, through pointing and gestures, have one of the other students in the group of three begin to give commands.

10) The teacher can and should pick students from the class to replace one of the three students at the front of the room so that a sufficient number of students can participate.

11) After this activity has continued for awhile, the teacher may divide the class into groups of three or so and let each of the groups begin the activity. If this is done, the objects should be placed in a central location so that they are accessible to all groups, or the objects can be divided among the groups.

d) *Additional Comments*—Obviously, this interactive activity is not just limited to the signs **me-GIVE-TO-you, you-GIVE-TO-me, you-GIVE-TO-him/her.** There are many other verbs which can be introduced with this activity—e.g. ____-SHOW-TO-____, ____-BRING-TO-____, ____-THROW-TO-____, ____-PICK-UP-____, ____-PUT-DOWN-____. Also, the objects or pictures of objects can be varied so that this type of activity can occur in every class period. As the students acquire more vocabulary, the complexity of the commands can increase. Even in the early stages, it is possible to have complex commands, e.g. **BOOK RED, CAR BLACK, you-GIVE-TO-me; BOOK RED, you-SHOW-TO-me FINISH, THROW-AWAY; BOOK BROWN, you-SHOW-TO-him/her FINISH, you-GIVE-TO-me.**

---

[3]Certain verbs in ASL indicate their subject and object by changes in the direction of movement. We have chosen to represent the subject and object by using lower case glosses. Thus, the verb ____-GIVE-TO-____ can be signed **you-GIVE-TO-me, me-GIVE-TO-you,** etc. For more information see **Grammar and Culture** text, chapter IX, Subjects and Objects.

Among the advantages of this activity (aside from not using spoken English) is the fact that the students are placed in a situation where they are expected to respond to a command or a question with a particular behavior. This gives the teacher a very easy means of evaluating the class performance and the overall effectiveness of the activity. Another advantage is that vocabulary is acquired and used in a somewhat meaningful context. The fact that the students begin to develop receptive skills and to demonstrate these skills before extensive expressive work is also an important advantage.

Although this activity may seem quite long and time-consuming, with practice and experience it can be done rapidly and conducted with a large number of students in less than half an hour. Because it requires the students to attend to the teacher and to work with new target items from context, the activity generally produces a high level of motivation and interest among the students.

2. Picture Description Vocabulary Development

The purpose of this activity is to enable students to develop vocabulary by direct association with pictures of objects, people, moods, actions, etc. In addition, this activity exposes students to the manner in which events are described in ASL. For this activity, cartoon-like drawings or slides are especially effective. All description and interaction is in the TL.

a) *Preparation* — The teacher has selected several pictures which portray a variety of specific actions and a variety of 'characters'. From these pictures, the teacher develops a list of target vocabulary items to focus on during the class period. The teacher may wish to make an overhead transparency of each picture or copies of them for the class if they are too small to be seen easily. For example, one of the pictures might depict a small boy being spanked by his mother.

The target vocabulary would then include items such as **BOY**, **MOTHER**, **CRY**, **MAD**, **SPANK**, **HURT**, etc.

b) *Initial Presentation* — The teacher displays the first picture on an overhead projector and/or distributes copies to the class. After allowing the class a few seconds to study the picture, the teacher goes through the following process:

1) The teacher points to one of the main 'characters' in the picture and makes the appropriate sign (e.g. BOY), perhaps repeating the sign two or three times.

2) Through the use of gestures and a slight movement toward the class, the students are encouraged to imitate the sign (e.g. BOY).

3) Steps 1 and 2 are repeated for each of the main characters. In the sample picture, the only two characters are BOY and MOTHER.

4) The teacher then points to the first character and, through gestures and a questioning facial expression, encourages the class to produce the sign BOY.

5) When the class has produced the sign (or when the teacher has given the sign again), the teacher points to the next main character in the picture and repeats step 4.

6) This process is continued at random until all main characters are easily identified and the class produces the appropriate sign for each one (e.g. BOY, MOTHER).

7) The teacher then begins to describe the characters in the picture, one feature at a time. One effective way to do this is to set up contrasts or comparisons whenever possible. Thus, the teacher might sign BOY SMALL, MOTHER TALL; MOTHER SPANK, BOY CRY; etc.

8) After each description (e.g. BOY SMALL), the teacher may encourage the class to imitate.

9) After the characters have been described, the teacher may ask a series of YES or NO questions to which the class is expected to respond appropriately. Thus, the teacher might ask BOY TALL (the answer is NO) or MOTHER SPANK (the answer is YES), etc.

10) This question-answer process continues until the class responds readily and quickly and until each of the characters and targeted descriptions have been used several times.

11) At this point the teacher may move on to the next picture and repeat steps 1-10 for that picture. Normally, three pictures are sufficient for a single class and will avoid overloading the students.

c) *Interactive Presentation* — Once the class has correctly mastered the initial presentation, the teacher can then produce a series of commands or questions which will reinforce the target vocabulary and introduce new items. The teacher now goes through the following process:

1) The teacher calls one student to the front of the room.

2) The teacher may give the student a series of commands (e.g. YOU CRY YOU, YOU MAD YOU), or the teacher may proceed to step 3. Usually the decision about whether to give commands or not will depend on the pic-

tures the teacher has chosen and the types of commands which are possible.

3) The teacher signs **BOY** and points to the boy, then **MOTHER** and points to the mother. (This process continues for all main characters in the picture(s).)

4) The teacher then signs **BOY, WHERE** and, with a questioning facial expression, points to all or several of the characters in the picture(s), and then signs **WHERE** again.

5) If the student does not respond by pointing to the boy, the teacher points to the boy and signs **BOY**.

6) Step 4 is repeated until the student correctly identifies all the characters by pointing.

7) The teacher should call several students to the front of the room, one at a time, to allow them to participate in the activity.

8) This process continues until the teacher is reasonably sure that the students can respond appropriately to the **WHERE** questions.

9) The teacher then calls one student up to the front of the room and signs **CRY, WHO** with a questioning facial expression.

10) The teacher then points to the boy and signs **BOY CRY**.

11) The teacher then signs **TALL, WHO** with a questioning facial expression.

12) As before, the student is helped until s/he responds appropriately to the **WHO** questions.

13) Steps 6 and 7 are repeated but focusing on **WHO** questions.

14) When the teacher senses that the class has mastered these questions, s/he may wish to call on students at random and ask both **WHO** and **WHERE** questions of those students.

15) The teacher may wish to divide the class into pairs and have them ask each other questions. This is very easy if the teacher has provided copies of the pictures for the students to use. If this is done, the process to be followed is basically the same as was described in activity B.1. (Object/Picture Vocabulary Development), steps 5-11, except that only two students are involved, not three.

d) *Additional Comments*—Obviously, the target vocabulary and the types of questions and commands which can be given will be determined by the pictures which the teacher uses. It may be difficult to find pictures which show specific actions or contain certain character types. Consequently, the teacher may have to sketch pictures or find a friend or colleague who has artistic talent. However, the Sunday comic strips or comic books often provide a wide range of very useful pictures.

If the teacher must sketch his/her own pictures, stick figures and some easily recognizable symbols can be used for these purposes. For example, the drawings seen on the next page can be easily recognized by most people as a church, a school, a bank, a man, and a woman.

The point is that the pictures do not have to be professionally drawn. It is more important that the pictures are clear to the students and that they can be used to expand the students' vocabulary. If the teacher has the time, it is also easy to 'stage' pictures and then take slides or photographs to be used in class. The pictures will be especially clear to the students if they involve familiar places or events.

Using a variety of pictures, one may introduce quite a range of vocabulary items for people (family, father, sister, brother, policeman, secretary, soldier, dancer, etc.), places (store, school, church, restaurant, theatre, etc.), actions (walk, run, buy, want, tell, drink, eat, come, go, etc.), and emotions (happy, sad, mad, lonely, worry, sorrow, love, hate, etc.).

By making sure that the pictures themselves are clear and unambiguous and by periodically reusing certain pictures, the teacher can be sure that the students are acquiring vocabulary in a meaningful manner without relying on the use of spoken English (or the students' NL). With careful use by the teacher, it is possible for the students to rapidly develop a sizeable, working vocabulary in an exciting, challenging way.

3. Picture Sequencing

The purpose of this activity is to enable students to expand their vocabulary base and to continue development of their visual memory. This activity also exposes students to longer sequences of ASL—in a narrative format. All descriptions and interactions occur in the TL.

a) *Preparation*—The teacher selects several pictures which form a sequence of events. The Sunday comic strips are a good source of such pictures, especially any comic strip in which there is little or no dialogue, or any comic strip in which the drawings convey a clear meaning apart from any written dialogue. (In any event, the teacher should cut out or remove any dialogue so that the picture is the central focus). Some examples of comic strips which are especially good for this activity are:

> *Henry* by Don Trachte
> (has no dialogue)
> *Peanuts* by Charles Schulz
> (dialogue must be removed)

Nancy by Ernie Bushmiller
(dialogue must be removed)

Blondie by Young & Raymond
(dialogue must be removed)

Dropouts by Howard Post
(dialogue must be removed)

The Lockhorns by Bill Hoest
(captions must be removed)

Berry's World by Jim Berry
(dialogue may have to be removed)

Of course these are not the only possibilities. A careful reading of the Sunday comic strips will reveal many more usable sequences of pictures. Comic books are also an excellent source of pictures for this activity. Not all of the pictures in a given story need to be used—the teacher can discard pictures which are very similar to ones already chosen. Ideally, the teacher will end up with a sequence of 6-8 pictures. From these pictures, the teacher develops a list of target vocabulary items. As before, the teacher may choose to make copies of the pictures for the students. If a comic strip is used, each frame is cut out and pasted on a separate index card.

b) *Initial Presentation*—The teacher randomly selects one picture from a specific sequence story and displays a transparency of the picture on an overhead projector or displays the picture in such a way that the entire class can see it. The teacher then goes through the following process:

1) The teacher follows steps 1-10 for activity B.2. (Picture Description) explained above.

2) These steps are followed for each of the pictures in the sequence. The teacher should select pictures from a specific sequence at random and not in their actual order. (The reason for random selection of pictures at this time is to avoid presenting them in their actual order since the students will be sequencing the pictures later. Also, the concern of the teacher at this point is the target vocabulary, not the sequencing.) Since the same character(s) are often involved in each picture, this process will move quite quickly.

c) *Interactive Presentation* —

1) When the teacher is reasonably sure that the class is familiar with the main target items, s/he calls one student to the front of the class.

2) The teacher then spreads out all of the pictures in a given sequence (generally there are about 6-8 pictures per sequence) on the desk or chalkboard ledge.

3) The teacher will then sign a brief, but full description of one of the pictures in the sequence (e.g. **CANDY, BOY SMALL EAT, WALK, EAT, WALK**) and through gestures (or perhaps signs like **you-PICK-picture**) and appropriate facial expression, encourages the student to choose the appropriate picture.

4) The teacher continues with step 3 for several pictures. In some cases, the teacher may add other target items that are new to the student. For example, in the description given in step 3, if there are no other instances of the boy walking or eating and the teacher has previously introduced the sign **EAT** (through step 1), then it is reasonable to assume that the student can select the appropriate picture from the description given in step 3. In addition, the student will be exposed to the sign **WALK** in such a way that it is relatively clear what the sign means.

5) The teacher should call up several students one-by-one to allow for maximum participation.

6) At this point, the teacher may wish to have the students give descriptions to each other. If so, the process is the same as B.2. (Picture Description), step 15 above.

7) When the teacher feels that the students are readily able to select single pictures from a brief description, s/he calls one student to the front of the room.

8) The teacher then signs the descriptions for two or three of the pictures in a sequence and, through gestures (possibly signs, by this time) and facial expression, encourages the student to select and arrange the pictures in the order described. (The order of description does not necessarily have to be the order of the actual sequence. However, the teacher must make sure that the order in which the student arranges the pictures is the same as the order of description.)

9) The teacher returns the pictures to their original positions. S/he then describes a new set of pictures for the student (or a different student). This time, however, the teacher increases the number of pictures described by one or two. So, if in step 8 the teacher described three pictures, s/he will now describe four or five pictures.

10) The process of increasing the number of pictures described continues until all the pictures in a sequence are used.

11) The teacher may then wish to call on a student to describe a particular sequence of three, four or more pictures. If so, the process is basically the same as described above.

d) *Additional Comments* — There are, of course, several variations to this activity. If the teacher has provided copies of the sequence of pictures to the entire class, then each student can select and/or arrange his/her own set of pictures according to descriptions given by the teacher. It is still helpful, in this case, for the teacher to call one student to the front of the class since this will provide a focal point for the activity. If students have their own set of pictures, the teacher should quickly check the class performance after each of the more difficult selection/arrangement tasks.

Since in most sequenced picture stories, the same 'character' appears in all frames, the class is encouraged to focus on any new or unusual action or behavior in each frame. This, in turn, will enable the teacher to focus instructional activity on those places where it is most likely that additional target items will be needed and noticed—the new or unusual action or behavior.

One of the major benefits of this activity is that students are exposed to longer segments of the TL and, because of the sequencing of pictures, can more readily and easily focus on new target items. In addition, if each student has a set of pictures, the entire class can become actively involved in the activity—which will increase attention, enthusiasm, and motivation.

4. Object Manipulation

The purpose of this activity is to expand the student's vocabulary base by direct association and manipulation of objects. In addition, a behavioral response by the student permits the teacher to gauge student comprehension. For this activity, a doll house with furniture, dolls, and other 'extras' are quite effective. The Fischer-Price Company manufactures several toy sets which are very helpful—e.g. sets with a house, gas station, farm, etc., as well as furniture, families of dolls, animals, cars, trucks, etc. A visit to any toy store will also supply the teacher with countless other possibilities to be used in this activity.

a) *Preparation*—After the teacher has purchased or borrowed a set of toys, s/he develops a list of target vocabulary which will include the various 'characters', places, actions, etc., which can be derived from the toy set. The teacher should also develop a list of descriptions of certain actions which the class will be able to act out by manipulating the dolls (e.g. **CAR, FATHER GET-INTO-CAR, CAR-DRIVE-AWAY**).

b) *Initial Presentation*—The teacher displays the toy set and all the objects on a table or desk so that the class can see them all. The teacher then goes through the following process:

1) The teacher picks up or points to one of the toy characters or places. If the class is familiar with the sign for that object (e.g. **BOY**), the teacher may ask the class to produce the appropriate sign.

2) If the class is not familiar with the sign or does not remember, the teacher produces the sign two or three times and encourages the class to imitate the sign.

3) Steps 1 and 2 are repeated until all objects and places have been identified or labeled. Occasionally, the teacher will want to go back to the beginning just to review for the class. It is helpful to do this several times to ensure that the class retains the signs for the various objects.

4) The teacher can, of course, provide a more detailed description of the characters (e.g. **GIRL, HAIR YELLOW, DRESS RED**). In fact, this may be necessary if there are two or more 'objects' which are similar in appearance.

5) The teacher can also use the **YES/NO** questioning technique which was discussed above. This technique, however, can be expanded. Instead of sim-

ply pointing to an object (e.g. a boy) and then asking the students a YES/NO question (e.g. **INDEX GIRL INDEX**), the teacher can ask more complex YES/NO, RIGHT/WRONG questions. For example, the teacher can place the 'mother' and 'dog' in the 'car' and ask **CAR, FATHER DOG THOSE-TWO INSIDE** and the class is encouraged to respond appropriately—NO or **WRONG**. Thus, the content of the question can become more complex.

c) *Interactive Presentation*—Once the class has correctly mastered the initial presentation, the teacher then produces a series of commands or statements which students are to 'act out' using the toys. This provides the opportunity for additional vocabulary development. The teacher goes through the following process:

1) The teacher calls a student to the front of the room.
2) The teacher has the student turn around so that s/he cannot see the toys.
3) The teacher then manipulates certain objects so that the rest of the class can see (e.g. the teacher might place the father and mother in chairs in front of a T.V. set).
4) The teacher makes sure that the class has seen this and then returns the objects to random positions on the table or desk.
5) The teacher then has the student turn around, facing the objects.
6) The teacher signs a command or statement to the student (e.g. **TV, FATHER MOTHER SIT they-LOOK-AT-tv**).
7) The teacher then encourages the student (through gestures or signs) to select and arrange the objects according to the command or statement.
8) If the student is correct, s/he turns around and steps 2-7 are repeated with a different command or statement.
9) If the student is wrong (e.g. s/he forgot that father and mother should be sitting), the teacher has two options:
   a. Either repeat the statement for the student, focusing on the portion that was forgotten or wrong; *or,*
   b. Ask other members of the class if the student is right or wrong. One member of the class is chosen to explain in sign what is wrong (e.g. **FATHER MOTHER SIT**).

   Since the class has seen the teacher manipulate the objects in the appropriate way (step 3), they are quickly able to focus on any errors, and since they have seen the teacher give the command or statement (step 6), they can quickly focus on that part of the statement which the student did not understand or which s/he forgot.
10) Through gestures or signs, the teacher encourages the student to manipulate the objects and give a command or statement (i.e. the student now assumes the role of teacher). This can be done by having the teacher point to the student and then gesture as if manipulating objects. The teacher can then point to him/herself and gesture that s/he will turn around.

11) The teacher turns around while the student manipulates the objects (as in step 3). At the appropriate time, the teacher turns back, facing the objects and the student. The student then signs a command or statement (as in step 6).

12) The teacher manipulates the objects according to the student's command or statement.

13) During this portion of the activity, the teacher may wish to deliberately make some errors in manipulating the objects. The reason for this is to encourage the student to re-state a portion of the command/statement. The teacher may also wish to re-state the student's command/statement just before manipulating the objects. This will give the teacher an opportunity to slightly change the command/statement as a way of checking or testing the student.

14) The teacher should replace the student periodically so that several students can participate in the activity.

15) After several students have participated, the teacher should call up two students to conduct the activity. One student will give commands/statements and the other will manipulate the objects. The students can alternate giving commands/statements. This will enable the teacher to observe the activity and make judgements about student performance.

16) If the teacher has a sufficient number of objects, the class can be divided into pairs so that the entire class can participate simultaneously.

d) *Additional Comments* —The definite advantage of this type of activity is that the teacher is provided with a quick and easy way of judging whether or not students comprehend the message. In addition, by using a variety of sets of toys, the teacher can provide a wide range of new and needed vocabulary items to increase the students' vocabulary base. As was mentioned earlier, there are a variety of toys that can be used in this activity. (A note of caution: while some board games can also provide similar interactive, response-manipulation activities, most of them take too long to play and the amount of interaction does not justify using them in most cases. In addition, the action with most board games is not fast enough to maintain class interest.)

The crucial factor for a teacher to remember in selecting a set of toys for this activity is that there must be a sufficient number of pieces or locations in the toy set so that a wide range of commands/statements is possible. If a large number of possibilities does not exist, then the activity can become boring and repetitious. However, a large number of possibilities will enable the students to use their creativity and spontaneity.

While the teacher may feel some initial reluctance at using an activity which involves the use of toys (doll houses, etc.) with adults, s/he will find that the students do not at all feel insulted or degraded by the use of such toys. In fact, most students will find this activity very enjoyable and non-threatening. In addition, the fact that student performance (either giving commands or statements or manipulating objects) is clearly visible to the class provides an excellent opportunity for each class member to test or evaluate his/her own skills. Certainly, the ability to self-evaluate is one mark of a successful language learner. Finally, any time an individual can influence the actions of other people, or any time that understanding another person's communication can be clearly demonstrated, then motivation and personal satisfaction are greatly increased.

5. Referential Tasks

The purpose of these activities is to place the student in a situation where s/he must duplicate a specific item from a set of items (either by selecting, drawing, or constructing that item) based only on a description. As with the object manipulation activity, this activity provides a concrete way for both teacher and student to readily measure the student's understanding of particular vocabulary items and grammatical constructions. There are three types of student responses — selection, drawing, or constructing. The type of response will depend upon the type of activity the teacher selects. Because of this, each type of activity will be described separately.

5.1 Referential Selection Task

a) *Preparation* — The teacher prepares a set of pictures or photographs — usually 10-12 pictures per set. Each of the pictures in the set should be as similar as possible but should differ from the others in only one way (e.g. 10 pictures of a group of people; in each picture the people are in a slightly different arrangement). This is to make sure that the students will focus on the total description and to make the task more challenging. The teacher makes a clear copy of this set of pictures. The teacher now has two sets of identical pictures. (Instead of pictures, the teacher can also use a set of objects such as glasses or books if they are similar in all respects but one.)

b) *Initial Presentation* — After the teacher has prepared two identical sets of pictures, photographs, or objects, s/he arranges each set in a random fashion on a table or desk. Between the two sets, the teacher places a 'blind' (a screen of some sort so that a person sitting in front of one set cannot see the other set). This can easily be done with the pictures, photographs, or objects arranged on a rectangular table (one set at each end) with a sheet of paper or cardboard placed in the middle. After placing the blind between each set, the teacher goes through the following process:

1) If many of the vocabulary items are new to the students and the teacher feels that the class will not be able to figure out the meanings of these items within the context of a description, then s/he will have to go through the

vocabulary introduction steps outlined for other activities (e.g. activity B.1., steps 1-7).

2) If the teacher feels that the students can handle the new vocabulary from context, or if the vocabulary is familiar to the students, or after the teacher has completed step 1, s/he then calls one student to the front of the room.

3) The student is seated at one end of the table in front of one set of pictures, photographs, or objects. The teacher stands at the other end of the table.

4) The teacher picks up one picture, photograph, or object and holds it near the blind (the piece of cardboard across the middle of the table) so that the class can see it, but the student seated at the other end of the table cannot see it.

5) The teacher puts down the picture, photograph, or object. Then the teacher signs a very detailed description of that picture, photograph, or object to the student who is seated while the rest of the class watches.

6) When the teacher is done, s/he encourages the student (through gestures or signs) to select the appropriate picture, photograph, or object from the identical set on the table in front of the student.

7) If the student selects the appropriate picture, photograph, or object, the teacher then holds up both the original and the student selection so that the student can see that s/he was correct.

8) If the student selects the wrong picture, photograph, or object, the teacher either repeats the description (in full or in part) or calls upon another student to repeat the description. Since the rest of the class has seen the targeted picture, photograph, or object (step 4), the description (step 5), and the picture, photograph, or object selected by the student, class members can easily focus on the reason(s) for the wrong selection.

9) The teacher then repeats steps 2-8 with the same student or with different students. Each time, the teacher selects a different picture, photograph, or object to describe.

c) *Interactive Presentation*—After several students have been involved in the initial presentation, the teacher calls two students to the front of the room and goes through the following process:

1) One student is seated at the end of the table. S/he will select the pictures, photographs, or objects.

2) The other student will give the descriptions and stands at the opposite end of the table.

3) The teacher then picks up a picture, photograph, or object for the student to describe (as in step 4 above) or allows the student to do so.

4) The remainder of the process is the same as above, except that the teacher is an observer.

5) As the activity continues (with different students involved periodically), the teacher should change sets of pictures, photographs, or objects in order to keep the activity stimulating.

5.2 Referential Drawing Task

a) *Preparation* — The teacher collects a set of 10-15 cartoon-like drawings (usually humorous drawings work best with this activity). After making sure that the students are familiar with most of the vocabulary, the teacher will arrange the pictures from the easiest to the most difficult (i.e. the simplest drawing to the most complex). The pictures should be as varied as possible and cover a wide range of activities and situations. The teacher should bring blank paper and pencils for the students to use. The teacher should make sure that the students do not see the pictures beforehand.

b) *Initial Presentation* — After the teacher has prepared a set of pictures, s/he then stands at the front of the room and goes through the following process:

1) The teacher distributes paper and pencils to the class.
2) Through gestures or sign, the teacher explains that s/he will describe a picture, the class is to watch the description and then draw the picture.
3) When the class understands the task, the teacher then chooses one of the easiest pictures and describes it in detail to the class. (The use of a file folder is helpful to prevent the class from seeing the picture before the description.)
4) When the teacher is finished, the class then draws the picture based on the description.
5) When the class is finished, the teacher shows the original picture to the class and compares it with the student drawings.
6) If appropriate, the class can discuss any misunderstandings or misinterpretations of the description.
7) The teacher describes three or four pictures in this manner.
8) The teacher then selects a picture, places it in the file folder and calls a student to the front of the room.
9) The student is instructed to describe the picture to the class.
10) The teacher should join the class in drawing what the student describes. This is a good check on the accuracy and level of detail of the description. The teacher should be careful to draw only what is described and not fill in any gaps in the description.
11) When the class is finished, discussion can occur on two levels: the appropriateness of the description and the level of understanding of the description.
12) Another student is chosen and steps 8-11 are repeated enough times to ensure maximum class involvement.
13) The teacher may wish to divide the class into pairs in order to increase the opportunity for class involvement. If so, the process is basically the same — i.e. one student describes, the other draws, and the teacher is free to monitor each pair.

5.3 Referential Construction Task

a) *Preparation* — The teacher obtains two sets of Tinker Toys, Lincoln Logs, Lego Blocks, or similar set of toys. With one set, the teacher builds a variety of objects or models. These objects or models should range from very simple to very complex ones. The teacher lists for him/herself the target vocabulary which the students are unlikely to acquire from context. The teacher then places all of the objects or models in a box so that they will not be seen by the class.

b) *Initial Presentation* — After the teacher has finished this preparation, s/he places the box with the objects or models on one end of a table and dumps out the remaining set of Tinker Toys, Lincoln Logs, or Lego Blocks at the other end of the table. The teacher then puts up a blind (a screen of some sort described above) in the middle of the table and goes through the following process:

   1) If there is any target vocabulary that the teacher feels cannot be acquired from context and must be pre-taught, s/he does so using steps described above.

   2) When step 1 is completed or if there is no vocabulary that must be pre-taught, the teacher calls one student to the front of the room.

   3) The student is seated at the end of the table in front of the scattered Tinker Toy pieces.

   4) The teacher takes one object or model from the box and holds it near the blind so that the student cannot see it, but the rest of the class can see it.

   5) The teacher then describes how to build the object or model step-by-step (e.g. the first step might be to collect all the pieces that will be needed, the second step might be to build the foundation, and so on).

   6) When the student is finished, both the original and the student-made model are held up so that the student can see if s/he was correct.

   7) The teacher calls several students up, one at a time, and repeats steps 3-6.

c) *Interactive Presentation* — After several students have participated in the Initial Presentation, the teacher goes through the following process:

   1) The teacher calls two students to the front of the room.

   2) One student is seated at the end of the table in front of the scattered Tinker Toy pieces. The second student stands on the other side of the blind.

   3) The teacher takes an object or model from the box (making sure that the student does not see the others in the box) and places it near the blind.

   4) Through gestures or signs, the second student is directed to describe step-by-step how to build the object or model so that the first student can build it.

   5) The teacher observes the activity and is able to make judgements and comments about student performance.

   6) Steps 1-5 are repeated with several students until there has been sufficient class participation.

   7) If the teacher has enough objects or models and enough Tinker Toy pieces, the class can be divided into pairs for the activity.

Additional Comments on Referential Activities:

As with any activity, there are many variations that are possible. For example, it is possible to permit the students who are selecting, drawing, or constructing to ask questions for clarification during the descriptions. It is certainly more difficult to do these tasks without asking questions. The teacher may begin by allowing questions and then, as the students become more skilled, prohibit any questions.

Another variation is the use of a third student as a 'blind'. Thus, for example, one student might be placed out in the hallway with a picture or model to describe; a second student in the classroom doorway, and the third in front of the chalkboard or Tinker Toy pieces. The student in the hall cannot see the student in front of the chalkboard or the Tinker Toy pieces. The student in the doorway must relay all messages between the two students. Apart from involving more students, this variation is a good way to check the memory and level of understanding of the student in the doorway. Also, since the class cannot see the student in the hall they are kept in suspense.

A third variation is that the teacher does not show the class the picture or model that is to be described. In other words, the teacher does not do step 4 of the Selection activity or step 4 of the Construction activity. This forces the class to focus on the description and keeps the class in a state of suspense.

The purpose of all of these referential activities is that there is a definite end product which the students must match based only on signed directions or descriptions from the teacher or another student. Other activities which have similar goals are equally helpful (e.g. one student gives directions for making a cake and another must follow those directions). The point is that the students are engaged in some type of communication which has a definite concrete, observable outcome. This enables self-analysis and evaluation and also maintains a high level of excitement and interest in the class.

C. Summary

The activities discussed above create structured situations in which the student is placed in some concrete communicative activity. His/Her level of comprehension is immediately recognized and can be immediately reinforced or corrected. Likewise, the student has the satisfaction of knowing that it is possible to understand and to demonstrate that level of understanding without the use of spoken English. The student can also express him/herself and then gain immediate feedback as to whether or not s/he can be understood by others.

Thus, the role of the teacher in all these activities is to structure situations in which the students have the *need* to communicate about something fairly concrete and in such a way that the communication results in some *observable action or behavior*. This creates an environment which motivates, encourages, and rewards the students for their attempts to communicate in ASL.

Chapter VI

Teaching ASL Without the Use of Spoken English: Dialogues and Drills

A. Introduction

Before discussing the preparation and presentation of a dialogue, it is useful to consider a few general characteristics of dialogues.

The main purpose of a dialogue is to enable the students to use freely and appropriately very common forms (both lexical and syntactic) of the TL in order to convey their own ideas. The basic process is that the students memorize and utilize a carefully developed set of TL sentences which form a natural, meaningful conversation. If the teacher focuses only on memorization and repetition, very little active, meaningful participation (and therefore very little attention) is required of the students. The teacher must be aware that memorization and repetition of a dialogue is simply a means to an end. That end is the students' use of sections of the dialogue in actual, meaningful situations with another person.

A dialogue is used in class for several reasons: to focus on a specific grammatical feature of the TL, to introduce new vocabulary, to focus on conversational behaviors in the TL, and to introduce certain cultural values of the TL community.

1) Grammatical Features

Since a dialogue, by definition, involves the use of sentences in a conversational format, it is quite obvious that certain grammatical features will have to be used in the dialogue. Generally, an attempt is made to focus on one main grammatical feature in each dialogue. (Of course, other grammatical features will have to be used, but the one that the dialogue focuses on should be the most frequently occurring feature). The reason for this is to provide the students with several realistic, natural examples of a specific TL feature which the students are likely to encounter and which they should know how to understand and use. The focus, then, is on a specific grammatical feature which occurs frequently in the dialogue.

In order to motivate the students, the dialogue should be composed of sentences which are natural and which represent the most useful aspects of a grammatical feature (i.e. those aspects with high functional yield) but not necessarily every possible example of its use. This means that if there are ten different uses of a specific grammatical feature, only the most frequent ones should be included in a dialogue (and possibly it will require several separate dialogues to do this). Those less frequent uses can be handled later when the student has had more experience in the TL. To attempt to include all uses of a grammatical feature in a dialogue will almost always result in an unnatural, artificial dialogue which will have little or no practical value for students. Also, such an attempt will result in a very unrealistic topic for the dialogue which will have little motivating value for the students.

In order to make sure that the students are aware of the meaning of the dialogue and have some understanding of the grammatical feature which the teacher wishes to focus on, it is necessary to provide some advance information to the students. This information should be of two types: first, a brief written explanation (in summary form) of the grammatical feature in the dialogue which the students should attend to, and second, a written summary of the dialogue.[1]

The written explanation of the grammatical feature is necessary so that students (most of whom will be adults) can begin to consciously apply what they already know about the TL to this particular feature. This explanation is also helpful because it provides the students with some general guidelines about specific grammatical features of the TL. Certainly, more detailed information can be given to the students at appropriate times. However, in order to deal with a dialogue, in-depth explanation is not needed and may only serve to confuse the students.

The written summary of the dialogue is necessary so that the students have an understanding of the context in which the dialogue occurs. Such contextual awareness is very important in helping students understand the appropriate uses of lexical items and grammatical features. If, for example, someone says in English "I think it came up yesterday", it is important to know the context to determine the appropriate meaning. That is, the sentence could have several meanings depending on the context—e.g. a hospital ('The swelling appeared yesterday'), an office ('The order was delivered yesterday'), a garden ('The plant grew yesterday'), etc. Thus, the written summary should provide the student with whatever level of detail is necessary to understand the context (e.g. peoples' names, roles, occupations, the place, time of day, the reason for the conversation or meeting).

If the teacher decides to distribute scripts of the dialogue, these scripts should be given to the students by using written English glosses for signs. There are several reasons for this: first, the use of glosses avoids the need for relying on English translations of ASL sentences. To translate one ASL sentence in a dialogue might require several English sentences in order to list all of the ways to express the ap-

propriate meaning in English (e.g. the ASL sentence <u>EAT FINISH, GO</u> *brow raise* might be translated 'When I'm done eating, I'll go', 'After I eat, I'll go', 'I'll leave when I'm done eating', 'I'll go when I've eaten', etc.). If all of these possibilities are not listed, then the student may formulate a very narrow, limited idea of the appropriate use and meaning of the ASL sentence. The use of glosses means that the teacher does not have to worry about providing all possible translations. Rather, the

---

[1]See pages 85–87 for an example.

student focuses on the meaning and not the ways that English might represent that meaning.[2]

A second reason for using English glosses instead of translations is that generally a gloss coupled with a detailed summary will provide the student with sufficient information to understand the dialogue. The student is, thus, encouraged to function as much as possible in the TL. Without having to deal with the NL as an intermediary step, the student is free to focus on how meaning is expressed in the TL in a clearly specified context.

A third reason is perhaps much more subtle but nonetheless extremely important. The use of translations in English may convey to many students the idea that there is a direct correspondence between ASL signs and English words. That is, students may begin to think that a sign represents an English word instead of representing a specific meaning. This is a common problem with many Sign Language books which are on the market. The student sees a drawing or illustration of a sign and is given an English word to represent that sign. However, the English word many times does not reflect the precise meaning of the sign. For example, in most sign books, the sign UP-TILL-NOW is generally labeled with the English word 'since'. However, this sign UP-TILL-NOW has a much more limited range of meanings than the word 'since'. For example, the sign does not mean 'because' (as in, 'Since you're so hungry, let's eat now'). Thus, the use of a gloss forces the teacher to be much more accurate in

UP-TILL-NOW

dealing with the meaning of signs and this, in turn, reduces possible confusion or misunderstandings on the students' part.

When using glosses, however, the teacher must inform the class (in writing) of the fact that glosses represent signs and not English. This point must be clearly stated, otherwise it is possible that students will think that glosses represent English and perhaps will develop inappropriate attitudes toward ASL ('ASL is bad English', 'ASL is broken English', etc.). To avoid this, the students must understand that glosses are used because, at present, there is no convenient, accurate way of writing ASL.

2) Introduction of New Vocabulary

A second reason for using a dialogue is to introduce new vocabulary. As was discussed earlier, students are more likely to retain and understand things that they must struggle to understand on their own. This is especially true of vocabulary items. A dialogue places the student in a situation where s/he is aware of the context

---

[2]Of course the use of glosses does not entirely solve this problem. Glosses, after all, are English words used in a somewhat specialized manner. As such, they have a built-in meaning for the person who reads them. Thus the gloss SUBSCRIBE might be appropriate when talking about magazines but that gloss is not accurate in English (although it is used) when talking about receiving a pension check or a Social Security check. However, the sign in ASL is the same in both cases. After some thought, it may be possible to find a more accurate gloss, e.g. RECEIVE-REGULARLY. But this often demands much thought and it is not always possible to find a gloss which is completely accurate.

and, in almost all cases, many of the vocabulary items. Given the detailed summary which should accompany any dialogue, the student is in a position to begin to make logical deductions about the meanings of vocabulary item s/he may not know. Consider the following example where contextual information can lead to understanding a new vocabulary item.

—a nurgek is very hard

(You now know that a nurgek is not a sponge, a foam rubber ball, chocolate pudding, or anything soft.)

—a nurgek is shiny

(You now know that a nurgek is not a blackboard, a tree, a rug, or anything dull.)

—a nurgek is very expensive

(You now know that a nurgek is not a plastic spoon, paper, milk, or anything that is inexpensive.)

At this point, you have narrowed the possible meanings of 'nurgek' to something that is very hard, shiny, and is very expensive. Although you may not know exactly what a nurgek is, you know what it is not. Thus, you are able to narrow the list of possible meanings by eliminating things that don't fit what you already know about a nurgek. With additional information you can finally decide what a nurgek is.

—a nurgek can cut glass

Now, what is something that is very hard, shiny, very expensive, and can cut glass? Of all things in the world, only one can fit all of those characteristics—a diamond. Thus, by providing more and more specific information about a new lexical item, it is possible to lead the student to the point where s/he can formulate the appropriate meaning(s) from available contextual information.

The point here is that instead of providing the students with a list of vocabulary items and their meanings, it is often much more effective to structure the context so that the student can figure out for him/herself the appropriate meanings and uses of vocabulary items. As was discussed above, this creative struggling on the part of the student leads to longer retention and a much more meaningful understanding of vocabulary items in the TL. In addition, forcing the student to derive meanings from context is excellent preparation for the student since s/he will be in similar situations when communicating in the TL outside the classroom. Certainly this ability to derive meaning from context is a skill which is vital to successfully learning any language. Even a native speaker of a language must rely upon this skill since it is impossible to memorize all the meanings and nuances of every vocabulary item in any living language.

Successful vocabulary learning occurs when the student is aware not only of the meaning(s) of specific vocabulary items but, just as importantly, is aware of when it is appropriate to use those vocabulary items. Knowing when to use certain vocabulary items is important for attaining native-like competence in any language. Aside from preventing some potentially very embarrassing situations, this knowledge is necessary to avoid misunderstandings. Consider, for example, the English expression 'Right on!'. A student who is learning English as a second language must learn not only what the expression means but also when it is appropriate to use it. Thus, a student who knows the meaning of this expression, but not when to use it, is likely to use it at the wrong times with the wrong people (an important business meeting, for example). The same is true for any language. Thus, the student of ASL must learn both the *what* and the *when* of vocabulary items. One way to accomplish both is through the use of carefully written, well-presented dialogues.

3) Conversation Regulators

Another reason for using dialogues is to help the students learn certain conversational behaviors in the TL which may be different than conversational behaviors in the student's NL. This is why the language needs to be demonstrated in as natural a context as possible. One such natural context is a conversation or dialogue. Indeed, the goal of communicative competence in ASL is measured by how well a student can participate in a conversation.

In order to use the language in this context, the student needs to learn a special set of eye and body behaviors, called "conversation regulators", which are used by Deaf people during conversations in ASL.

Conversation regulators are specific behaviors that people use to signal to each other what they want or plan to do during the conversation—e.g. keep talking, interrupt, etc. Most people are not aware that they and others are using these signals. Yet, if someone is not appropriately responsive to these signals or does not use them correctly, conflicts may arise in which people become uncomfortable or angry with each other.

For example, in conversations between English speakers, if the person who is talking ends a statement with what is called 'open inflection' (i.e. the pitch is level, neither raised or lowered) and does not look at the listener (the Addressee), this signals the Addressee that the person who is talking is not finished and wants to continue. If the Addressee is not responsive to this signal and instead, begins talking, the Speaker feels 'cut off'. If the Addressee does this repeatedly during the conversation, the Speaker may become angry and feel that the Addressee is not interested in what the Speaker has to say.

Conflicts can easily occur between Deaf and hearing participants in a conversation because they may be unconsciously using different kinds of regulators and, therefore, are not responsive to each other's signals. For example, many signals used by hearing people involve the voice (e.g. 'clearing one's throat' to show you want to begin talking) and, thus, are not effective in conversations with Deaf people. Hearing people need to learn the regulators used by Deaf people—signals geared to vision, rather than sound.

There are two sets of conversation regulators—those used by the Speaker[3] and those used by the Addressee. Obviously, since people 'take turns' in conversations, they frequently switch roles back and forth between being the Speaker or Addressee

---

[3]In this context, the word 'Speaker' refers to the person who is signing.

and use the regulators that are appropriate for their role. Speakers use regulators to signal that they want to (a) begin a conversation, or (b) continue their turn and not be interrupted, or (c) end their turn and the Addressee can begin a turn. Addressees use regulators to signal that they are willing to (a) let the Speaker begin a conversation, or (b) remain 'silent' while the Speaker continues his/her turn, or (c) that they want to begin a turn. Addressees also use regulators to show that they are following the conversation and to signal how they are responding to the communication of the Speaker.

What are some Speaker and Addressee regulators used by Deaf people during conversations? As explained below, understanding how Deaf signers take turns in a conversation requires an awareness of where their eyes are looking and where their hands are located. Unlike conversations between hearing people, communication cannot take place unless the Addressee is watching. This single fact makes eye gaze the most powerful regulator in signed conversations since it determines when a person can 'speak' *and* be 'heard'. The location of the hands is also very important since signs are made in a specific area, called the "signing space". This area approximates a circle extending from the waist to about 6″ above the head, with the diameter determined by the signer's lax arm spread on both sides, as illustrated below. Thus, moving one's hands toward or into the signing space (especially the area in front of the body) signals a desire to begin or continue a turn. Moving one's hands away from the signing space or keeping one's hands out of the signing space signals a desire or willingness to be the Addressee.

Signing Space

How does a signer begin a conversation? Since a signer can't communicate until the potential Addressee is watching, the signer must first get his/her attention.

There are several ways to do this. When the desired Addressee is relatively close by, the signer may wave a hand up and down in the direction of the Addressee or lightly touch his/her arm and then wait until the person looks toward the signer (initiator). If seated at a table, the initiator may tap the table so that the vibrations get the Addressee's attention. If the Addressee is further away, the initiator may use a larger hand wave (either sideways or up-and-down) or may get the attention of someone else near the desired Addressee and that 'third person' will then get the Addressee's attention and point to the initiator so that the Addressee knows who wants to talk with him/her. When there is a large group of people and the initiator wants to get everyone's attention, s/he may flick the light switch or get several people's attention through handwaving and then ask them to help in getting everyone else's attention. This 'facilitation' by other people in helping to get someone's attention is very common in the Deaf community.

There are several types of errors commonly made by hearing people with respect to getting someone's attention. In the beginning, before the hearing person really understands that it's useless to sign if no one is watching, s/he may just begin signing without trying to get the Addressee's attention or may unsuccessfully try to get the Addressee's attention and then begin signing. Either way, no communication is taking place and the hearing person then feels frustrated and, perhaps, foolish. Another common error involves the use of attention-getting devices which may be inappropriate, such as stamping on the floor, overly aggressive jabs at the Addressee, or unnecessary 'flailing' at the Addressee (Deaf people are generally sensitive to movement and usually do not require frantic waving!), or waving a hand right in front of the Addressee's face (which is considered rude). Finally, because hearing people are generally unaccustomed to having to 'work' to get another person's attention (i.e. usually just beginning to speak is adequate), they frequently become impatient when initially unsuccessful in getting the other person's attention. Sometimes that person is involved in doing something else, and the initiator will have to wait until the desired Addressee is ready to give his/her visual attention to the initiator. Here it is important for the hearing person to understand that it's more demanding to require one's visual attention than one's auditory attention (i.e. it usually disrupts any other activities the Addressee may be involved in, since many daily activities require vision), and the hearing person needs to become sensitive to this difference.

When the initiator (Speaker) has been successful in getting the Addressee's attention, the Addressee will maintain constant eye gaze toward the Speaker (on the face) until they switch roles or something interrupts them[4].

---

[4]Since many daily activities require vision, there is some give-and-take in this "constant eye gaze". For example, if the Addressee is eating, s/he may momentarily look down—at which point the Speaker should pause until the Addressee looks up again. However, apart from such occurrences the Addressee is expected to maintain constant eye gaze on the Speaker's face, using peripheral vision to 'read' the manual signs.

How does the Speaker signal that s/he wants to continue 'speaking' (without interruption) after a short pause? Sometimes during a conversation, the Speaker needs to pause for a moment to think about what to say next, and does not want to lose the 'floor' (the turn). To signal this intention, the Speaker will not look at the Addressee (so the Addressee cannot begin signing/communicating) and will keep his/her hands in the signing space in front of the body. The Speaker may also either hold the last sign made or may 'fill' the pause with facial or hand movements that indicate thinking, such as furrowing his/her brow or wiggling his/her index finger or all the fingers.

How does the Addressee signal that s/he is paying attention and that the Speaker may continue? Addressees need to give feedback to the Speaker that they are following and responding to what is being signed. To do this, the Addressee will maintain eye gaze on the Speaker while using various facial or head movements to show how s/he is responding. Occasionally, the Addressee may also offer short signed feedback, such as **RIGHT, WOW,** or **TRUE** which do not interrupt the Speaker, but act as a response. (However, generally, the Addressee will keep his/her hands out of the signing space (or resting on the body) so as not to distract or 'threaten' the Speaker with any indication that s/he may try to interrupt.)

How does the Speaker signal that s/he is about to finish (or has finished) speaking? Speakers signal that they are finishing their signing turn by looking back at the Addressee (so that the Addressee can begin signing) and by moving their hands out of the signing space. The Speaker may also decrease his/her signing speed. In addition, the Speaker may call for a response from the Addressee by (a) lowering his/her hand(s) with the palm facing up, (b) pointing to the Addressee with a questioning facial expression, (c) raising and/or holding the last sign made (if a question has been asked), or (d) simply looking at the Addressee with a questioning expression.

How does the Addressee signal that s/he wants to begin signing? Addressees signal their desire to begin a turn by moving their hand(s) (and possibly head or body) toward or into the signing space. Positioning the hand(s) with the palm up also signals a desire to speak. Addressees may also point at, touch, or wave a hand in front of the Speaker if the Speaker does not stop signing. If the conversation is animated and they are competing for turns, the Addressee will likely look away from the Speaker as soon as s/he has the Speaker's attention and begin signing. Now the Addressee has become the Speaker and 'holds the floor' by not looking at the new Addressee (until s/he wants to check for feedback). Another aggressive way to 'get the floor' is to start signing, repeating the first few signs until the Speaker looks over, and then immediately looking away while continuing to sign.

Except among good friends while joking, an Addressee should never try to grab the Speaker's hands to keep them from signing in order to 'get the floor'. This is considered quite rude and is like putting one's hand over a hearing person's mouth!

Problems with 'Mixed' Groups —Special problems often arise when several Deaf and hearing people are interacting in Sign together because they have learned somewhat different sets of conversation regulators and because these regulators are fairly unconscious behaviors and, therefore, hard to control. One all-too-frequent problem arises when a hearing person uses his/her voice to signal a desire to speak either before or as s/he begins signing (e.g. saying 'Yeah' or 'Uh . . .'). This attracts the attention of the other hearing people who then look at the hearing initiator. However, since the Deaf people do not hear the vocal signal, they miss the beginning of that person's comments and are hindered from being able to effectively follow the conversation. Often a Deaf person may begin a turn, thinking that s/he has the floor, only to find that a hearing person has already claimed it by using his/her voice. Clearly, the way to avoid such problems is for the hearing people to learn and use *visual* signals only, and not use vocal signals.

However, some Deaf people who are accustomed to interacting with hearing people have developed ways of taking advantage of those people's hearing when competing for the floor! That is, the Deaf person knows that sound will attract the hearing person's attention. So the Deaf person may say something (getting the hearing person's attention) and look away, continuing to sign so that the hearing person will be forced to stop signing and watch! (Here we leave it to the hearing person to complain, laugh along, or learn to ignore sounds while signing!)

An awareness of the conversational regulators used by Deaf people is important if the student is to achieve communicative competence in ASL. This awareness will help to avoid embarrassing moments and will help to lessen student frustration. One effective way for the students to learn to recognize and use these regulatory behaviors is through the use of dialogues.

4) Cultural Awareness

The fourth reason for using a dialogue is to introduce certain cultural values of the TL community to the students. A language is shared by a group of people who, for the most part, also share the same culture. The customs, habits, ideas, knowledge, beliefs, etc., of a group of people has a definite impact on the language of that group of people. This is obvious in such different things as the vocabulary of a language, the general topics of conversation, the humor of a group, etc.

Before it is possible to appreciate and fully use the TL and to communicate effectively and easily with the TL community, a student must have an awareness of, and a respect for, the TL culture. Without respect for a community and its culture, it is not possible to become truly competent in the language of that community.

This means that students of ASL must become aware of the many people, organizations, events, etc., which influence the Deaf community. Some of these are: state schools, the NAD, the *Deaf American*, TTY's, the NTD, interpreters, captioned films, deaf clubs, attitudes toward hearing people, etc.

By using some of these as topics of dialogues, students not only acquire exposure to and practice in ASL, but also begin to learn some of the cultural values of the Deaf community. Of course, the only really effective way to learn about the culture of a group of people is to spend a large amount of time with members of the community. By doing this, the 'outsider' may become accepted as a member of the community (i.e. s/he may be enculturated). When, and if, this happens, the individual begins to share in and learn more about the culture of the community. However, before an individual can be accepted by a particular group, s/he must be trusted by that group of people. Certainly one way to indicate trustworthiness is to have a high degree of respect for the TL and the TL culture.

B. Writing a Dialogue

It is important for the teacher to realize that dialogues must be carefully prepared and practiced before they can be effectively used in class. This is to ensure that the students will obtain maximum benefit from the dialogue and that the teacher is aware of what crucial elements should be focused on in the class. The following guidelines are suggested for preparing dialogues.

1) As much as possible, a topic for the dialogue should be selected which relates to the TL culture in order to make the dialogue meaningful and helpful to the students.

2) If the dialogue is used to focus on a specific grammatical feature, then that feature should occur several times throughout the dialogue. This is to enable students to have multiple exposures to that feature in context.

3) The dialogue should be as natural as possible. This means that the topic of the dialogue and the grammatical features used must be presented in as natural a way as possible. In other words, do not try to force too many different things into the dialogue or it will become obviously artificial. In addition, all vocabulary items should be used and produced as naturally as possible (which is not necessarily the way the signs are illustrated in books). In short, the dialogue should be about things that people really communicate about, presented in the way people really communicate.

4) Only two signers should be used for the dialogue. At more advanced levels it is possible to have prepared group dialogues, but generally the two-person dialogue works best. This is because it is easier for the students to follow (and thus to focus on the targeted grammatical features) and, as will be discussed later, it is easier for the teacher to present.

5) The dialogue should be divided fairly evenly between the two signers. This is to ensure that a true dialogue (and not a monologue) will take place. Also this ensures that certain regulatory behaviors can be demonstrated through the dialogue.

6) For dialogues with beginning students, the sentences should be fairly short until the students are ready for longer and more complex sentences. In addition, the dialogue itself should be fairly short for beginning students. An appropriate length is about five turns (not necessarily five sentences) for each signer. This is an average of 10 turns per dialogue.

7) The teacher should develop this dialogue in ASL. This means that the teacher should *not* first write the dialogue in English and then translate it to ASL.

Such an approach most often results in sentences which are more like English than ASL.

8) The dialogue should be written using glosses in order to assist the teacher in the presentation stage (and the students if the teacher decides to hand out the glossed script).

9) After the dialogue has been glossed, the teacher should try to verify the dialogue with a consultant—a native Deaf signer. This is to ensure that the dialogue is valid and represents a natural dialogue. This 'second opinion' is important (even if the teacher is Deaf, and especially if the teacher is hearing) in order to make sure that the dialogue is a natural, fair sample of ASL. Of course, all consultants should be compensated for their services.

10) A brief summary of the dialogue, explanation of the context, and other needed pertinent information should be written and given to the students (along with the glosses if the teacher wishes).

C. Presenting a Dialogue

In presenting a dialogue, there are several basic steps which must be followed, as well as several optional steps. Of course, access to videotape equipment is desirable since the dialogues can be taped and then can be viewed several times. Also two signers can be used in making the tape which will expose the students to different signing styles. If, however, the teacher does not have access to videotape equipment, then the next best thing is a live consultant who can present the dialogue with the teacher in front of the students. If either of these two options are not possible, then the teacher must present the entire dialogue him/herself. This is not the most desirable situation, but through the use of space and body shifts, it can be clear to the students that the teacher is playing both parts of the dialogue. In any event, it is vital that the teacher (and any consultants that might be used in the presentation) thoroughly rehearse and memorize the dialogue so that it can be presented as naturally as possible. In presenting the dialogue in class, the following steps should be taken:

1) Teacher hands out the written summary of the dialogue (and the script in gloss—if desired) and gives the class time to read through the summary.

2) If the dialogue is on tape, the full dialogue is shown to the class. If a consultant is used, then s/he assumes the role of one signer in the dialogue and the teacher assumes the other. If the teacher must assume both roles, this can be done by appropriately shifting the body when assuming each role (e.g. shift to the left when becoming signer A, and to the right when becoming signer B). Regardless of which option is used, the full dialogue is presented to the class at a normal rate of speed. This is very important because a slower rate of speed will tend to distort the rhythm and other production factors. Also, the students must begin to develop their receptive skills for ASL produced at normal rates.

3) When the full dialogue has been presented, the teacher signs the first sentence. The class then imitates the teacher. It is important that the teacher not use too much time at this point trying to correct every production error the students might make. The correction will come in successive stages. When the class produces a reasonable approximation of the first sentence, the teacher signs the second and class imitates. This process continues for the full dialogue.

4) When the class has completed step 3, the teacher calls one student to the front of the room. The teacher shows the student a gloss script of the dialogue (or the student brings his/her own). The teacher then starts the dialogue with that student. The teacher signs the first turn, the student the second and so on. At this point the teacher can make a few suggestions to help correct any errors. The teacher should repeat this process with several students and should alternate roles (i.e. with the first student the teacher signs part A; with the second, the teacher signs part B, and so on). The rest of the class watches in order to continue to develop their receptive skills.

5) When several students have participated in step 4, the teacher calls two students to the front of the room and assigns each one a role in the dialogue. At this point, the teacher can step back and watch more intently for possible errors. If the teacher notices errors, they should be handled at the end of the particular sentence by simply signing the full sentence correctly and having that student repeat.

6) When several students have participated in the dialogue in front of the room, the teacher can divide the class into pairs. Each person is given a specific role in the dialogue—either A or B. The teacher is free to move from pair to pair making corrections and offering suggestions on an individual basis.

7) After a sufficient amount of time, and after each student has practiced his/her role in the dialogue two or three times, the students should then switch roles and again practice the dialogue two or three times.

Additional Comments—If the teacher has access to videotape equipment, it is highly desirable to videotape the particular dialogue the class will be working with beforehand. If this is done, native Deaf signers should be used as models whenever possible. In videotaping a dialogue, both signers should be visible throughout the conversation. This will enable the students to see the conversation regulatory behaviors which were discussed earlier. As an additional variation, the teacher may wish to tape only one half of the dialogue to allow students to practice with the tape. If so, the following process is used:

1) Both of the models sign the dialogue at a fairly normal rate of speed. (With videotape the students can view the same dialogue several times; so speed is not a significant factor if the image is clear.)

2) The camera should focus on only one of the signers (e.g. signer A) and should be framed so that it appears that the signer is communicating directly to the

viewer. The best way to achieve this effect is to tape signer A by placing the camera slightly to the right or left of signer B and as close as possible. Thus, signer A is fully visible but signer B is only partially visible on the screen. A fairly natural time period is built into the tape when students respond with the other half of the dialogue (e.g. signer B's part).

3) The process should be repeated but this time the other half of the dialogue is taped with signer B in full view and signer A in partial view.

The use of the half-dialogue technique allows the students to interact with the videotape in a somewhat controlled situation. Since the time allotted for a response has been 'built-in' by a native Deaf signer, the student has an indication of whether s/he is approaching conversational rate. In addition, since only one signer is seen fully on the screen, this allows for a more direct dealing with certain regulatory behaviors (even if the signer starts before the student finishes, this can be a valuable experience for the student—learning to anticipate turn-taking). Such 'half-dialogues' can be used with the class as a whole, with small groups, or with individual students. In using the tape the teacher basically follows the process in steps 3 and 4 above. The advantage of the tape is that the teacher is free to focus on student production and to make any necessary suggestions or comments.

Sample Dialogue:

A. Synopsis:

Pat and Lee are having dinner at a restaurant. Pat asks Lee if s/he has read the *Deaf American* magazine. Lee replies that his/her subscription stopped last year and s/he hasn't paid to renew it. Pat says that Lee should renew the subscription because now the cover of the magazine is new—the artwork and the color. It's different than the old magazine. Lee asks to see it. Pat replies that s/he left it home. This morning s/he read it for a half an hour and hasn't finished yet. Lee says that maybe next week s/he will join the National Association of the Deaf (NAD) and subscribe to the *Deaf American*. Pat states that after joining the NAD then Lee can go to the convention which is held every two years. Lee says that s/he has gone occasionally and that s/he will go to the convention two years from now. Pat asks why. Lee responds that at the convention two years from how, the NAD will have a centennial (100 year) celebration.

B. Cultural Information:

The *Deaf American* is a magazine that is published monthly (except a joint July-August issue) by the NAD. This national magazine contains items of interest to the Deaf community such as: interviews with Deaf persons, sports results, general interest articles, legislation-related projects and activities, etc. This publication, along with newsletters published by state NAD chapters or local clubs, helps members of the Deaf community keep up with what is happening in the community on a national and local level.

The National Association of the Deaf (NAD) began in 1880 at the First National Convention of Deaf-Mutes in Cincinnati, Ohio. The first president of the NAD was Robert P. McGregor of Ohio. In 1952, the NAD opened its first home office in Chicago. In 1960, the Junior NAD was established to provide Deaf young people with training in citizenship and leadership. In September, 1964 the home office of the NAD was re-located to Washington, D.C. The name of the NAD publication was changed from the *Silent Worker* to the *Deaf American*. In 1964, the NAD decided to hire a full-time Executive-Secretary — Frederick C. Schreiber. In 1969, the NAD began publishing books and articles on deafness, the education of deaf people, manual communication, etc. In 1973 the NAD moved into its present location, the Halex House, in Silver Spring, Maryland. Currently, the NAD has 17,000 members.

C. Dialogue[5]

(Pat) 1.   *q*
       FINISH READ-*paper* DEAF AMERICA YOU

           neg   *t*
    (Lee) 1. ONE-YEAR-PAST, ME RECEIVE-REGULARLY,

                        t   *neg*
       STOP,, ME me-PAY-TO-rt, AGAIN

(Pat) 2.   *t*
       SHOULD,, NOW DEAF AMERICA COVER, NEW +,,

                t
       ART, COLOR, DIFFERENT*

    (Lee) 2. SEE-SEE +

(Pat) 3. *neg*
       LEAVE-*deaf american-rt* HOME INDEX-*rt*,

       MORNING ME READ-*paper* HALF-HOUR,,

                  neg
       NOT-YET FINISH

---

[5]In the transcription of this dialogue, we have used several notation conventions which are explained in detail in the companion text on grammar and culture. In brief, words in capital letters stand for signs. When the letters in a word are separated by hyphens, it means the word is fingerspelled. When words are separated by hyphens, it means the ASL sign requires more than one English word to translate it; those hyphenated words represent one ASL sign. The letters '*rt*' stand for 'right'; '*lf*' for 'left'. The letters or words written above a line refer to non-manual grammatical signals that occur with all of the signs transcribed below the line. Seen in this dialogue, the letter '*q*' represents the signal for a 'yes-no question'; '*neg*' for 'negation'; '*t*' for 'topicalization'; '*br*' for 'brow raise'; '*nod*' or '*nodding*' for those head movements; '*mm*' for a particular non-manual adverb; and '*wh-q*' for 'wh-word question'. Other symbols seen in this dialogue are: a comma—used to indicate a clausal boundary; a double comma—used to indicate a sentence boundary; a plus sign—used to indicate repetition of a sign; an asterisk—used to indicate stress on a sign; and '*(2h)*'—meaning the sign is made with two hands.

$$\overline{}^{\,t}$$
(Lee) 3. ONE-WEEK-FUTURE,

MAYBE ME   *me*-PARTICIPATE- IN-*cntr* N-A-D,,

$$\overline{}^{\,nodding+br}$$
ME RECEIVE-REGULARLY D-A

(Pat) 4. $\overline{\text{PARTICIPATE-IN-}nad \text{ FINISH,}}^{\,nodding\,+br}$ $\overline{\text{CAN}}^{\,nod}$

(gaze rt   ) $\overline{\text{RIGHT}}^{\,nodding\,+q}$
GO-TO-rt MEETING EVERY-TWO-YEAR,,

$$\overline{}^{\,nodding\,+\,mm}$$
(Lee) 4. ME GO-TO-*lf* ONCE-IN-A WHILE,,

$$\overline{}^{\,t}$$
TWO-YEAR-FUTURE, ME GO-TO-*lf*

(Pat) 5. $\overline{\text{TWO-YEAR-FUTURE, WHY}wg}^{\,wh\text{-}q}$

$$\overline{}^{\,t}$$
(Lee) 5. THAT-ONE-*lf* TWO-YEAR-FUTURE, N-A-D
        *(2h)*THRILL ONE HUNDRED YEAR CELEBRATE

(Pat) 6. $\overline{\text{"THAT'S-RIGHT"}*}^{\,nod}$

Notice how this dialogue meets the criteria for successful dialogues discussed earlier:

1) The topic relates to the TL culture.
2) The specific grammatical feature—Time Signs—occurs at several places in the dialogue.
3) The dialogue is fairly natural and likely to occur.
4) Only two signers are used—Pat and Lee.
5) The dialogue is evenly divided between the two signers.
6) The sentences are relatively short.
7) The dialogue was developed in ASL—not translated from English.
8) Glosses are used to aid the teacher.
9) The dialogue has been verified with a native, Deaf consultant.
10) A summary and other pertinent information have been provided.

If the teacher decides to distribute copies of the dialogue to the class, then it is advisable to provide the students with the summary and dialogue on one sheet of paper. The cultural information should be on a separate sheet of paper. This will greatly facilitate matters when and if the students need to 'read' the dialogue.

The targeted vocabulary includes not only lexical items which relate to the structural feature (i.e. Time Signs) but also several new items. Thus, introduction of new vocabulary is not limited to items which relate to the targeted structural feature. In addition, each of the sentences in the dialogue can be used in a variety of additional class activities, such as dialogue-related drills.

D. Dialogue-related Drills

With any motor skill and with any second language, a certain amount of guided repetition and practice is helpful in attaining proficiency. This may be especially true with ASL since, as was mentioned before, the majority of students will be required to use their bodies in ways which are unfamiliar and strange to them. Guided repetition and practice can help students gain the muscular coordination and comfort level needed to become proficient in ASL. Drills are one type of activity which provide this guided repetition and practice while still maintaining class interest and motivation.

In using drills, there are several general principles which the teacher should remember. These principles are basically intended to help the teacher (and student) gain the most benefit from any time spent in a drill situation.

General Principles: Drills

1) Although helpful, repetition alone cannot and does not lead to communicative competence in any language. Communicative competence implies the creative use of a language while repetition is simply imitation of something created by someone else. Thus, the teacher must not rely upon any form of drill as the sole source of reinforcement or practice. Drills should supplement a wide range of other classroom activities.

2) If the teacher repeats a sign (to help students correct production problems), then the repetition should occur within the context of a sentence in order to be most beneficial to students. This means that the teacher must avoid any approach which focuses only on the repetition of isolated signs. Students' interest and motivation is generally much higher when they are presented with meaningful situations and contexts—things that they can make sense of and know will be helpful in conversations outside the classroom.

3) Repetition should be presented so that it demands a fair amount of student attention. However, tasks or activities which are very predictable or are conducted in a predictable fashion generally do not require much attention and therefore lead to boredom. The teacher must make sure that any drills used do not become boring.

4) Increased attention takes energy. This means that a properly conducted drill will lead to a certain amount of student fatigue. When the students reach that point of fatigue in a given class period, drills lose their effectiveness and the teacher should shift to a different type of activity. This means that the teacher must be sensitive to student responses—not only the accuracy of the response but also the students' alertness and quickness to respond.

5) As much as possible, drills should be based on material covered elsewhere in the lesson. In this way, students begin to view drills as supplemental and not

as something completely unrelated. Also, by using sentences from a dialogue, for example, as the starting point for a drill, the teacher helps to unify that lesson for the student.

These are general principles which apply to all types of drills. Depending upon the particular drill-type, there are additional principles which the teacher should be aware of. In brief, however, the basic aim of any drill is a certain amount of practice with a specified grammatical feature and targeted vocabulary items in as controlled and rapid a way as possible.

There are two general types of drills: mechanical drills and manipulative drills. *Mechanical drills* are highly controlled and structured and are used to practice certain forms or structures in the language. In mechanical drills, there is generally only one correct response. This means that students do not create their own responses but rather focus on and imitate responses created by the teacher. Mechanical drills provide feedback for the teacher on some important areas of production in the TL. In such cases, the focus is on the students' ability to respond quickly and accurately.

Manipulative drills are controlled to some extent, but the student must rely on his/her knowledge of the TL to respond correctly. Generally, there is more than one correct response although one response may be more appropriate than others. The general goal is that the response be grammatically correct and be meaningful in that context. In order to accurately complete these drills the student must be aware of the grammatical structures used and the content of the message. This means that some short, grammatical explanation (in printed form) may be necessary for manipulative drills.

1) **Mechanical drill types:**

a) *Simple repetition:* The students repeat the target sentence (the cue) exactly. The teacher signs a sentence and the class repeats it as a group, for example:[6]

T (Teacher): $\overline{\text{YESTERDAY ARRIVE HOME}}^{\,t}$, TIRED

C (Class): $\overline{\text{YESTERDAY ARRIVE HOME}}^{\,t}$, TIRED

T: $\overline{\text{TOMORROW}}^{\,t}$,   GO-TO NEW-YORK

C: $\overline{\text{TOMORROW}}^{\,t}$,   GO-TO NEW-YORK

etc.

Notice that the sentences are not necessarily related to each other except that they both involve the use of an initial time indicator. This type of simple

---

[6]In the companion **Grammar and Culture** text, the sign glossed here as YESTERDAY is glossed as ONE-DAY-PAST; the sign glossed here as TOMORROW is glossed as ONE-DAY-FUTURE.

repetition is helpful, for example, in going through a dialogue or in first introducing a new grammatical structure. Another approach is for the teacher to
randomly call on individual students and have them repeat the target sentence, e.g.:

$$\overline{\hspace{7cm}}^{\,t}$$

T (Teacher): YESTERDAY ARRIVE HOME, TIRED

$$\overline{\hspace{7cm}}^{\,t}$$

S₁ (Student): YESTERDAY ARRIVE HOME, TIRED

$$\overline{\hspace{2cm}}^{\,t}$$

T: TOMORROW,   GO-TO NEW-YORK

$$\overline{\hspace{2cm}}^{\,t}$$

S₂: TOMORROW,   GO-TO NEW-YORK

etc.

For more advanced students, simple repetition drills may seem rather boring. However, they can be challenging if the length of the target sentence is
increased and if the teacher includes a short lead-in sentence to provide some
context for the repetition. The student does not have to repeat the short lead-in
sentence:

T: **NOW SUMMER VACATION**

$$\overline{\hspace{2cm}}^{\,t}$$
TOMORROW, DRIVE-TO NEW-YORK,

STAY-THERE ONE-WEEK

$$\overline{\hspace{4.5cm}}^{\,mm}$$
TOUR-AROUND SIGHT-SEE

$$\overline{\hspace{2cm}}^{\,t}$$
S₁: **TOMORROW,   DRIVE-TO NEW-YORK,**

STAY-THERE ONE-WEEK

$$\overline{\hspace{4.5cm}}^{\,mm}$$
TOUR-AROUND SIGHT-SEE

$$\overline{\hspace{3cm}}^{\,cs}$$
T: FEW-DAYS-AGO ME SICK,

$$\overline{\hspace{5.5cm}}^{\,t}\ \overline{\hspace{1cm}}^{\,rhet.q}$$
YESTERDAY ARRIVE HOME, TIRED, WHY,   WALK++

$$\overline{\hspace{5.5cm}}^{\,t}\ \overline{\hspace{1cm}}^{\,rhet.q}$$
S₂: YESTERDAY ARRIVE HOME, TIRED, WHY,   WALK++

etc.

In presenting repetition drills, the teacher should have a prepared list of target
sentences (10-12 is usually sufficient). The teacher should also move through the

drill rather quickly and not use too much time trying to correct every error. There will be ample opportunity for the students to gradually improve their performance in a less frustrating manner. If a particular student is having difficulty, the teacher may sign the target sentence again and have the student repeat it again, but then should move to the next target sentence.

b) *Single Slot Substitution:* This type of drill requires both class (C) and individual student (S) response. As such, it is a good way for the teacher to get feedback on individual student performance while still involving the class. In a single slot substitution drill, one item or slot is chosen by the teacher and the students go through a process of replacing or substituting other items in that slot, e.g.:

$$t$$
T: $\overline{\text{YESTERDAY ARRIVE HOME}}$, **TIRED**

$$t$$
C: $\overline{\text{YESTERDAY ARRIVE HOME}}$, **TIRED**

T: **ANGRY**

$$t$$
S_1: $\overline{\text{YESTERDAY ARRIVE HOME}}$, **ANGRY**

$$t$$
C: $\overline{\text{YESTERDAY ARRIVE HOME}}$, **ANGRY**

T: **HUNGRY**

$$t$$
S_2: $\overline{\text{YESTERDAY ARRIVE HOME}}$, **HUNGRY**

$$t$$
C: $\overline{\text{YESTERDAY ARRIVE HOME}}$, **HUNGRY**

etc.

This drill should also move quite quickly. If the teacher notices a student (e.g. S_1) has a problem either in production of the sentence or in where to make the appropriate substitution, the teacher should sign the full sentence with the appropriate substitution so that the student can imitate. Then the teacher should signal the class to imitate. Later in the drill, the teacher may wish to call on that student again.

In writing a single slot substitution drill, the teacher should make sure that the cues (the words used to substitute) are clear and unambiguous. For example, in the English sentence 'Girls like sports', the cue 'boys' is not clear because a student could respond either 'Boys like sports' or 'Girls like boys'. Both choices are correct, but the teacher may not have wanted or expected one of them. Such ambiguity can be confusing to students. In mechanical drills there should only be one correct, logical response.

Finally, the last substitution should result in the same sentence that was used to start the drill. This helps the teacher and the students to know when the drill with that sentence is finished. It also prevents one sentence from being over-used (generally 8-10 substitutions per sentence is sufficient). The target sentence may be chosen from a dialogue or in some other way related to other class activities.

Sample Single Slot Substitution Drills:

Target (or Head) Sentence:

$$\overline{\text{YESTERDAY,}}^{\;t}\quad \text{FATHER ARRIVE HOME,}\quad \text{TIRED}$$

Cues: ANGRY
                                                                                     HUNGRY
                                                                                     DIRTY
                                                                                     HAPPY
                                                                                     SAD
                                                                                     SICK
                                                                                     THIRSTY
                                                                                     TIRED

Target (or Head) Sentence:

$$\overline{\text{ONE-WEEK-PAST MOVIE,}}^{\;t}\quad \overline{\text{NOT-LIKE (ME)}}^{\;neg}$$

Cues: BOOK
               DRAMA
               SCHOOL
               MEETING
               WORK
               MOVIE

With more advanced students, of course, the item which changes can be longer and more complex. The process is the same as above; however, the task becomes appropriately more challenging for more advanced students.

c) *Double Slot Substitution:* This drill type is identical to Single Slot Drills (b) except that instead of replacing only one item, two somewhat related items are replaced. The process of presenting the drill is the same as above except that the teacher gives both cues to a single student. In writing a double slot drill, the teacher must be aware of the need for clarify in the cue items, for example:

Target (Head) Sentence:

$$\overline{\text{HOUSE,}}^{\;t}\quad \text{MOTHER WANT PAINT RED}$$

Cues:
CAR   WHITE
FENCE   BROWN

ROOM	**YELLOW**
BOAT	**GREEN**
TABLE	**ORANGE**
CAR	**BROWN**
CHAIR	**PURPLE**
HOUSE	**RED**

Notice that the elements can occur more than once if they are in different combinations. Thus, **CAR** occurs twice — once in combination with **WHITE** and once with **BROWN**; **BROWN** occurs twice — once in combination with **FENCE** and once with **CAR**. Not all sentences can become Target (Head) Sentences for a double slot substitution drill, unlike single slot substitutions where almost any sentence can become a target sentence.

d) *Multiple Slot Substitution:* This drill involves the replacement of one item at a time in the target (head) sentence, as in the single slot drills. The difference is that the cue item may occur in a different 'slot' with each response. The process of presenting the drill is the same as above. As each new item is substituted, the sentence changes and remains that way until a new substitution is made in that slot. The target (head) sentence may be drawn from a dialogue or other class activity, e.g.:

Target (Head) Sentence:

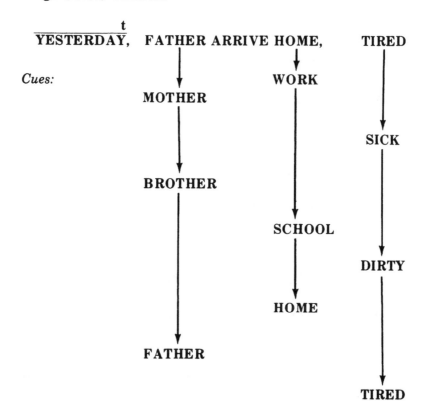

As with all drills, the teacher should make sure that the cues are clear and unambiguous. Also, with movable slot drills, the teacher must make sure that the sentence continues to make sense as substitutions are made. In the example above, the fourth substitution produces the sen-

tence $\overline{\text{YESTERDAY}}^{\;t}$, BROTHER ARRIVE WORK, SICK (remember the sentence continues to change with each new substitution). This sentence does make sense and is likely to occur in a natural context. If any cue will produce a sentence that does not make sense or is unlikely to occur naturally, it is a bad cue and should not be used.

2) **Manipulative Drill Types:**

a) *Expansion drills:* The student is required to take a target sentence (modeled by the teacher) and to restructure the sentence to include new information (supplied by the teacher). These drills are especially helpful in dealing with time signs, adjectives, adverbs, and certain questions. The presentation process is essentially the same as it is for substitution drills, except that the cue is not substituted but rather added to the target sentence. The student relies upon his/her knowledge of the TL to add the cue in the appropriate location in the target sentence or to re-state the sentence to fit the information provided by the cue, for example:

T: $\overline{\text{INDEX GIRL}}^{\;t}$,   HAVE BALL

C: $\overline{\text{INDEX GIRL}}^{\;t}$,   HAVE BALL

T: **RED**

S_1: $\overline{\text{INDEX GIRL}}^{\;t}$,   HAVE BALL RED

C: $\overline{\text{INDEX GIRL}}^{\;t}$,   HAVE BALL RED

T: **CUTE**

S_2: $\overline{\text{INDEX GIRL CUTE}}^{\;t}$,   HAVE BALL RED

C: $\overline{\text{INDEX GIRL CUTE}}^{\;t}$,   HAVE BALL RED

etc.

The student must rely upon his/her knowledge of the TL in order to formulate a meaningful sentence. If the student produces a non-meaningful sentence or one which is syntactically incorrect, the teacher models the correct sentence and has the student imitate before the class imitates.

Sample Expansion Drills:

Target (Head) Sentence:

$$\overline{\underset{\text{BOY,}}{\overset{t}{\rule{2em}{0.4pt}}}}\quad \text{WANT BICYCLE}$$

Cues:	BLUE
	RIDE
	ONE-WEEK-PAST
	SMALL
	SAD
	TWO

Target (Head) Sentence:

$$\overline{\underset{\text{BROTHER,}}{\overset{\qquad t}{\rule{4em}{0.4pt}}}}\quad \text{ARRIVE HOME}$$

Cues:	ONE-WEEK-PAST
	ANGRY
	TUESDAY
	TWO
	YOUR
	SMALL

The teacher has two options with an expansion drill—either the sentence can become longer as each new element is added appropriately or the new element can simply be added to the target sentence only. Thus in the first sample drill, the second expansion could be either **BOY WANT RIDE BLUE BICYCLE** or **BOY WANT RIDE BICYCLE**. If the teacher decides to use the longer expansion drill, then s/he must make sure that the sentence makes sense at all points and that none of the cues are ambiguous.

b) *Completion drills:* In completion drills, the teacher provides a cue which is a partial sentence. The student must then complete the sentence with something that makes sense for that sentence and that is syntactically correct. These drills help the student to move from highly structured drills where s/he has no control of response content to a situation where the student can begin to express his/her own thoughts. These drills are most helpful in dealing with contrasts of time or certain structural patterns. In the beginning levels, the completion can consist of a single sign, and for more advanced levels, it can be an entire phrase.

The process can be the same as other drills: $T \rightarrow S_1 \rightarrow C \rightarrow T \rightarrow S_2 \rightarrow C$, etc., or the teacher can eliminate the class response and simply have individual students complete the sentence cues. The only criteria for an acceptable response are that it must make sense and it must be syntactically correct, for example:

Sentence Cues:

$$\overline{}^{t}$$
T: TOMORROW,   ME GO-TO *(student response)*

$$\overline{}^{t}$$
S₁: TOMORROW,   ME GO-TO *NEW-YORK*

$$\overline{}^{t}$$
T: ONE-YEAR-PAST,   ME BUY *(student response)*

$$\overline{}^{t}$$
S₂: ONE-YEAR-PAST,   ME BUY *HOUSE*
etc.

Sample Completion Drills:

Sentence Cues:

$$\overline{}^{t}$$
MY MOTHER,   HAVE COOKIE

$$\overline{}^{t}$$
TOMORROW,   MY SISTER BIRTHDAY

$$\overline{}^{t}$$
GIRL SMALL,   WALK HOME

YESTERDAY ME SEE BIRD

$$\overline{}^{t}$$
ONE-YEAR-PAST,   JOHN BUY CAR

BROTHER ENJOY PLAY BASKETBALL

$$\overline{}^{nodding}$$
MARY WANT JOIN BUT STUCK SICK

JOHN SKILL BASKETBALL,   BASEBALL LOUSY

$$\overline{}^{rhet.q}$$
BABY CRY,   REASON,   MOTHER SPANK

M-A-R-Y AGE 35,   DISBELIEVE ME DISBELIEVE

$$\overline{}^{t}$$
KNOW-THAT JOHN,   WANT MOVE-TO CALIFORNIA

$$\overline{}^{t}$$
YESTERDAY FEEL SICK,   TODAY,   HEADACHE DISAPPEAR

The length of the item which completes the sentence is dependent on the creativity and skill of the students. With more advanced students, the teacher can encourage longer and more complex responses. Again, the minimal criteria of acceptable performance is that the response be syntactically correct and that it make sense in that context.

c) *Transformation drills:* In transformation drills, the student is required to take the cue sentence and transform (change) it so that it has a different meaning. The teacher must stipulate how the students are to transform the cue sentences. The process of presentation is basically the same as discussed above. The teacher specifies a particular transformation (change) that the students must produce (e.g. question, negation, command, etc.). From that point on, the process is essentially $T \rightarrow S_1 \rightarrow C \rightarrow T \rightarrow S_2 \rightarrow C$, etc. The teacher can then change the required transformation and repeat the process. Obviously, the students must possess some knowledge of the various structures that they will be asked to produce. This means that transformation drills can only occur after the students have had exposure to (and possibly explanation of) some grammatical feature. An example of the process involved in conducting a transformation drill is:

Feature: Negative Transformation:

Sentence Cues:

T: <u>TEXAS,</u> (t) ME WANT GO-TO

S₁: <u>TEXAS,</u> (t) ME <u>NOT-WANT GO TO</u> (neg)

C: <u>TEXAS,</u> (t) ME <u>NOT-WANT GO-TO</u> (neg)

T: <u>MY CAR,</u> (t) SMALL

S₂: <u>MY CAR SMALL,</u> (q) <u>NOT</u> (neg)

C: <u>MY CAR SMALL,</u> (q) <u>NOT</u> (neg)

etc.

Sample transformations and sample sentence cues:

Feature: Negative Transformation:

Sample Cues:

<u>MY FATHER,</u> (t) HAPPY

<u>TOMORROW,</u> (t) MOTHER COME HOME

<u>YESTERDAY,</u> (t) WALK HOME (ME)

<u>ONE-YEAR-PAST,</u> (t) FAMILY GO-TO EUROPE

<u>SATURDAY,</u> (t) WATCH FOOTBALL T-V

Feature: Question Transformation:

Sample Cues:

$$\overline{\text{MY FATHER,}}^{\;t}\quad\text{HAPPY}$$

$$\overline{\text{YESTERDAY,}}^{\;t}\quad\text{JOHN WORK ALL-DAY}$$

$$\overline{\text{ONE-YEAR-PAST,}}^{\;t}\quad\text{FAMILY GO-TO EUROPE}$$

$$\overline{\text{JANE,}}^{\;t}\quad\text{WANT JOIN GROUP}$$

$$\overline{\text{BOSS HIS CAR,}}^{\;t}\quad\text{BREAK-DOWN}$$

Notice that some of the same cues can be used for different transformations. This is not always possible but, when it is, it is helpful to the students because it will focus attention on the particular syntactic structure in question. Of course, a teacher will not be able to use all possible transformation drills at any one time. The drills are useful to reinforce particular behaviors that the teacher wishes to focus on in a specific class. For example, the question transformation drill above is helpful in reinforcing the particular non-manual behaviors that are needed for forming questions in ASL.

Transformation drills can vary from relatively easy ones as shown above to much more complex transformations (e.g. **WHO, WHAT, WHEN, WHERE, HOW,** etc.). The level of difficulty will be determined by the sentence cues which the teacher provides and the results which the students are expected to produce.

These are just a few of the major types of drills. Some of the texts in the bibliography contain additional types of drills which are worth investigating (e.g. question-answer drills, guided reply drills, two and three stage drills). Regardless of which type of drill the teacher uses, there are a few general principles which should be remembered:

a) Mechanical drills are intended to help a student practice a particular pattern.
b) Mechanical drills should be conducted at a rapid pace.
c) Mechanical drills should involve the whole class in responses as much as possible.
d) Mechanical drills are well suited for homework assignments.
e) Manipulative drills cannot be conducted at a rapid pace since the students are focusing on content *and* meaning, not just form or a pattern.
f) The teacher should insist on a full statement (not just a phrase) as an acceptable response in a manipulative drill.
g) In certain manipulative drills, the teacher should react to student responses in a natural manner.

The main goal of dialogues and drills is to have students practice specific patterns with as little teacher signing as possible. When the teacher does sign, a normal signing speed should be used. If the teacher has to slow down for some reason, s/he should immediately repeat the sentence at a normal rate.

It is also helpful in some cases for the teacher to use a student's name sign before introducing the next cue. This will keep the activity moving and also alert the student to his/her turn. In any event, the teacher should take whatever steps are needed to keep the dialogue or drill moving rapidly. This will maintain class interest and make the activity much more exciting for the class.

E. Summary

Dialogues and drills provide one means of placing students in a structured situation in which, for the most part, the content is controlled. This enables the students to focus on what a particular syntactic feature(s) looks like and how it should be produced. Dialogues also provide one means for the teacher to introduce cultural information about the Deaf community as well as key conversational behaviors. In writing dialogues and drills, it is important that the teacher check or verify them with at least one native signer. This will insure that the model which the teacher presents is reflective of actual ASL usage. Finally, the teacher must remember that imitation and memorization alone will not give the students communicative competence. However, imitation and memorization, if used appropriately, can help to supplement and reinforce the skills needed to attain communicative competence.

Chapter VII

Teaching ASL without the use of Spoken English: Conversational Activities

A. Introduction

The overall goal of conversational activities is to give the students a chance to use what ASL they have learned in an environment where they can express ideas and opinions and take part in a somewhat free-flowing conversation. There are several-types of activities which can provide such an environment. Here we will discuss three major types: simulations, guided conversations, and direct experiences. Certainly, these activities are more easily conducted with advanced students; however, even with beginning students, the teacher will be able to make appropriate adjustments which will make these activities both meaningful and enjoyable for the students.

The value of such activities is that the students are, in a very real sense, in control of their own communication. In addition, during these activities, new vocabulary will be acquired in meaningful ways. The teacher assumes the role of facilitator in most activities, serving to clarify (if needed) or to help students if they become stuck or bogged down.

B. Simulations

Simulations are basically an advanced type of role playing. The value of simulations is that they provide students with an opportunity to learn when and with whom it is appropriate to use the grammatical patterns and the vocabulary they have acquired. Thus, certain socially-determined rules concerning use of the TL can be acquired and experienced by the students.

Unlike dialogues, in simulations the responses are not memorized or rehearsed. Rather, the students rely upon their own creativity and perceptions to interact with each other. Generally, the teacher will describe a specific situation and then, after choosing the appropriate number of students, will assign specific characters to each student. In assigning characters, the teacher should provide certain background information (in writing) that will help the student develop his/her character (e.g. age, feelings at the moment, reason for being in the situation, etc.).

1) **The Job Interview:**

Situation — The ABC Company has a job opening for a _____ (should be a job type that students are likely to be familiar with). Mr/Ms. Hall is interviewing applicants for the job. Two people have applied. Mr/Ms. Hall must interview each applicant and decide who is the best choice for the job.

Characters —Mr/Ms. Day: young, about 25 years old; just graduated from college with a degree relating to the job— _____; very eager and enthusiastic; tries to impress the interviewer with his/her intelligence.
—Mr/Ms. Knight: middle-aged, 40-45 years old; never attended college; has 15 years experience as a _____ ; very much in control of him/herself; emphasizes his/her experience.
—Mr/Ms. Hall: personnel manager of the ABC Company; very businesslike; approximately 50 years old; must decide who to hire.

Props —Sufficient job application forms so that each student in class has two— one for Mr/Ms. Day and one for Mr/Ms. Knight. These forms can usually be obtained from the personnel office of any company, college, etc.

Task —Mr/Ms. Hall must complete the application form on each applicant based on an interview and then decide which one to hire. The class should also fill out application forms so that some discussion can occur after the simulation. (The teacher may decide not to have the interviewer or the class fill out a specific application form. In this case, the teacher should supply Mr/Ms. Hall with a list of interview questions (e.g. qualifications, personal information, references, background).

Procedure—The teacher prepares a handout describing the situation and the task, but not the characters. The teacher then asks for volunteers (or selects the appropriate number of students). Each volunteer is given an index card with a description of his/her character. The students should not read each other's cards. Mr/Ms. Hall is seated behind a desk or table. The two applicants leave the room. A chair for the applicant is positioned so that his/her responses can be seen by the interviewer and the class. One of the applicants is called into the room (the other stays outside) and is interviewed. Mr/Ms. Hall and the class record the responses of the applicant. When this is completed, s/he leaves and the second applicant comes in.

When both applicants have been interviewed, Mr/Ms. Hall announces who will be hired. Then the class discusses this choice. The teacher should not interfere during the interviews but should take notes which can be presented during the discussion period. These notes should include things like needed vocabulary, remarks on student performance, use of grammatical patterns, inappropriate uses of vocabulary or grammatical patterns, etc.

2) The Party:

Situation—Four or five people meet at a party; they don't know each other and attempt to find out as much information about each other as possible. At the end of the simulation, the class tries to provide as complete a biography of each character as possible.

Characters—M. (Mike or Mary) Smith: young, about 20 years old, going to college out of town at the University of _____; is majoring in Special Education; wants to teach Deaf children; grew up locally; college is the first time away from home; very bright but tries to monopolize the conversation; talks about anything and has an opinion on everything.

—S. (Susan or Sam) Jones: about 30 years old; graduated from high school and started working as a _____; is married and has two children—a boy and a girl; his/her spouse works as a _____; grew up locally, has never left the town; is very proud of him/herself and the family; tends to be quiet unless asked a direct question; is also a very nervous person by nature.

—B. (Bob or Betty) White: about 35 years old; recently moved to the city; is recently divorced; has no children; owns his/her own business as a _____; has never lived in one place more than 2 years; dropped out of high school to travel; has a great sense of humor; never takes anything seriously; is always teasing others; tries to be 'the life of the party'.

—P. (Patty or Peter) Jones: about 30 years old; is married to S. Jones; is very proud of the new house they just bought; proud of the family; works as a _____; met S. Jones in high school; never left the hometown; tends to be very talkative; belongs to a bowling league; is always talking about something; tends to 'hang onto' his/her spouse.

—J. (John or Jane) Williams: about 35-40 years old; has lived in the city for 25 years; well liked and respected by everyone; recently got out of the hospital after an operation; sells cars; is married, but his/her spouse is at home sick; is chairperson of the local _____ committee; is very well-read and generally takes his/her time answering questions; wants to talk about the experience in the hospital; is always patting people on the back trying to be friends with everyone.

Task—The five characters are to interact with each other based on their assigned personalities and backgrounds. They are to mingle with the other characters and not form one large circle. The characters are to try to find out about each other— background, hobbies, etc. The class is to observe the behaviors of the characters and focus on the information which is shared. The class will be asked to describe each character after the simulation.

Props — In order to simulate actual party behaviors, it is helpful to give each character a cup or glass or a small dish. This enables the students to practice signing with only one hand and provides the rest of the class an opportunity to practice reading signs under such conditions. One or two chairs should be provided so that some characters sit and others must stand.

Procedure — The teacher prepares five index cards with one character sketch per card. Any blanks should be filled in with appropriate jobs or names that the students are familiar with. A description of the situation and the task is prepared and handed out to the class. No character descriptions are given out. The teacher can ask for volunteers but it is generally better if the teacher 'type casts' the party. That is, the teacher should pick people who will be able to carry out a specific role in a realistic fashion.

The teacher then gives each student his/her character card. The students are not to read each others' cards. The teacher may select one person to be the host/hostess. If so, this should be on the character card. The students are then given a cup, glass, or other prop, and the party begins.

After a sufficient time, the party is stopped. The teacher selects one character at a time, and the class must give a 'biography' of that character in ASL. The other characters can contribute also. This continues for each character.

The teacher may decide to provide input (vocabulary, social behavior information, grammatical information, etc.) at this time or wait until the biography sketches are completed.

There are, of course, a wide variety of simulations which can be devised by the teacher (e.g. a car accident, seeking information, etc.). However, it is crucial that the teacher try to provide simulations which will enable students to produce samples of ASL that will have meaning and application in real life. In any event, there are certain portions to any simulation which the teacher should provide:

> *the situation description:* This basically explains the situation and the specific task(s) to be done by the characters and the class. If the class is more advanced, the task can be quite complex.
>
> *the character descriptions:* These include characters' names, personality, experience, problems, hobbies, etc. The description should be adequate enough to permit the student to use his/her own creativity but not too detailed to inhibit student independence. The aim is that the student is able to develop his/her own character through the brief description given.
>
> *useful expressions:* In some simulations, the teacher may find it helpful to provide glosses on each character card for certain expressions which that character is likely to use during the simulation. This is a good way to help students focus on new vocabulary and patterns or on new uses of vocabulary and patterns.
>
> *background information:* In some simulations which may require some common, shared knowledge by the characters (e.g. a meeting, a culturally related simulation), the teacher should provide some background information — either a short handout, a film, lecture, etc. This will help the students respond appropriately during the simulation.

C. Guided Conversations

Guided conversations are essentially free discussions by the class about a topic which has been pre-selected by the teacher and for which the class has done some preparation. Two basic types of guided conversation seem to be most helpful — problem-solving activities and information/idea exchanges. The goal of guided conversation activities are essentially to place students within a commonly shared framework where they can agree, disagree, and argue with each other in the TL.

The teacher must be aware that some students will tend to monopolize such a situation. Thus, the teacher must act as monitor (or appoint a student to monitor) in order to ensure that all students are encouraged to participate and have the opportunity to participate. Of course, seating arrangement is crucial since each student must be able to see and be seen by the other students.

1) Problem-Solving Activities:

These activities are essentially ones in which the student is given a problem (for which there may be no right or wrong answer). Each student, acting alone or in a small group, must formulate a possible solution to the problem with reasons for that solution. Then class discussion and exchange of possible solutions takes place. The following two examples will illustrate this type of activity.

a) *The Lifeboat:*

Situation — You are captain of a large yacht. There are 11 passengers on board. The yacht is in the middle of the Pacific and starts to sink. There is one lifeboat, but it can only hold 6 people. Since you are the only person with any experience at sea, you must be one of the 6 survivors. Thus 5 of the 11 passengers can be saved. In all probability, the 6 survivors will find an island and have to live on it for several years before they are rescued. Anyone not chosen will die.

Task — As captain, you must decide which 5 passengers you will save, and the 5 people most able to survive and establish a viable society. You must be able to justify your choices.

Passengers:

Mary — 30 years old; 6 months pregnant; has two children at home.

John — 70 years old; retired doctor; has no family.

Susan — a famous artist; is quite rich; well-liked.

Mike — a carpenter; a loner, does not get alone with others.

Alice — a well-known lawyer; likes to garden.

Sam — excellent swimmer; a born trouble-maker.

Cathy — highly educated; well-read; a leader; overweight.

Jim — a minister; has good organizational skills; a thinker.

Barbara — a politician; likely to be the first woman President of the U.S.

David — a teacher; former Eagle Scout; one arm is paralyzed.

Helen — gourmet cook; authority on plant life; allergic to fish.

Procedure—The above information (the situation, the task, and the passenger descriptions) is handed out to the class. The class is instructed to rank order all 11 passengers and to circle the first 5 (the 5 passengers they intend to save). After a few minutes during which the students make their choices, the teacher begins the discussion. The ultimate aim is for the class to reach agreement on which five passengers will be saved.

In order to get maximum discussion (and thus maximum opportunity for the students to interact in the TL), the teacher should avoid taking votes but rather should encourage the students to try to convince each other through discussion. In other words, the teacher should try to push the students into discussions as often as possible because the actual point of the activity is not so much agreeing on 5 passengers but rather the discussion process.

b) *The Camping Trip:*

Situation—You are scheduled to take a one-week camping trip. You must select the food and equipment that you will take with you. You can only carry a maximum of 30 pounds. You cannot split up any of the items listed below.

Task—Select the equipment and food you will take with you on the trip. You cannot split items (i.e. take ½ an item). The total weight you can take is 30 pounds.

Equipment/Food	Weight
—sleeping bag	5 lbs.
—pillow	1 lb.
—swimming suit	½ lb.
—extra shoes	3 lbs.
—water	5 lbs.
—camera	3 lbs.
—plates, cups, utensils	1 lb.
—cooking pots	2 lbs.
—flashlight	1 lb.
—toothpaste, toothbrush	½ lb.
—fishing gear	4 lbs.
—extra clothing	5 lbs.
—backpack	4 lbs.
—soap, towel	½ lb.
—matches, knife, axe	4 lbs.
—rain gear	1 lb.
—food for 1 week	6 lbs.
—maps, compass	1 lb.
—tent	5 lbs.

Procedure—The above information (the situation, the task, and the list of equipment/food) is handed out to the class. The class is instructed to circle and rank order the items they would select. The process is the same as in the Lifeboat problem—i.e. discussion by the class, explaining and justifying their choices. The point is the process, not so much the end product.

Other simulations such as the two described above can be developed by the teacher. If the teacher decides to do so, then s/he should remember that the crucial element of such simulations is that individuals (or the group) are put in a situation where limited choices must be made from a large number of relatively plausible options. Very often simulations like this can be found in books which focus on group dynamics or group processes.

2) Context-Specific Discussions:

These discussions are activities in which students are placed in a situation where they have done background reading on a specific topic and then are called to participate in a conversation about the topic. Generally, conversations involving a large group of people (ten or more) who are not prepared tend to be monopolized by a couple of individuals who may have more background or knowledge about the topic. By providing some basic preliminary reading material, the teacher ensures that all members of the class share some common information about the topic.

The topics for discussion, as often as possible, should fit into one of two categories: either something related to the TL culture (deafness, education of deaf children, attitudes toward hearing people-etc.), or something that the class is interested in (some civic issue, a topic related to students' backgrounds, etc.). This means that there must be a certain amount of planning on the teacher's part for this activity to be successful.

The teacher actually must perform several tasks in this type of a guided conversation activity:

Select a topic —This can be done by locating an article (or series of articles) which is thought-provoking and perhaps even controversial in nature. Such articles can come from several sources—the *Deaf American,* local Deaf newsletters, local newspapers, magazines, etc. It is preferable that the topic be related to the TL culture in order to provide the students with more input on the TL culture. However, another source of topics is the students themselves. If they share some common experiences (e.g. are students at a college) or some common interests (e.g. are all interested in politics), then the teacher can draw upon these factors in choosing a topic.

Provide background reading material —Once a topic has been selected, then the teacher must locate an article or two relating to that topic. The article does not have to be long, but it must provide the students with certain information which can become the focus of the discussion. The teacher must make sure that all of the students have a copy of the article or have access to the article.

Arrange the environment —If the conversation/discussion is to occur in the classroom, then it is important that the environment be arranged so that all of the students can see and be seen by each other. Usually a circle is the best arrangement for this. It is also helpful to find a location for the activity which is conducive to casual discussion and conversation. A lounge area or a living room provides a natural setting for this type of activity. This change in physical environment (from the classroom) provides an atmosphere which is much less formal than a classroom and is more like what students may encounter in future interactions with the TL.

Facilitate the discussion—This means that it is the teacher's job to keep the discussion moving—not by monopolizing the conversation, but rather by making sure that no one monopolizes the discussion. It also means that the teacher should have a prepared list of questions which can be asked if the discussion starts to die. These should be questions which have a variety of possible answers—not simply factual questions or Yes-No questions. In addition, the teacher may have to play the 'Devil's Advocate'. That is, if the conversation is dying, the teacher may have to make statements or express ideas which are clearly wrong or unpopular in order to stir up the conversation. This requires some planning on the teacher's part.

There are, of course, other variations of the guided conversation presented above. Each of them, however, requires preparation on the teacher's part. Some of these variations may be more appropriate than others depending on the skill level of the students.

a) *Debate*—The debate is an opportunity for a small number of students (usually 2-4) to discuss a controversial topic and to try to convince the rest of the class that a particular viewpoint is correct. This requires planning on the part of each 'team' (2 students per team) and the selection of a topic that has a fairly good balance between the sides—pro and con. A debate is an excellent opportunity for students to begin to learn and develop persuasive skills in the TL as well as learn more about the community itself. For example, the topic "Deaf children receive a better all-around education if they are mainstreamed" is one which has strong pro and con points of view.

b) *Small group discussion*—This is essentially the same as was described above for the full class except that the class may be divided into groups of 5-6 students, enabling more student involvement. However, this means that the teacher may have to pick one person per group to act as facilitator and provide that person with questions for discussion. The teacher is then free to move from group to group and monitor their progress, and to assist where needed.

c) *Fishbowl discussion*—Instead of one large group discussion, the teacher selects 4-6 students who are then seated in a semi-circle in front of the class. These 4-6 students engage in a discussion of the assigned topic. These students are 'in the fishbowl'. Any of the other students may join the discussion and enter the fishbowl by simply replacing one of the original 4-6 students. (Generally it is a good idea to have some pre-arranged cue such as tapping on the shoulder.) This variation is an excellent way for the teacher to gauge the overall receptive skills of the students. If a student joins the fishbowl and makes initial comments unrelated to the preceding discussion, then the teacher may have an indication of that student's receptive skills.

d) *Incomplete dialogue* — An incomplete dialogue is one in which the teacher supplies the class with a written English gloss for only half of a dialogue. The students are then given time to prepare appropriate responses which will complete the dialogue. Generally, the portion of the dialogue which is given to the students consists of a series of somewhat related questions. It is necessary to provide the students with written glosses so that they have an opportunity to prepare responses. After the students have prepared their responses (in class or at home), the teacher can call students one at a time to engage in the conversation or can divide the class into pairs. Thus, the students have an opportunity to express their own ideas within certain controlled limits.

The point of guided conversation activities is to provide the students with an opportunity to begin expressing their own ideas and thoughts in a somewhat prepared situation. Such activities can provide the teacher with valuable information relative to student progress and assimilation of principles of the TL.

3) Direct Experiences:

Direct experiences are those in which the students leave the classroom and interact in an environment other than the classroom. In a very real sense, the community becomes the classroom. In arranging for field trips or direct experiences, the teacher needs to carefully select the site and probably needs to visit that site before taking the class there. That way the teacher can make any necessary arrangements with appropriate personnel to accommodate the class.

The teacher (and ultimately the class) should view such trips as opportunities for acquiring new vocabulary, for acquiring a new level of TL awareness, and for applying what has been learned in the classroom. These trips should *not* be viewed as times for the students to 'play Deaf' or 'act Deaf', but rather to use ASL in much more realistic situations than the classroom. Encouraging students to 'play Deaf' or 'act Deaf' may lead to certain negative, stereotyped behaviors on the part of the students. In addition, it is generally not possible for most students to do this in a positive way. Rather, the teacher should encourage the students to interact in ASL in a particular situation. This may seem like a fine distinction, but it is crucial in terms of the attitude which is conveyed.

Some suggested direct experiences or field trips are:

a) *Buying a house* — The class meets at a model house or apartment, and the teacher assumes the role of a person trying to sell the house. Students are encouraged to ask the types of questions that a buyer might ask.

b) *The grocery store* — Students meet at a grocery store and the teacher can assign teams of students to locate, price, or purchase certain food items.

c) *The bus station/train station/airport* — Students meet at one of these locations, and the teacher has the students plan trips, figure out the fastest way to get to a certain place, etc.

d) *The restaurant* — Students meet at a restaurant for dinner or lunch and must place their order through the teacher who supplies or corrects needed vocabulary or syntax and who places the group's order with the waiter/waitress.

There are a large number of other places that are appropriate for such direct experiences (museums, stores, parks, playgrounds, etc.). The only limiting factors are the particular locale of the class and the creativity of the teacher. Certainly such direct, firsthand experience will reinforce vocabulary acquisition far better than attempts at creating these environments in the classroom.

D. Summary

In order for students to acquire conversational competence in ASL, two basic conditions must be satisfied: first, the students must have sufficient exposure to ASL, and second, the students must be placed in situations where ASL is the expected means of communication. These last three chapters have presented detailed explanations and descriptions of a variety of activities and tasks that can be used to create or simulate situations which can be conducted entirely in ASL (without the use of English). Perhaps the most important principle that the teacher of ASL must be aware of is that any time s/he uses English, the students are not exposed to ASL, nor are they placed in a situation where they can realistically be expected to use ASL.

The activities and tasks presented in the last three chapters fall into three main categories: (a) those in which there is an observable, concrete means of detecting receptive or expressive success (picture description, object manipulation, etc.), (b) those in which there are certain constraints on student performance (dialogues and drills), and (c) those in which students control both content and form (simulations, discussions). Certainly the activities and tasks presented are not a complete listing of all possible tasks. However, they do serve as examples of the types of tasks and activities which the teacher can use to develop the students' conversational competence in ASL. In addition, these tasks can be modified so that they are applicable to students at all skill levels.

Chapter VIII

Evaluation of ASL Skills

In discussing evaluation, it is important that the teacher separate two very important issues: 'What to evaluate' and 'How to evaluate'. Very often these issues are not separated, and the result is that the teacher is often not sure of what skill was evaluated and whether or not it was appropriately evaluated. Another important issue that is often confused with these two issues is 'How to report evaluation results'. This chapter will discuss these three issues as they relate to evaluating expressive and receptive skills in ASL.

A. What to evaluate

Obviously, in an ASL class the teacher needs to measure how successfully the students have learned what was covered in the classroom. Presumably what was covered in the classroom is ASL. If this is true, then by measuring what was covered in the classroom, it is possible to assess the students' ASL skills at a specific level — the level of skill targeted for that particular course. This relationship between what was taught or covered in the class and what is evaluated is called "relevance".

In an instructional situation such as an ASL class, the evaluation must have a high degree of relevance. If, in a specific class, the teacher covers certain information and skills but the evaluation measures different information and skills, then the evaluation has no relevance. Thus, it is important that the evaluation for any ASL course be carefully planned and be designed with a high degree of relevance. With such an evaluation, the teacher can gain two types of information: information about student progress and information about instructional effectiveness. Both types of information are very important in program planning and modification. However, such information is only possible if the evaluation itself is relevant to the instruction. If, for example, a significant number of students do poorly on a specific test, then there are two possible explanations:

1) the instructional program was inadequate (the teacher's fault); or
2) the test measured skills which were not covered adequately in class (the test developer's fault).

If the first possibility is true, then the teacher knows that s/he must revise and repeat certain parts of the course because a significant number of students did poorly. In this case, the test did measure what was covered in class but the results show that it was not covered well enough. In the second case, the teacher needs to re-examine the test since what the test measured was not sufficiently covered in class. Therefore, the results cannot have much value for the teacher because the test was measuring a different set of skills than what the students were taught. Thus, what should be measured in an instructional setting are those skills which the course and the curriculum are designed to give the students.

B. How to evaluate

Any evaluation that is effective must be dependable. This means that the teacher (or whoever is evaluating) must be consistent in how s/he rates student performance. This consistency is called "reliability".

In certain types of situations, high reliability is very easy to obtain. For example, in a properly designed true-false test, certain answers are true and certain answers are false. If 15 people are given the answer key and the same set of papers to grade, they will all give each student the same score. These raters will have very high reliability (in fact, perfect reliability) since they are all using the same criteria in the same way to evaluate student performance. Indeed, anyone using this test and the answer key will evaluate students with the same reliability. If the evaluation is consistently scored the same way, it is *reliable*. If the test is relevant but is inconsistently scored, the test is *unreliable*.

Thus, an evaluation must be constructed so that there are certain clearly defined criteria which the evaluator can use in scoring. Without such criteria, there is no guarantee that two evaluators will evaluate in a similar fashion. If each evaluator has his/her own individual criteria for evaluating, a student might receive a high score from one evaluator and a low score from another. This inconsistency can also occur with only one evaluator (e.g. a teacher) who might rate two students very differently even though their performance was very similar.

The use of such criteria is very important in making an evaluation more objective. This is crucial in a program where a student may have several teachers in a course or several courses from different teachers. If there are some criteria which the teachers agree to use in their evaluations and if they use these criteria in the same way, then the student should obtain reliable feedback on his/her progress, and the teachers will obtain reliable input for program improvement. Thus, it is important that the evaluation be as objective as possible.

C. How to report results

Assuming that a relevant test has been developed and is scored in a reliable fashion, the teacher must now decide how to report the results of the evaluation to the students. Generally, there are two approaches that can be used:

1) The results are reported in relation to the other students taking the test. This approach is called a "norm-referenced approach" and basically tells the student what percentage of the other students learned less than s/he did.

2) The results are reported in relation to what should have been learned in the class. This approach is called a "criterion-referenced approach" and basically tells a student what skills s/he has mastered and what skills s/he has difficulty with.

Norm-referenced reporting is used in tests such as the College Boards or the Scholastic Achievement Test. This means that the results indicate how well a person performed in comparison with a specific group of people taking the same test. Criterion-referenced reporting is used, for example, in reporting results of written driving tests. This means that results indicate how well a person performed in comparison with what would be total or perfect mastery of that knowledge or skill.

Usually, if the test is designed appropriately, it is more helpful for language learners to receive criterion-referenced results. These results can tell a student where s/he has specific weaknesses in relation to targeted mastery of a skill or body of knowledge. Norm-referenced results are probably less helpful for the individual but may be very helpful for a program coordinator who must allocate teachers and classroom space. The decision of whether to report criterion-referenced or norm-referenced results is, in part, determined by how the test results will be used. There are some contexts in which norm-referenced results are as meaningful for students as criterion-referenced results.

The ideal evaluation process, then, is one in which a relevant test is scored reliably and results are reported to students in a meaningful manner. Before examining these issues in relation to the evaluation of ASL skills, it will be helpful to examine some common errors which are made in testing students. These errors can be listed briefly and are rather obvious. The reason for listing them is to help the reader gain an appreciation for how much time and thought must go into successful test development. These common errors are:

1) use of irrelevant tests
2) over-reliance on subjective judgement
3) blaming students and not the test or the course
4) delaying test preparation until the last minute
5) tests which are inefficient or too short
6) ambiguous test items
7) inappropriate student response format

The sections which follow attempt to provide some ideas and suggestions which will help teachers of ASL avoid these mistakes in evaluating their students.

D. What to evaluate in ASL

Assuming that the ultimate aim of an ASL course is to provide the students with a certain level of conversational skill in ASL, then it is obvious that conversational skills must be evaluated. However, the category "conversational skills" is very broad and needs to be sub-divided into specific behaviors. For example, the teacher needs information about the students' vocabulary development, knowledge of grammatical structures, and use of conversational behaviors. These distinctions will enable the teacher to provide much more direct and useful information to the student as well as to discover strengths and weaknesses in the instructional program. Within each of these three sub-divisions (vocabulary/lexical, grammatical, conversational), there are specific factors which need to be evaluated. These are described below.

1) Vocabulary:

Within the area of vocabulary, an evaluation needs to measure the production, selection, and comprehension of those lexical items which are targeted for a given course.

Production: Traditionally, Sign Language evaluations have used terms like "clarity" and "accuracy" to deal with the production of vocabulary. However, these terms are rarely well-defined and thus are almost always measured subjectively. This presents problems with the reliability of ratings from teacher to teacher. For example, what is "clear" to one person may not be "clear" to another. In addition, the level of information which can be provided to the student is ambiguous at best. All that can be reported is something like "Pat, you have difficulty with the clarity of your signs". This does not provide the student or teacher with specific enough information to begin to correct any difficulties.

A more helpful means of evaluating production is to use a factor analysis approach — i.e. what factors are important in the production of lexical items in ASL? The obvious answer to this question is found in Chapter IV: the four parameters of sign production. Thus it is possible to evaluate how a student makes a sign in terms of its handshape, location, movement, and orientation. This level of evaluation can provide both student and teacher with information about certain tendencies or difficulties that a particular student might have and thus help them make decisions about future instruction and attention. It is much more helpful to know that a student has problems with the handshape or movement of signs than to say that s/he lacks clarity or accuracy.

Another factor which must be evaluated is the specific non-manual behaviors which accompany certain signs. Consider the facial behavior needed for the following signs: **FAT, THIN, HAPPY, SAD, MAD, CARELESS, PUZZLED,** etc. Each of these signs has a particular non-manual component which is not just 'extra' or 'added on', but is part of the sign itself. For example, normally the sign **FAT** has a puffing of the cheeks and the sign **THIN** has a pursing of the lips.

Thus, the production factors on the lexical level which should be evaluated are: handshape, movement, location, orientation, and non-manual behaviors.

Selection: Another lexical area which must be assessed is whether or not the student knows and uses the appropriate vocabulary to express his/her ideas. There are two factors here which the student and teacher need to examine. First, does the student know the sign(s) to express a particular idea and, second, does the student use the sign(s) appropriately to express a given meaning.

These two factors are quite different in the type of information which they provide the student and teacher. The first indicates the extent and depth of a student's vocabulary base. That is, what meanings can the student express and what meanings can't s/he express via signs. The second factor indicates whether the student knows the appropriate uses and limits of the signs s/he knows. Somewhat different instructional techniques may be required for each case. In the first case, the teacher must focus on developing vocabulary which the student needs to express certain meanings. In the second case, the teacher may have to devise situations in which the student can un-learn certain uses of signs and become aware of their semantic limits. For example, a student may know how to produce the sign USE-ASL,

USE-ASL

but may use it when referring to the use of any variety of manual communication. This is clearly a case where the student, although s/he knows *how* to make a particular sign, does not know *when* to use it.

Thus, an evaluation should assess the student's knowledge of specific vocabulary items, including the appropriate contextual use of those items.

Comprehension: The third major lexical area which must be evaluated is the student's ability to comprehend or understand the meaning of specific lexical items. There are two quite different types of comprehension which should be measured by an evaluation. The first relates to the student's ability to recognize and understand the meanings of signs which have been included in the curriculum or have been specifically taught in the classroom. These are vocabulary items which the student should understand with no hesitation and with complete accuracy.

The second area is a student's ability to figure out the meanings of certain signs from the context in which they are used. Thus, if a student understands everything in an ASL sentence except one sign, then s/he should be able to make a reasonable guess as to the meaning of that sign. An evaluation should measure the student's ability to use context to determine (or try to determine) meanings of items not specifically taught in class. This is a crucial skill for any language learner.

Thus, factors which must be evaluated in the area of vocabulary are:

(a) **Production:**

      Manual behaviors: handshape
                         movement
                         location
                         orientation
      Non-manual behaviors

(b) **Selection:**

      Knowledge
      Appropriate usage

(c) **Comprehension:**

      Sight recognition
      Contextual understanding

2) Grammatical Structure:

The factors of Production, Selection, and Comprehension have been discussed only as they relate to vocabulary. However, it is also necessary to consider these factors as they apply to the syntactic structure of ASL. The companion text on grammar and culture provides an in-depth discussion of certain syntactic features of ASL which should be evaluated. Any meaningful evaluation will provide both student and teacher with information about a student's production, selection, and comprehension of these features. (As more research on the structure of ASL becomes available, the teacher should incorporate this information into the evaluation). For example, one of the chapters in the **Grammar and Culture** text describes the grammatical structure of signs referring to "time". Within this topic, there are many categories which the teacher needs to evaluate (when appropriate in the curriculum):

TIME

a) the location and movement of signs along the "time line"
b) the incorporation of number on time signs
c) the non-dominant hand as a reference point
d) the modulation of time signs to indicate "regularity"
e) the modulation of time signs to indicate "duration"
f) the modulation of time signs to indicate "approximate" or "relative" time
g) the modulation of time signs to indicate "repetition" and "duration"
h) time signs that indicate "tense"
i) non-manual adverbs that indicate relative time

As was stated above, an evaluation should measure the Production, Selection, and Comprehension of each of these features. One possible result of such an evaluation is a matrix which provides detailed information about a student's ability to produce, use, and comprehend specific structural features of ASL. The following is an example of this matrix for some of the features of ASL that relate to time.

	Production		Selection		Comprehension	
	manual	non-manual	knowledge	usage	recognition	contextual
time line						
number incorporation						
non-dominant hand						
regularity						
duration						
approximate time						
repetition & duration						
tense						
non-manual						

Of course, each of the grammatical features listed to the left can be even further divided (e.g. number incorporation on the time signs HOUR, DAY, WEEK, MONTH, etc.) The advantage of this type of schema is that a teacher can be fairly specific about a student's ability to use grammatical features of ASL and can begin to see if there are patterns in the performance of a given student or of a class. For example, if none of the students in a class can productively demonstrate number incorporation on time signs (e.g. TWO-WEEK, THREE-HOUR), this probably indicates a gap in the instructional program. If, on the other hand, this inability is found in only one student, then more individualized instruction may be needed in this area.

In addition, the teacher can be fairly specific about certain weaknesses of the students. Under the manual portion of the production category, for example, a teacher can indicate which parameter a student is using incorrectly. Thus, in the feature concerning movement along the "time line", the teacher may note that a particular student consistently does not use an outward movement to indicate future time. This level of information is quite helpful to both teacher and student in identifying possible causes of this type of error, especially if it is a recurring error (e.g. the student may have a visual discrimination problem or s/he may have some physical motor control problem).

This level of in-depth evaluation is vital in order to help the teacher monitor class performance and instructional effectiveness. It is also vital because it provides the student with some specific, in-depth information as to what aspects of the language are problematic. However, this analytic information merely indicates that a student can produce and comprehend certain features of ASL. It says nothing about a student's actual performance in a conversational setting. Therefore, it is also necessary to evaluate certain conversational behaviors.

3) Conversational behaviors:

The evaluation schema presented above is helpful in identifying those features of ASL which the student has or has not mastered. However, since the ultimate goal of most students is to attain conversational competence, it is necessary to determine how well a student can apply his/her knowledge of and skill in these lexical and grammatical features to a conversational situation. In addition, there are certain conversational features which must be evaluated in order to provide appropriate feedback concerning the student's conversational competence. These conversational features include:

(a) *Conversational openers:* These are specific lexical items which are used to start a conversation in ASL. These lexical items serve to get the attention of a potential addressee. An evaluation should measure whether or not a student can produce and use these items correctly as well as recognize them. Some of these conversational openers are: **THRILL, AWFUL, WOW, DISGUST, KNOW-THAT, YOU KNOW,** etc. The expected response is that the potential addressee will be interested in knowing what is 'awful', 'disgusting', etc., and will attend to the signer. Then the conversation begins.

(b) *Attention-getting behaviors:* These are specific linguistic or non-linguistic ways which signers use to get the attention of another person. Conversational openers are one type of attention-getting behavior. However, the student should know when and how to use other types of attention-getters. Some examples are: waving his/her hand, a gentle touch or tap, tapping on a table, flicking a light switch, asking another person to get someone's attention, etc. The evaluation should measure whether or not a student knows how to use these devices as well as when it is appropriate to use each of them.

(c) *Establishing eye contact:* Before any conversation can occur, the addressee must be looking at the signer. Thus, the teacher should evaluate whether or not the student waits until such contact has been established before beginning a conversation.

(d) *Topic maintenance:* This refers to the student's ability to comprehend a particular message and, generally, contribute to the conversation by making relevant statements or asking appropriate questions pertaining to the topic of conversation. This can also refer to the student's ability to shift or change the topic of conversation at appropriate times. The exact content of the student's response is not important (i.e. the student can agree, disagree, challenge, make erroneous statements, etc.) as long as it pertains to the topic or appropriately initiates a new topic.

(e) *Turn-taking:* This refers to the student's ability to know when it is appropriate to begin signing (i.e. when it is his/her 'turn'), how to hold the floor, and how to interrupt the signer, if appropriate. Basically, this is the skill of maintaining a smooth flow in the conversation by appropriately alternating turns with the other participant(s).

(f) *Addressee feedback:* This refers to the use and comprehension of manual or non-manual signals which indicate to the signer that s/he is being understood. Signs such as **RIGHT, WOW, TRUE,** etc., head movements (nods or shakes), and various facial expressions are used to provide feedback to the signer. The student should be able to use and comprehend these signals.

(g) *Seeking clarification:* This refers to the student's ability to ask for clarification of specific signs or statements which s/he does not understand. This skill is very important since it is probable that the student will encounter lexical items that s/he does not understand or statements which do not seem to make sense to the student. In order to understand such messages, the student must be able to ask for clarification.

(h) *Use of space:* This refers to the student's ability to use space appropriately in a conversational setting. This means knowing where to locate (or 'set up') new information, using previously established locations for referents, etc. The use of space and consistency in referencing is important for maintaining clarity and intelligibility in a conversation.

(i) *Pausing and Phrasing:* This refers to the student's ability to present information in a conversational setting in meaningful idea-units. Thus, it is important that the student use appropriate pausing and phrasing devices (e.g. 'holding' a sign, use of space, etc.). These are very important in helping the addressee comprehend the intended meaning.

(j) *Speed/rate:* This essentially refers to the student's ability to sign at an appropriate rate for the addressee. The addressee's reactions are important in determining the appropriate rate. A rate which is too slow may be boring and unintelligible, a rate which is too fast may be unclear and unintelligible. This also refers to the student's ability to vary his/her signing speed at appropriate times (e.g. faster when excited, slower for dramatic effect).

(k) *Style Variation:* This refers to the student's ability to use appropriate lexical items and even syntactic structures to fit a variety of conversational situations. Very often the participants in a conversation will determine whether a person should sign more formally or informally (e.g. school principal *vs* best friend). Thus, the student should be evaluated on his/her conversational skills in a variety of settings with a variety of participants.

The preceding description of specific types of skill and knowledge within the categories of vocabulary, grammatical structure, and conversational behaviors now makes it possible for us to partially answer the question: "What should be evaluated in ASL?". It is necessary to evaluate the production, selection, and comprehension of lexical items and grammatical features of ASL and to evaluate the use and comprehension of key conversational behaviors. Notice that the intent is not to measure or evaluate how much a student knows *about* certain structural features of ASL or conversational behaviors of ASL signers (i.e. whether or not a student can explain or describe certain features or behaviors). Rather, the focus of the evaluation is on *usage* — production, selection, and comprehension. This is because the ultimate goal of the course(s) is that the student will attain conversational or communicative competence. If the goal of the course(s) was that the student would attain a theoretical understanding of the structural features of ASL, then it would be important for the student to be able to explain or define those features. There is, however, a vast difference between knowing *about* a language and knowing *how to use* that language. Simply knowing about the features of a language does not at all guarantee any fluency in that language. While it is true that explanations and descriptions are quite helpful to students, these explanations and descriptions are simply a means to an end. It is that end—communicative competence—which must be evaluated.

The following is a list of those areas which should be evaluated in ASL. Within each area, the factors of Production, Selection, and Comprehension should be evaluated.

I.   **Lexical/Vocabulary**
       — vocabulary items targeted for receptive and expressive mastery for a given course

II. **Grammatical Features**
       — sentence types
       — time
       — pronominalization
       — subjects and objects
       — classifiers
       — locatives
       — pluralization
       — distributional aspect
       — temporal aspect

III. **Conversational Behaviors**
       — conversational openers
       — attention-getting behaviors
       — establishing eye contact
       — topic maintenance
       — turn-taking
       — addressee feedback
       — seeking clarification
       — use of space
       — pausing and phrasing

—speed/rate
—style variation

As has been discussed earlier (Chapter I), the language teacher has a responsibility to provide certain cultural information to the students. Certainly one means of incorporating this information into class activities is through the use of carefully developed dialogues (Chapter VI). The type and extent of the cultural information provided will be determined, in part, by the curriculum. The teacher should be sensitive to the local Deaf community and include appropriate, pertinent information about the local Deaf community in the class (e.g. educational, social or political factors which are unique to the local Deaf community). In general, this cultural information may consist not only of printed materials but also certain behaviors and attitudes which the student must demonstrate in order to successfully interact with the community.

To summarize the discussion of "What should be evaluated in ASL?", we can say that the teacher should assess the following:

(a) student's skills in production and comprehension of lexical and grammatical features of ASL and conversational behaviors;

(b) student's awareness of and knowledge of certain cultural values and features of the Deaf community;

(c) student's mastery of specific course objectives not related directly to (a) or (b)—(e.g. readiness skills).

E. How to evaluate ASL skills:

Once the teacher has determined what lexical, grammatical, conversational, and cultural areas are to be covered in a given course, all of these areas should be evaluated. This section will be devoted to explaining certain evaluation techniques for measuring the lexical and structural areas. Since the cultural area is in large part, knowledge and awareness, much of it can be measured through the use of techniques such as discussions, question/answer periods, written reports, in-class presentations, and field trips.

One general principle which should be remembered is that all vocabulary must be evaluated in context. This means that students should not be presented with a list of glosses and then asked to sign them. Nor should they be presented with a list of signs and then asked to write the glosses. The reason for avoiding this approach has been discussed in detail elsewhere (Chapter V). Briefly, however, the student must be able to produce and comprehend signs *in context,* not in isolation, in order to achieve conversational competence. The production or reception of single, isolated signs not only lacks relevance, but it also does not provide the teacher with any additional information which could not be obtained from a contextual approach to evaluation.

In discussing some evaluation techniques, we will examine three main categories: Receptive, Expressive, and Receptive/Expressive. Certainly these discussions will not identify all possible means of evaluating student performance. However, they will provide the teacher with some ideas about fairly objective ways to make evaluations. Given an objective means of evaluation, reliability will be very high. What is meant by an "objective means of evaluation" is that the student's response can be matched with an expected behavior which can be clearly and accurately stated and then rated by the teacher. The following techniques illustrate a range of expected student behaviors which are useful in assessing ASL skills.

Receptive Assessment Techniques:

1) *True-False Task:* The teacher first selects several pictures and then for each picture, s/he develops 4-5 statements in ASL. Some of the statements are true and some are false. During the evaluation, the teacher shows the class the first picture (displaying it so that it can be seen by everyone during the evaluation). Then the teacher signs the first statement and the class is to write T or F (or circle a T or F on a pre-typed sheet). Since the students can see the picture, their task is to consider the teacher's statement and see if it matches the picture. If it does match, they indicate T; if it doesn't, they indicate F. The teacher then signs the next statement for that picture. The process continues until all statements for the first picture have been used. Then the teacher shows the second picture and the process is repeated.

Because there is one factor constant for all students (the picture), the teacher can gauge how well the class understood various statements about that picture. The problem, of course, is that because the students only have two choices (T or F), there is a good possibility that some students could achieve high scores simply by guessing. The next technique partially solves this problem.

2) *Multiple-Choice Task:* In order to reduce the guess factor with True-False questions, it is helpful to have several choices. However, if the teacher signs the choices and has the students select the correct one, there is a problem with memory. That is, the student will have to remember all of the choices as they are signed. Errors could then be due to a faulty memory, rather than a lack of knowledge. To avoid this memory problem and still provide choices, the following technique is suggested.

The teacher gathers several sets of similar (but not identical) pictures. Each set should have at least 5 pictures in it, and the teacher should clearly number each picture, 1 through 5. The teacher then develops a certain number of true statements (or brief descriptions) for each picture in each set. Thus for one set of 5 pictures, the teacher may have 15 true statements—3 per picture. During the evaluation, the teacher displays all 5 pictures in the first set so that they are clearly seen by all of the students. Then the teacher signs the first statement. The student's task is to identify which picture the statement refers to by writing the number of the appropriate picture or by circling the appropriate number on a prepared answer sheet.

Because there are five possible choices for each statement, the possibility that a student could be right simply by guessing is greatly reduced.

3) *Command Responses:* The teaching technique described in Chapter V ("object manipulation") can also be used very nicely as an evaluation technique. There are several possible variations:

(a) The teacher gives a certain number of commands (e.g. 10) to one student at a time and records whether or not the command was properly carried out by marking "yes" or "no" on a score sheet.

(b) The teacher gives all of the commands (e.g. 25) to one student, and the teacher and the rest of the class record that student's performance. This is actually a test of the whole class since they too must understand the command in order to record the results appropriately. This is similar to the True-False Task discussed above, except that the students are responding to an action and not to a picture.

(c) The teacher arranges for another person (not a student) to manipulate the objects. The teacher and this person decide beforehand which commands will be incorrectly performed. The class then records the performance of this outside person.

(d) The teacher can provide the class with a black and white line drawing of a picture and instruct the class to color the picture according to specific commands which the students couldn't guess (e.g. 'color the sky purple'). This has limited application for assessing color terms and whatever items are in the picture.

4) *Question/Answer Tasks:* These tasks require that the students make a judgement as to whether the response to a given question is appropriate or not, or that the students provide a non-linguistic response to a given question.

(a) The teacher signs a question in ASL and then signs a response to that question (almost like a mini-dialogue). The students then indicate in writing whether the response is "appropriate" or "inappropriate" or by circling A or I on a prepared response sheet. A response may be inappropriate either because the content is totally wrong or because certain structural features of the response were incorrectly used.

(b) The teacher provides the class with a sheet of blank clock faces. Then the

teacher makes a statement in ASL (e.g. $\overline{\text{WORK FINISH, TIME}}^{\,t}\ \overset{\frown}{\text{NINE}}$) and

asks the class a question related to the time in that statement

(e.g. $\overline{\text{WORK FINISH, TIME "WHAT"}}^{\,wh\text{-}q}$).

The class must then draw the hands of the clock so that the appropriate time is indicated.

5) *Description Comprehension Tasks:* These tasks require that the students draw scenes based on the teacher's description of a picture or based on the teacher's narration.

(a) The teacher describes a picture (in whole or in part) and the students draw the picture. This can then be rated on accuracy (which may be an assessment of memory) and comprehension.

(b) The teacher describes a scene not taken from a picture and the students draw the scene. This may also be used to test accuracy and comprehension.

(c) The teacher describes a series of events and the students must draw a series of appropriately sequenced pictures.

6) *Narrative Comprehension:* These tasks require the student to make certain judgements about statements which relate to a particular narrative given by the teacher.

(a) The teacher signs a narrative and then makes a series of statements relating to that narrative. The statements can be true or false or inappropriate for that narrative. The student must indicate in writing whether each statement is true, false, or inappropriate by circling the appropriate letter (**T, F, IA**) on a pre-typed sheet.

(b) The teacher signs a narrative and then asks a series of questions about that narrative. The questions should be answerable in short phrases. The students then indicate their response by circling the right answer from 4 or 5 choices on a prepared sheet. Note that the students are not required to write their responses in English, but merely circle the correct phrase or short answer. The similarity of the choices will determine the difficulty of the task.

7) *Retention Tasks:* These tasks require the students to match a written choice with a signed stimulus. Because the students must remember the signed stimulus, these may be testing retention or memory more than comprehension.

(a) The teacher signs two sentences in ASL and the students must indicate whether the sentences are the 'same' or 'different' by circling S or D on a pre-typed answer sheet.

(b) The teacher signs two sentences (each consisting of two parts such as a conditional sentence or a compound sentence). The students must identify which sentence makes the most sense by circling the appropriate number (1 or 2).

(c) The teacher signs two or three sentences. Each sentence begins the same way but has a different ending. The students must indicate which of the sentences is most appropriate (i.e. which 'ending' best finishes the sentence). The students circle their choice on a pre-typed answer sheet.

8) *Grammatical Identification Tasks:* These tasks require the students to match a written choice with a signed stimulus or to select a written explanation for a signed stimulus.

(a) The teacher signs a sentence and the students must select which grammatical feature did not occur in the sentence from a pre-typed list of four or five possible grammatical choices.

(b) The teacher signs a sentence and the students must indicate which grammatical features did occur from a pre-typed list of four or five possible syntactic choices.

(c) The teacher signs a sentence and the students must indicate whether the sentence appropriately used a specific feature by circling the correct choice on a pre-typed sheet. The choices are: **A** = appropriate, **I** = inappropriate, **NU** = not used in the sentence.

The tasks described above all share two features which are essential to measuring students' comprehension in ASL:

a. All of the tasks avoid having the students write an English translation or gloss for an ASL sentence. This process of writing an English equivalent for an ASL utterance is, in fact, a test of a person's interpreting ability and has been discussed earlier. Since it is possible for a person to understand an utterance in ASL (or any language) but not be able to interpret that utterance, tests which require that type of response are not simply testing comprehension. (A student who fails such a test may have failed for one of two reasons: (a) s/he did not understand the sentence, or (b) s/he understood the sentence but could not interpret it.) In order to evaluate comprehension, it is necessary to require that the students respond in non-English ways. Thus, drawing, circling choices, and behavioral responses are a much more accurate measure of student comprehension.

b. All vocabulary is tested in context. Given carefully thought-out test items, it is possible to say that a student who did not get certain items correct, did not comprehend certain vocabulary items or certain grammatical features. For example, in the task described in (2) above (Multiple-Choice Task), the statements or items can be prepared so that certain vocabulary items must be understood in order to get the test item correct. If those items are wrong, the teacher can be fairly sure that the student did not understand certain vocabulary items. An evaluation task which requires students to write a gloss for a single, isolated sign does not measure the student's ability to comprehend that sign in context. It also does not measure the student's ability to comprehend that sign with the various changes that may occur when it is used in different contexts.

Expressive Assessment Techniques:

1) *Imitation task* — The student is required to imitate a sentence which is first signed by the teacher. Since the student is not responsible for generating the content of the sentence, s/he can focus on how the sentence is to be signed. The teacher is then able to evaluate the various production factors (manual and non-manual) discussed above.

2) *Memorization Task* — The student is given a dialogue or short story to memorize and prepare. The teacher can then evaluate the production factors (manual and non-manual) discussed above. If a dialogue is used, the teacher may wish to assign one role or character to one student and the second character to another student. Again, the content has already been pre-determined by the teacher so the student is free to focus on production.

3) *Substitution Drills* — The teacher can use substitution drills (described in Chapter VI) as a means of assessing production factors and to begin assessing grammatical awareness. Since the content of the drill has been pre-determined, the

student can focus on production of the sentence and on the appropriate slot in which to substitute the targeted sign. Unlike the first two tasks (imitation and memorization), this task requires a certain amount of receptive skill since the student must be able to understand the sentence to know where to make the appropriate substitution.

4) *Directed Questions/Answers* — This task places the student in a situation where s/he must spontaneously and appropriately respond to specific questions. In the tasks described so far, the student has had a model (complete or partial) to match; the focus has been on sign production factors and not on a student's ability to use certain grammatical features. With this task, the focus is on the student's production *and* selection of manual and non-manual behaviors used in spontaneously replying to specific questions. Depending upon the question, certain grammatical features can be predicted as acceptable responses. There are, however, two important considerations which the teacher should remember. First, the questions should be developed so that they require two or three short sentences as a response. Yes/No type questions should be avoided. Second, the questions should not test specific content, but be general in nature and, whenever possible, relate to areas or topics that the students are very familiar with. A simulated job interview (Chapter VII) is a good example of the directed question technique.

5) *Command and Description Tasks* — These tasks essentially provide the student with a non-linguistic stimulus which s/he must describe or explain. The student's response to these tasks will require the use of certain predictable grammatical features and vocabulary items. Since the student is spontaneously generating the description or explanation, the teacher can assess not only production factors, but also selection and grammatical factors.

(a) *Picture description* — The student is given a picture to describe (Chapter V), and is evaluated on how accurately s/he describes the picture. Depending on the class, the teacher may wish to evaluate the receptive skills of the other students by having them draw what the student describes. The content of the picture must be analyzed beforehand by the teacher to determine what structural features and vocabulary the student should use to accurately describe the picture.

(b) *Object manipulation* — The student is placed in front of a set of objects. The teacher manipulates the objects and the student must describe how they were manipulated. Again, an analysis of the various settings the teacher creates will reveal what lexical and structural features should be used by the student. In addition, the receptive skills of a second student can be evaluated if s/he has not seen the teacher manipulate the objects but must manipulate them according to the description given by the first student.

6) *Dialogues* — The student is given a printed summary of a specific situation and then is assigned a role in the dialogue. The teacher (or another student) assumes the second role. The dialogue is spontaneously created by the two participants. This differs from memorized dialogues in that the student is given the situation but not his/her actual lines in the dialogue.

7) *Story completion*—The student is shown a portion of a film, film-strip, or videotape which provides the beginning of a short story. At an appropriate, climatic moment, the film or filmstrip is stopped and the student must finish the story.

Expressive/Receptive Assessment Techniques

The above techniques have attempted to isolate either receptive or expressive skills for the purposes of evaluation. In reality, however, this is very difficult to do and, in fact, some of the techniques mentioned above require some receptive skills in order to obtain samples of expressive ASL (e.g. dialogues). Since the ultimate aim of acquiring ASL skills is generally that the student achieve conversational competence, and since conversations require both receptive and expressive skills, it is appropriate to consider techniques which can assess both skills simultaneously. Essentially, these tasks will require that a student understand a signed message and then produce an appropriate response. If the response is appropriate, then the teacher has a measure of the student's receptive skills and can then assess the expressive portion of the task. In fact, even if the response is inappropriate, the student's expressive skills can still be assessed at certain levels.

1) *Cloze tasks*—A cloze task is one in which the student must 'fill in the blank' in a signed sentence with the appropriate form of a given sign. The teacher signs an ASL sentence but indicates a blank at some point (e.g. where the verb should be). At the end of the sentence the teacher provides the citation form of the sign which 'fills' that blank (e.g. ＿＿＿-GIVE-TO- ＿＿＿). The student's task is to provide the appropriate form of that sign for the sentence (e.g. *you*-GIVE-TO-*me*).

2) *Focused conversations*—Some of the activities described in Chapter VII (e.g. the Lifeboat, the Camping Trip) provide situations in which the student's receptive and expressive skills can be assessed. These situations are much more like actual conversational situations that students will encounter than are some of the more controlled situations which have been described above.

3) *Half-Conversations*—This task involves the use of videotape. (See next section.) Basically, the teacher arranges for two Deaf, native signers to hold a conversation. The only stipulation is that one of the participants, **A**, is told to ask the other participant, **B**, some questions. The questions can be determined by that individual, **A**. The teacher may specify a topic or provide some background information to the participants. While the two signers are conversing, the teacher videotapes participant **A**. This videotape is then used for evaluation purposes. One-at-a-time (preferably out of sight of the other students), the students view the tape and 'become participant **B**'. That is, the students have a conversation with the videotape. Student responses to questions will indicate whether or not they understand (measuring their receptive skills), and the answers they provide will indicate their expressive skills.

The Use of Videotape in Evaluations:

One of the difficulties in designing a reliable test of Sign Language competency is that very often the tests are administered 'live'. This causes problems since it is very difficult to ensure that the same test is given to different groups of students—i.e. the teacher may vary his/her performance slightly when administering the test at different times. These variations can mean that, in fact, two different tests are being given. This is also true in assessing expressive skills. Teacher memory and fatigue play important roles in 'live' assessments. As a result, the teacher may be using different standards and scoring criteria from student to student. While there are times when the teacher will want to conduct 'live' evaluations (such as when the task is simple, clear, and objectively-rated—e.g. the student did or did not manipulate the objects correctly), by and large it is much more desirable to videotape stimuli for the receptive tasks and to make at least one recording of the students in some expressive task. Such recordings have several advantages:

a) Receptively, the teacher is sure that all students from class to class and year to year are presented the same stimuli. This makes comparison of results possible.

b) The teacher can videotape a variety of signers (hopefully native, Deaf signers) who might not always be available for 'live' presentations of test material.

c) The teacher is able to review and re-examine student performance—which is not possible with 'live' testing.

d) The teacher can have other individuals evaluate and rate student performance—which is not always possible with 'live' testing.

Given the fact that these advantages make videotape testing much more objective and consistent, the teacher should determine the most appropriate time(s) to use videotapes. However, there are several important factors which teachers need to be aware of in order to use videotapes effectively.

a) Videotapes (black and white, or color) essentially present a flat, two-dimensional image to the viewer. As such, there is a certain lack of depth on videotapes which does not occur with 'live' signers. Therefore, the students should become accustomed to viewing signing on videotape before being placed in a testing situation using videotape.

b) In order to provide some sense of depth, it is generally helpful if there is a slight angle (20°-30°) when making the videotape. That is, do not videotape 'head-on', if possible, but slightly to one side. If the signer is right-handed, then the camera should be at a slight angle to the signer's left. This provides a sense of depth for the viewer.

c) Since a camera provides no feedback, it is quite likely that normal non-manual behaviors (which constitute an important part of ASL) will be altered when trying to sign only to a camera. Therefore, it is necessary that there be an 'audience' of three or four people for the signer.

d) Since a T.V. monitor presents a smaller image than a live signer, it is generally felt that a maximum of 10 viewers per monitor is appropriate for allowing equal viewing. With more than 10 viewers, distance and angle become serious problems. Thus, it may be necessary in larger classes to arrange for two T.V. monitors connected to the same videodeck to allow everyone equal viewing opportunities.

e) Lighting is especially important during the production of videotapes. It is important to reduce shadows and at the same time make sure there are no 'hot spots' (i.e. reflections of light off shiny surfaces—watches, rings, noses, foreheads, etc.). Lighting is also an important consideration in viewing videotapes. The teacher must make sure that there is no glare from overhead lights or windows on the T.V. screen itself.

The following test tasks are appropriate for videotape. Since they have been described above, they are simply listed here. Tasks which are not listed here are either too complex to be videotaped without a lot of equipment (e.g. group conversations) or are better done by the teacher in a 'live' situation (e.g. Command responses).

1) **Receptive Tasks**
   —True/False picture statements
   —Multiple-Choice task
   —Description Comprehension
   —Narrative Comprehension
   —Retention tasks
   —Grammatical Identification

2) **Expressive Tasks**
   —Memorization tasks
   —Directed Question/Answer
   —Commands and Descriptive
   —Dialogues
   —Story Completion

3) **Expressive/Receptive Tasks**
   —Cloze procedure (stimulus only)
   —Half-Conversation (stimulus only)

F. How to score and report results

Before describing how to score evaluations and how to report results, it is necessary to first consider a very basic, but often overlooked question: 'How will the results be used?' Another way of stating this question is 'What is the purpose of this evaluation?' This question has been briefly discussed above. What follows is a more in-depth discussion of this issue.

There are several reasons for evaluating a person's ASL skills—to place a student in an appropriate course, to determine areas of strength and weakness, to determine whether a student has completed certain course requirements, etc. Each of these is a valid reason for assessing students' skills. However, different types of information are required in each case. If the evaluation is to be used for placement purposes, then items or tasks in the evaluation must represent and measure a range of 'basic' to 'fluent' skills in order to determine the most appropriate and comfortable placement for the student. This can be viewed as a "screening" or "performance-type test". If, on the other hand, the evaluation will be used to determine the student's strengths and weaknesses (and thus influence future instructional activities), then the items or tasks in the evaluation must include a fairly complete sample of the range of skills which the student should possess. This can be viewed as a "diagnostic test".

As a general rule, it is much more helpful to have an in-depth diagnostic evaluation than just a screening evaluation. With just a screening test, it is not possible to obtain the detailed level of information about the student's competence that is revealed in diagnostic tests. In addition, a screening test can be rather easily developed from a diagnostic test by using those items or tasks on the diagnostic test which best predict student performance.

Perhaps an analogy will help to illustrate the difference. Your car is not running properly, so you take it to a gas station. The mechanic looks at it and says, 'Yup, there's something wrong with your car. It's either the carburetor, alternator, battery, the timing, or something else". The mechanic has conducted a screening-type test—s/he has confirmed that something is wrong and has somewhat narrowed down the possibilities. But you still don't know what to fix or what to work on. If, on the other hand, you take your car to a place that does automotive diagnostic testing, you receive specific information about how well the carburetor, battery, alternator, etc., are functioning and whether or not they are functioning at peak efficiency levels. By examining the report, you are able to focus on the problem area(s) and work on it.

In much the same fashion, simple screening tests generally confirm what a teacher already knows or suspects—i.e. that a particular student has difficulties. But, generally, screening tests do not pinpoint the nature of the difficulty. This creates a situation where two students could, theoretically, obtain the same score on a screening test but may have completely different sets of problems. Consider the following example:

> Students are given a receptive test in which there are 10 sentences, 5 signs each (total 50 points). The students are supposed to write an English translation for each sentence. (Note: this testing method is **not** considered valid or relevant for reasons noted above, but does represent an approach used by many teachers.) The teacher then awards up to 5 points per sentence. Student X correctly translates the first 5 sentences but does not attempt the last 5. His/her total score is 25. Student Y correctly translates ½ of each sentence and is given 2½ points per sentence. His/her total score is 25.

In this example, both students received the same score, although their performance was quite different. To place these two students in the same class or to assume that these two students are similar in ability would be unfair and, in fact, inappropriate. A more diagnostic approach to evaluation might have revealed that Student X performed perfectly with a particular type of sentence, but did not perform well with other types of sentences. Student Y, on the other hand, consistently glossed the subject of each sentence but was unable to deal with the verb. With this type of information, both teacher and student are better prepared to focus energies in areas of needed improvement.

As a general rule, an analysis of the stimulus items on an evaluation provides the teacher with a listing of specific vocabulary and structural features of ASL which the student must understand or produce in order to score correctly on that item. Without such an analysis, the teacher is only capable of making general statements about a student's strengths or weaknesses and, more importantly, no information can be provided to help measure instructional effectiveness.

Let us apply this general rule of analysis to a specific task. Consider the task described above in which the student must select the appropriate picture from a set of 5 very similar pictures based on a stimulus sentence signed by the teacher. Assume that one set of five pictures is as follows:

> 1) a teacher helping a doctor
> 2) several teachers helping a doctor
> 3) a doctor helping a teacher
> 4) several doctors helping a teacher
> 5) a lawyer helping a doctor

Suppose the teacher signs the following test item:

(gaze rt   )   (gaze lf   )   (gaze rt   )
DOCTOR-*rt*,   TEACH AGENT-*lf*   *teacher*-HELP-*doctor*

'The doctor, the teacher helped him/her.'

In order to correctly select or identify the picture which shows a teacher helping a doctor (#1), the student must understand the following lexical and structural features:

Lexical: **TEACH AGENT , DOCTOR , __-HELP- __**

Structural: Verb Directionality—the doctor could help the teacher (picture #3) but the direction of the verb indicates that this is not the case.

Thus, if a student correctly selects picture #1, the teacher can reasonably assume that the student understood all of the lexical items and structural features in that item. Of course, simply getting one test item correct is not adequate proof that a student *fully* understands all of the lexical items and structural features in that item. For example, the feature of verb directionality should be tested several times using different sets of pictures and different lexical items (__-GIVE-TO-__, __-SHOW-TO-__, __-THROW-TO- __, etc.). If the student can understand the use of directionality with several different lexical items on the test, the teacher can safely assume that the student has receptively mastered that structural feature. If, on the other hand, the student does not perform these items correctly, then the teacher knows that there are two possible explanations: the student did not understand the lexical items, or the student did not understand the structural feature of verb directionality. If the teacher cross-checks to see if the student performed correctly on other test items which use that lexical item but do not use verb directionality, then the teacher can determine which of these two explanations is correct.

Examine the following six sentences which might be used as part of a receptive test using this picture selection task. There might be three different sets of five pictures each (one set of five pictures for sentences 1 and 2, one set for sentences 3 and 4, and one set for sentences 5 and 6).

(1) **TEACH AGENT-*rt*   DOCTOR-*lf*   *teacher*-HELP-*doctor***
(2) **TEACH AGENT-*rt*   DOCTOR-*lf*   *doctor*-HELP-*teacher***
(3) **BOY SMALL-*rt*   DOG-*lf*   *boy*-LOOK-AT-*dog***
(4) **BOY SMALL-*rt*   DOG-*lf*   *dog*-LOOK-AT-*boy***
(5) **NURSE-*rt*   LAW AGENT-*lf*   *nurse*-HIT-*lawyer***
(6) **NURSE-*rt*   LAW AGENT-*lf*   *lawyer*-HIT-*nurse***

Before administering the test, the teacher would analyze each test item for the lexical items and grammatical structures in each item. The teacher can then prepare an analysis sheet which represents a perfect score on all test items. An analysis sheet for the six items above is seen in Figure 1 (p. 133).

In this analysis, the plus mark (+) represents a lexical item or structural feature which a student must understand in order to get the item correct. (Note: for sake of explanation, the only structural feature examined here is verb directionality. However, given different pictures and different statements several structural features could be tested. Also the test items are arranged so that they form pairs of similar items. This is done here for clarity's sake. On an actual test a more random order is suggested.)

The teacher prepares an analysis sheet such as this for the entire test and makes sufficient copies so that s/he has one for each student. After the test is given the teacher collects the students' answer sheets (on which the students have written a number for each test item or circled the correct number). The teacher then analyzes the students' responses using one copy of the analysis sheet for each student. If the student's response is correct, the teacher simply indicates this under the column "student choice". If the student's response is incorrect, the teacher indicates which picture was selected and which items or features were in that picture by making a circle in the appropriate column.

A sample analysis sheet of one student's performance on the six item test above is seen in Figure 2 (p. 134).

Fig. 1–TEST FACTORS

TEST ITEM			LEXICAL								STRUCTURAL	
	Correct Response (picture #)	Student Choice (picture #)	TEACH⌢AGENT	DOCTOR	BOY	SMALL DOG	NURSE	LAW⌢AGENT	-HELP-	-LOOK-AT-	-HIT-	Verb Directionality
#1	1		+	+					+			+
#2	3		+	+					+			+
#3	2				+	+				+		+
#4	4				+	+				+		+
#5	3						+	+			+	+
#6	5						+	+			+	+

Fig. 2– SAMPLE RECEPTIVE ANALYSIS SHEET

TEST ITEM			LEXICAL									STRUCTURAL	
	Correct Response (picture #)	Student Choice (picture #)	TEACH⌢AGENT	DOCTOR	BOY	SMALL	DOG	NURSE	LAW⌢AGENT	-HELP-	-LOOK-AT-	-HIT-	Verb Directionality
#1	1	1	+	+						+			+
#2	3	①	+	+						+			⊕
#3	2	④			+		+				+		⊕
#4	4	4			+		+				+		+
#5	3	3						+	+			+	+
#6	5	②						⊕ DOCTOR	+			+	⊕

An examination of this analysis sheet reveals the following information about this student's performance:

1) all verbs were understood on the lexical level.
2) generally, all nouns were understood (the one exception—confusion of DOCTOR for NURSE—would need to be checked in further test items.
3) the structural feature of verb directionality was understood only 50% of the time across all verbs.

Through this type of analysis, the teacher now knows that verb directionality is a serious problem for the student and that the problem is not confined to one verb only. Vocabulary, in general, does not seem to be a problem for this student. Given another student who performed differently, the teacher would have a different analysis and a different set of results.

Notice that if this type of test were scored as a screening test (i.e. student's score is the number of pictures correctly identified), then the score would be 50%. But such a score would fail to reveal the information given above.

A similar approach can also be taken with expressive tasks. In these cases, the teacher must structure the test situation so s/he can reasonably predict which lexical items and structural features the student must use to correctly carry out the task. With this type of preparation, the teacher can then determine whether or not the student performed correctly.

Consider the picture selection task just discussed. If the teacher selects pictures which correspond to the six sentences given above, the teacher then knows what lexical items and structural features the student should use to briefly describe each of the pictures. As before, the analysis sheet can be prepared in advance using plus marks for what should be done for each test item. The teacher can then fill in each sheet based on student performance. In addition, the teacher must include ratings of production, selection, and non-manual factors. (Note: At this point, non-manual behaviors are considered in general. However, as more research becomes available it will be possible to be more specific with this rating category.)

Figure 3 (p. 136) shows the expressive analysis sheet for the six test items discussed above. In this sheet, the plus marks (+) indicate the expected student performance to correctly describe the picture and the circles are errors or incorrect performance.

Given these results, the teacher is in a position to make the following statements about this student's performance:

1) production seems to be a problem for both nouns and verbs.
2) movement difficulties comprise the largest type of production error.
3) selection was appropriate in all cases except one (DOCTOR instead of NURSE) which should be checked in other test items.
4) non-manual behaviors were appropriate except for a single instance of inappropriate use of the eyes.
5) in general, 75% of all lexical items were correct. Production errors accounted for almost all of the problems with lexical items.
6) directionality was correctly used only 50% of the time.

Fig. 3–SAMPLE EXPRESSIVE ANALYSIS SHEET

TEST ITEM	Production	Selection	Non-Manual	TEACH AGENT	DOCTOR	BOY	SMALL	DOG	NURSE	LAW AGENT	-HELP-	-LOOK-AT-	-HIT-	Verb Directionality
				LEXICAL									STRUCTURAL	
#1	+	+	+	+	+						+			+
#2	⊕ movement	+	+	+	+						+			⊕
#3	+	+	+			+	+	+				+		+
#4	⊕ orientation and movement	+	⊕ eyes not directional			+	+	+				⊕		⊕
#5	⊕ handshape	+	+						+	⊕			+	+
#6	⊕ movement	⊕	+						⊕ DOCTOR	+			+	⊕

Given this level of information, the teacher can begin to structure specific instructional activities which will focus on the two main problems of this student: production and directionality. Again, notice that if this type of task were scored only on a right-wrong basis, then the student's score would have been 50%.

Once a teacher has given and rated evaluations of this type, results can be reported back to the student in several formats. For example, the rating sheets themselves could simply be given to the student. This way the student obtains rather in-depth information about his/her receptive and expressive skills. Another option is that the ratings can be transformed into percentage scores. A profile can be produced which would consist of the rating categories (in as much detail as the teacher wishes) and a percentage scale.

If the teacher wishes, s/he can formulate a profile which is as detailed as the evaluation sheet, listing all of the lexical items. However, if percentages are used to report results, a perfect score (i.e. 100%) does *not* mean that a student has completely mastered that category. Rather that score (or any score) simply indicates the student's performance in that category on a specific set of test items.

There are, of course, other approaches to evaluating ASL skills. Perhaps the most common is the use of rating scales. These scales generally use the numbers 1 to 5, with 1 being the lowest score and 5 being the highest. There are, however, several problems with such scales which prevent them from providing the in-depth level of information given by the approach outlined above.

First, the rating categories are generally not clearly defined and are open to subjective interpretation. Thus, terms like 'clarity', 'rhythm', and 'rate' mean different things to different people and will be rated differently.

Second, the points on the scale are generally not well-defined. For example, a '3' on most scales is 'average', but there is no detailed, objective description given as to what is meant by 'average' performance. Again the use of the scale is open to subjective interpretation.

Third, since the mid-point in odd-numbered scales generally represents 'average' (and since there are no clear, objective distinctions made between a '2' and a '3', or a '3' and a '4'), when in doubt, raters most often give a '3'. This "tendency toward the middle" means that the student's score may not truly reflect his/her actual performance.

Fourth, because of the above factors, the reliability of people using such scales tends to be quite variable. This means that what one teacher rates as 'excellent', another may rate as 'average'.

In short, such rating scales do not generally provide a detailed linguistic description of student performance which can be used by the classroom teacher, curriculum developer, or other staff. In addition, the numerical rating generally does not provide the in-depth analysis needed for effective feedback to the instructional program. The advantage of an in-depth diagnostic approach to evaluation such as the one discussed above is that it does provide this in-depth information in a manner which can be reliably measured.

In addition, a summary or composite "profile" can be developed by the teacher to see how the class as a whole performed on the test. This summary can be developed by averaging student scores for a particular category. This information is very helpful in determining which areas should be stressed in different courses.

Such in-depth information can also be used to determine whether or not a student should move on to the next class. That is, certain criteria can be established for entry into other than a basic level class (e.g. a student must have a certain "profile" before being admitted into the next level class).

One objection to such a detailed level of testing is that it is time-consuming. However, the question of time is generally not a factor when considering receptive testing since many of the techniques suggested above are group-administered and since the scoring and analysis is done by the teacher after the test has been given. While it is true that the expressive testing techniques are somewhat time-consuming because they are individually adminstered, there are certain steps which can be taken to reduce the required time.

For example, the teacher can use tasks which require expressive skills of one student and which then provide receptive test stimuli for the rest of the class (e.g. the picture description task described above). Or, the teacher can use videotapes which provide both expressive and receptive test data (e.g. half-conversations on tape). While there is no way to avoid the fact that assessing expressive skills is, and must be, an individualized task, the teacher should be aware of approaches which will make maximum use of the time given for expressive testing. Regardless of the time involved, the teacher should make every effort to give the type of evaluation which can be scored and reported back to the student in the most meaningful and helpful way possible.

To summarize this section on evaluation, there are several questions which must be addressed when constructing or administering any evaluation:

A) Why is the evaluation being given? There are several possible answers to this question (e.g. placement, screening, diagnosis, achievement). The answer to this question will influence the answers to the remaining questions and the evaluation design.

B) What is being evaluated? Obviously, the answer is ASL skills, but the depth of the evaluation is determined by the responses to question A.

C) What assessment approaches best fit the responses to A and B? The response to this question must not only consider the responses to questions A and B, but also the response to question D.

D) What is the most helpful type of information to report to the student? The response to this question is obviously dependent upon the response to question A, but will have some bearing on question C—concerning test format.

The answers to these questions are crucial in order to design, develop, and administer an evaluation which is meaningful and effective. Of course, before an evaluation can be developed, curriculum goals and objectives must be determined because the evaluation needs to have a high degree of relevance vis-a-vis the instructional program. This level of care and depth is needed so that the information received from evaluation is beneficial to the program and the teacher but, most importantly, to the student.

Chapter IX

Curriculum Guide for ASL

The purpose of this chapter is to present and discuss a curriculum guide for teaching ASL. This curriculum guide is intended as a model; modifications may be necessary when applying it to specific programs. However, before examining the curriculum guide, it will be helpful to discuss exactly what a curriculum guide is and what is involved in the development of a curriculum guide.

A curriculum guide is basically a series of statements listing what students should know or be able to do by the end of a given course or program. If these statements are somewhat general (e.g. "The students will gain an appreciation of the history of ASL"), then they are called *goals*. If they are more specific (e.g. "The students will write a one-page report on the following article: 'Notes for a Psycho-History of American Sign Language' by Harlan Lane"), then they are called *objectives*. Notice that the difference between a "goal" and an "objective" is that the teacher can easily determine whether or not a student has met an objective (e.g. the student turned in the one-page report); determining whether or not a student has met a goal is much more difficult (e.g. how do you measure "appreciation"?). For this reason, most curriculum guides are basically a carefully sequenced series of objectives.

In writing an objective, it is generally agreed that the teacher should include some means of determining whether or not the student has accomplished the stated task. This means that the objective should include some visible, measurable means of determining student performance. Consider, for example, the following objective:

"The student will read the play *Sign Me Alice*."

This objective clearly states the expected performance ("read the play") but does not include a way of measuring whether or not the student has, in fact, read the play. In order to evaluate the student's performance, the teacher needs to include a phrase which states the criteria for successful accomplishment of the task. The following objectives illustrate several observable ways to determine student performance:

"The student will read the play *Sign Me Alice* and write a three-page report on the play."
"The student will read the play *Sign Me Alice* and give a ten-minute report in class."
"The student will read the play *Sign Me Alice* and participate in a group discussion of the play."
"The student will read the play *Sign Me Alice* and participate in a dramatic rendition of the first act."

In each of these examples, the teacher is able to determine whether or not the student has read the play through some visible behavior on the student's part. Objectives which include this type of observable, behavioral criteria are called *behavioral objectives*.

There are many advantages to using objectives in designing a curriculum. Some of the most important advantages are:

1) They provide a means for teachers to know whether or not students have mastered specific goals in a given course;
2) They provide a means for students to know what is expected of them in a given course;
3) They enable both student and teacher to see the relationships between courses;
4) They provide a means of placing students in appropriate courses;
5) They force the teacher and curriculum developers to begin to think more analytically about sequencing skills, information, etc.

In addition to the general behavioral objectives discussed above, there is another level of *sub-objectives*, or *enabling objectives*, which is equally important. Not all of the skills necessary for conversational competence in ASL can be neatly stated in one behavioral objective. Oftentimes a single objective may require four or five sub-objectives. These sub-objectives should be clearly stated in behavioral terms. For example, consider the following objective:

> "The student will demonstrate expressive readiness for ASL by successfully completing all assigned tasks relating to body awareness, body comfort, and the use of space."

As stated here, this behavioral objective is satisfactory as a general objective for a course. But, the teacher must also be aware of the fact that there may be five or ten tasks which are related to body awareness, body comfort, and the use of space. It is necessary, then, for the teacher to list these tasks in behavioral terms so that both student and teacher know what is meant by demonstrating expressive readiness for ASL. For example,

> "The student will demonstrate expressive readiness for ASL by successfully completing all assigned tasks relating to body awareness, body comfort, and the use of space.
>
> 1) To develop body awareness and body comfort, the student will accurately perform the Facial Strings activity.
> 2) To develop body awareness, body comfort, and the use of space, the student will accurately perform the Picture Drawing activity.
> 3) To develop appropriate use of space, the student will accurately perform the Proper Positions activity.
> 4) To develop body awareness, body comfort, and appropriate sensitivity to space, the student will accurately perform the Change the Stick activity.
> 5) etc."

If the sub-objectives are carefully developed and are comprehensive enough, then, when the student correctly performs or masters all of the sub-objectives, the teacher can say with confidence that the student has mastered the main objective. Of course, it may not be necessary for the student to complete all of the sub-objectives in order to demonstrate mastery of the main objective. Some of the sub-objectives may be hierarchically arranged (for example, if the student can perform sub-objective 7, s/he already has the skills required for sub-objectives 1-6). It is not always possible to develop or arrange sub-objectives in this fashion. When it is possible to do this, then the teacher has a "developmental" listing of all of the factors involved in a particular major objective.

There are, however, certain areas of language teaching and learning which cannot be written in terms of behavioral objectives. For example, the teacher might write a behavioral objective which requires that all of the students attend a play given in ASL. However, the teacher cannot write a behavioral objective which requires that all of the students enjoy the play. Good behavioral objectives are written using words such as 'show', 'demonstrate', 'write', 'discuss', etc. Good behavioral objectives avoid words such as 'like', 'enjoy', 'appreciate', 'respect', etc., because these things cannot be directly measured. Thus, there may be certain areas in a curriculum guide which cannot be written in behavioral terms. However, these areas should still be included and should be written as clearly as possible.

Another helpful feature to include in a behavioral objective is a specific mastery criterion. This means including a statement that indicates what the student must do to 'pass' the objective. For example, consider the following objective: "The student will demonstrate receptive mastery of pluralization processes in ASL by obtaining a score of 90% on a test of such pluralization processes." This objective includes a specific passing level—90%—as well as the specific behavior required of the student—a test of pluralization processes. Whenever possible, it is helpful to include such a criterion. There are, of course, many places where this is not possible and the teacher must use other means of determining success.

A note of caution is needed at this point. In establishing criteria for objectives, the teacher must be realistic. While it may be desirable for all students to obtain 100%, this is not a realistic expectation. Criteria—especially percentages—must be carefully selected and, if necessary, adjusted over time. A teacher may set 90% as a criteria for mastery and then feel that it should be adjusted to 85%. These adjustments should be made after the teacher considers the following factors: the task, the instructional support, the level of proficiency required, the students' capabilities, program constraints, etc. In this way, the criteria that are selected can be fair and realistic. The teacher must also bear in mind that when a student 'passes' or masters a certain objective, that does not necessarily mean that the student has mastered all that is involved in a particular area. This only means that the student has mastered those areas covered in the sub-objectives. For example, a student who 'passes' or masters a particular objective relating to pluralization processes in ASL has only mastered those particular processes written into sub-objectives. However, there may be pluralization processes which the teacher has not included in the sub-objectives which the student knows nothing about. Thus the term "mastery" is a somewhat relative term that refers to the content and performance level set by the teacher.

A curriculum guide, then, is a carefully sequenced series of major course objectives. There are, however, different approaches to arranging a curriculum guide. For our purposes, we can contrast two such approaches: a *linear* curriculum guide and a *spiraling* curriculum guide. Most other approaches are variations of these two basic approaches.

A linear curriculum guide is a series of objectives which, once they are mastered in a given course, are never dealt with in that course again or, never dealt with specifically in more advanced courses. For example, if one were to adopt a linear approach to ASL instruction, it would be necessary in one course to cover everything the student needed to know about pluralization since that topic would not be covered again in future courses. For the most part, linear curriculum guides are not appropriate for language teaching and learning. This is because the nature of language learning demands that as the student becomes more and more skilled, s/he begins to deal with aspects of the language at a deeper and deeper level. In general, courses which are vocabulary courses tend to rely on a linear curriculum approach ("This week Chapter 1, next week Chapter 2, etc."). Most contemporary language learning and teaching curricula use a spiraling approach.

A spiraling curriculum guide is a series of objectives which require deeper and deeper levels of a skill at different points in a single course or across several courses. To use the example of pluralization in ASL again, in a first course the objectives might require that the student master only one or two ways of indicating plurality. In subsequent courses, additional strategies for indicating plurality would be covered. In this way, as the student gains more skill in the language, s/he can handle and assimilate more complex structures in a meaningful manner. Thus a spiraling curriculum provides limited exposure to a wide range of language features and then returns at a later date (i.e. "spirals back") to deal with those language features at a deeper level. This spiraling process may continue for several courses, thus providing reinforcement for the student for what s/he has already learned as well as providing instruction at appropriate places for more complex material. It is generally believed that the spiraling approach is a more effective way to teach a language because languages are so complex. In the curriculum guide which follows, we have used a spiraling approach.

The curriculum guide which follows is designed for a six-course program in ASL. It is intended for classes which meet three times a week for one and one-half to two hours each meeting. It is intended as a guide and, therefore, certain adjustments and modifications may be necessary to fit the constraints of specific programs.

The curriculum guide contains only major course objectives with a brief statement of the rationale for each particular course. No sub-objectives are given since it is felt that these can best be developed by individual teachers in a way which reflects their own teaching style. There are, however, certain factors which are mentioned in the rationale and discussion which should be included in the sub-objectives. At the end of the chapter, a curriculum matrix is presented which shows the relationship of the various objectives.

The reader will note that the labels "beginning", "intermediate", and "advanced" are not used in the course titles. Instead, a simple numerical label is used: ASL I, ASL II, etc. The reason for this is that, at present, there exists no research data on ASL learning and teaching to support the distinction between "beginning", "intermediate", and "advanced" skills. In fact, these divisions are often quite arbitrary and differ substantially from program to program.

Before examining the curriculum guide and the following discussion of the objectives, there are two things which the reader should be aware of. First, the division of the objectives into four major categories (Cultural Awareness, Grammatical Features, Vocabulary, and Conversational Skills) is intended to help clarify and organize the objectives. There are certain objectives which could appear in more than one of these major categories (e.g. an objective dealing with exposure to short stories and narratives could easily be written to fit in the grammatical feature category as well as the conversational skills category). Consequently even though an objective appears in only one category, it may presuppose or include content from one or more of the other categories.

Second, the objectives for a given course are not always dealt with in the order in which they are presented below. For example, the students need to receive written information throughout an entire course, not only in the beginning of a course. Once the teacher has developed the specific sub-objectives for each of the major objectives, then s/he must decide which sub-objectives will be dealt with in each class. Thus the sub-objectives become very important in planning each lesson. In other words, one lesson may include sub-objectives from four or five of the major objectives (e.g. a short story or narrative may provide information about the Deaf community and may also focus on specific grammatical features and vocabulary items which the teacher has targeted for a specific lesson).

The obvious focus of the entire curriculum is the development of communicative competence in ASL. For that reason, the objectives in the four major curriculum categories—Cultural Awareness, Grammatical Features, Vocabulary (Lexicon), and Conversational Skills—are designed to foster interaction and conversation as much as possible. As was mentioned above, some of the course objectives in one category imply or require skills which logically might fit into another category. Teachers will need to work out these implied or prerequisite skills and interrelations when preparing their own behavioral sub-objectives.

ASL I

A. Cultural Awareness:

1) The student will receive written information on the following topics: the history of ASL, the Deaf community, ASL and its relation to other forms of signing on the diglossic continuum.
2) The student will write a two-page report reacting to a book or article which relates to the Deaf community and is assigned by the teacher.
3) The student will attend at least one social function at which members of the Deaf community are present (but not a Deaf club).
4) The student will demonstrate receptive readiness for acquiring ASL.
5) The student will demonstrate expressive readiness for acquiring ASL.

B. Grammatical Features:

1) The student will demonstrate receptive mastery of targeted, context-specific commands, questions, and statements in ASL.
2) The student will demonstrate expressive mastery of targeted, context-specific commands, questions, and statements in ASL.
3) The student will be exposed to short dialogues in ASL.

C. Vocabulary (Lexicon):

1) The student will receive exposure to a targeted set of vocabulary items.
2) Given a set of targeted vocabulary items drawn from class activities, the student will demonstrate receptive mastery of these vocabulary items.
3) Given a set of targeted vocabulary items drawn from class activities, the student will demonstrate expressive mastery of these vocabulary items.

D. Conversational Skills:

1) The student will demonstrate receptive and expressive mastery of targeted conversation-facilitating behaviors (AGAIN, SLOW, "WHAT", etc.).
2) The student will demonstrate receptive and expressive mastery of targeted conversation regulating behaviors (attention-getting devices, turn-taking signals, etc.).
3) The student will be exposed to short narratives, stories, etc., in ASL that are told by the teacher and by Deaf users of ASL.
4) The student will demonstrate the ability to initiate, conduct, and terminate a short context-specific conversation with Deaf users of ASL other than the teacher.

ASL II

A. Cultural Awareness:

1) The student will receive written information related to culturally significant topics in the Deaf community.
2) The student will write a short paper (approx. 5 pages) on a specific aspect of the Deaf community that is assigned by the teacher.
3) The student will attend at least one social function at which members of the Deaf community are present (but not a Deaf club).

B. Grammatical Features:

1) The student will receive appropriate written information on all targeted grammatical features of ASL covered during the course.
2) Given a set of specially prepared ASL dialogues, the student will demonstrate receptive mastery of those features of ASL targeted in the dialogues.
3) Given a set of specially prepared ASL dialogues, the student will demonstrate expressive mastery of those features of ASL in the dialogues.

C. Vocabulary (Lexicon):

1) The student will be exposed to a targeted set of vocabulary items.
2) Given a set of targeted vocabulary items (including fingerspelled loans) drawn largely from specially prepared dialogues, the student will demonstrate receptive mastery of these vocabulary items.
3) Given a set of targeted vocabulary items (including fingerspelled loans) drawn largely from specially prepared dialogues, the student will demonstrate expressive mastery of these vocabulary items.
4) Given a set of targeted vocabulary items (including fingerspelled loans), the student will demonstrate receptive and expressive mastery of appropriately selected stylistic, regional, social, ethnic, and age-related variations of these vocabulary items.

D. Conversational Skills:

1) The student will demonstrate receptive competence for relatively short narratives, stories, etc., in ASL that are told by the teacher and by Deaf users of ASL.
2) The student will demonstrate the ability to express self-generated short stories, short narratives, etc., in ASL.
3) The student will demonstrate the ability to initiate, conduct, and terminate context-specific conversations of medium length with Deaf users of ASL other than the teacher.

ASL III

A. Cultural Awareness:
1) The student will receive written information concerning culturally significant topics in the Deaf community.
2) The student will attend at least two social functions at which members of the Deaf community are present (but not a Deaf club).
3) The student will sign a short (2-3 minutes) report in class using ASL on a teacher-assigned topic related to the Deaf community.

B. Grammatical Features:
1) The student will receive appropriate written information on all targeted grammatical features of ASL covered during the course.
2) Given a set of specially prepared ASL dialogues, the student will demonstrate receptive mastery of those features of ASL targeted in the dialogues.
3) Given a set of specially prepared ASL dialogues, the student will demonstrate expressive mastery of those features of ASL in the dialogues.

C. Vocabulary (Lexicon):
1) The student will be exposed to a targeted set of vocabulary items.
2) Given a set of targeted vocabulary items (including fingerspelled loans) drawn largely from specially prepared dialogues, the student will demonstrate receptive mastery of these vocabulary items.
3) Given a set of targeted vocabulary items (including fingerspelled loans) drawn largely from specially prepared dialogues, the student will demonstrate expressive mastery of these vocabulary items.
4) Given a set of targeted vocabulary items (including fingerspelled loans), the student will demonstrate receptive and expressive mastery of appropriately selected stylistic, regional, social, ethnic, and age-related variations of these vocabulary items.
5) The student will demonstrate receptive and expressive mastery of the manual alphabet and the use of fingerspelling in ASL.

D. Conversational Skills:
1) The student will demonstrate receptive competence in understanding medium-length stories, narratives, etc., in ASL that are told by the teacher and by Deaf users of ASL.
2) The student will demonstrate the ability to express self-generated stories, narratives, etc., of medium length in ASL.
3) The student will demonstrate the ability to initiate, conduct, and terminate rather lengthy conversations with Deaf users of ASL other than the teacher.
4) The student will demonstrate the ability to successfully participate in context-specific, teacher-directed group discussions.

ASL IV

A. Cultural Awareness:

1) The student will receive written information on culturally significant topics in the Deaf community.
2) The student will subscribe to the *Deaf American* and any local newsletter of the Deaf community.
3) The student will attend at least two social functions at which members of the Deaf community are present (but not the Deaf club).
4) The student will make one teacher-arranged visit to a Deaf club.
5) The student will sign a medium-length report (3-5 minutes) in class using ASL on a teacher-assigned topic related to the Deaf community.

B. Grammatical Features:

1) The student will receive appropriate written information on all targeted grammatical features of ASL covered during the course.
2) Given a set of specially prepared ASL dialogues, the student will demonstrate receptive mastery of those features of ASL targeted in the dialogues.
3) Given a set of specially prepared ASL dialogues, the student will demonstrate expressive mastery of those features of ASL in the dialogues.

C. Vocabulary (Lexicon):

1) The student will receive exposure to a targeted set of vocabulary items.
2) Given a set of targeted vocabulary items (including fingerspelled loans) drawn largely from specially prepared dialogues, the student will demonstrate receptive mastery of these vocabulary items.
3) Given a set of targeted vocabulary items (including fingerspelled loans) drawn largely from specially prepared dialogues, the student will demonstrate expressive mastery of these vocabulary items.
4) Given a set of targeted vocabulary items (including fingerspelled loans), the student will demonstrate receptive and expressive mastery of appropriately selected stylistic, regional, social, ethnic, and age-related variations of these vocabulary items.
5) The student will demonstrate receptive and expressive mastery of targeted fingerspelled items.

D. Conversational Skills:

1) The student will demonstrate receptive competence in understanding lengthy stories, narratives, etc., in ASL that are told by the teacher and by Deaf users of ASL.
2) The student will demonstrate the ability to express self-generated lengthy stories, narratives, etc., in ASL.
3) The student will view and discuss the 1910-1920 films made for the preservation of Sign Language by the NAD.
4) The student will demonstrate the ability to successfully participate in non-context-specific group discussions.

ASL V

A. **Cultural Awareness:**
   1) The student will subscribe to the *Deaf American* and any local newsletter of the Deaf community.
   2) The student will attend at least two social functions at which members of the Deaf community are present (but <u>not</u> a Deaf club).
   3) The student will make at least one teacher-arranged visit to a Deaf club.
   4) The student will spend approximately 25% of the course (at least one class every two weeks) interacting with members of the Deaf community (outside the classroom, if possible).

B. **Grammatical Features:**
   1) The student will demonstrate receptive mastery of all grammatical features of ASL in all course activities.
   2) The student will demonstrate expressive mastery of all grammatical features of ASL in all course activities.

C. **Vocabulary (Lexicon):**
   1) The student will receive exposure to a targeted set of vocabulary items.
   2) Given a set of targeted vocabulary items drawn from class activities, the student will demonstrate receptive mastery of these vocabulary items.
   3) Given a set of targeted vocabulary items drawn from class activities, the student will demonstrate expressive mastery of these vocabulary items.
   4) Given a set of targeted vocabulary items (including fingerspelled loans), the student will demonstrate receptive and expressive mastery of appropriately selected stylistic, regional, social, ethnic, and age-related variations of these vocabulary items.
   5) The student will demonstrate receptive mastery of socially restricted signs.

D. **Conversational Skills:**
   1) The student will do an in-depth reading, analysis, and discussion in ASL of the play *Sign Me Alice*.
   2) The student will successfully participate in non-directed group discussions relating to experiences in interacting with members of the Deaf community.

ASL VI

A. Cultural Awareness:

1) The student will subscribe to the *Deaf American* and any local newsletter of the Deaf community.

2) The student will spend approximately 50% of the course interacting with members of the Deaf community outside the classroom, if possible (e.g. by joining a bowling league, a captioned film club, athletic events, religious functions).

3) The student will make at least one teacher-arranged visit to a Deaf club.

B. Grammatical Features:

1) The student will demonstrate receptive mastery of all grammatical features of ASL in all course activities.

2) The student will demonstrate expressive mastery of all grammatical features of ASL in all course activities.

C. Vocabulary (Lexicon):

1) The student will receive exposure to a targeted set of vocabulary items.

2) Given a set of targeted vocabulary items drawn from class activities, the student will demonstrate receptive mastery of these vocabulary items.

3) Given a set of targeted vocabulary items drawn from class activities, the student will demonstrate expressive mastery of these vocabulary items.

4) Given a set of targeted vocabulary items (including fingerspelled loans), the student will demonstrate receptive and expressive mastery of appropriately selected stylistic, regional, social, ethnic, and age-related variations of these vocabulary items.

D. Conversational Skills:

1) The student will demonstrate the ability to successfully participate in non-directed group discussions on student-generated topics.

2) The student will exchange a videotaped "letter(s)" in ASL with a student at a similar skill level in another ASL class in another part of the country.

The following discussion provides an explanation and a rationale for several of the objectives in the curriculum and for the sequencing and placement of certain objectives. Before discussing these, however, it will be helpful to point out some general characteristics of the proposed curriculum. This general discussion will provide an appropriate framework for dealing with specific courses and objectives.

The first general feature of the curriculum is that it is designed to provide students with conversational competence in ASL. Thus in every course, the students are either exposed to certain types of conversational behaviors or are expected to demonstrate receptive and/or expressive skills in certain types of conversational behaviors—e.g. dialogues, group discussions, signed reports. These objectives are crucial since they provide the student with opportunities to develop and practice those skills which will be most useful in interacting with the Deaf community.

Second, vocabulary is drawn from meaningful contexts—e.g. dialogues, stories, conversations. The teacher can, of course, list all the lexical items or the minimum number of lexical items targeted for each course by studying the dialogues, stories, narratives, or other activities which are planned for the course. The vocabulary taken from these sources should be listed in three categories: *exposure*—students are not held accountable for these items in a specific course but may be held accountable in a later course; *receptive*—students are expected to be able to demonstrate receptive mastery of these items, but not necessarily expressive mastery; *expressive*—students are expected to be able to demonstrate both receptive and expressive mastery of these items. In tabulating targeted vocabulary, the teacher should remember that an item which appears in the expressive list must also appear in the receptive list, but some items may only appear on the receptive list or exposure list and not on the expressive list. This approach avoids using an arbitrary number (e.g. 500 signs, 750 signs) or an arbitrary categorization (e.g. the first 8, 9, or 10 chapters of a given text) when identifying the target vocabulary for a given course.

Third, the formal introduction to and study of the manual alphabet and fingerspelling is delayed until the third course. This provides ample time and opportunity for the student to experience success and satisfaction in communicating with signs. More specific reasons for delaying fingerspelling have already been discussed in Chapter III. The students will, of course, be exposed to and be held accountable for certain fingerspelled loan signs (#WHAT, #JOB, #CAR, etc.) in the first two courses.

Fourth, the first teacher-arranged visit to a local Deaf club does not occur until the *fourth* course. By that time, the students should have developed sufficient competence to make the visit an enjoyable and satisfactory experience for them and for the Deaf individuals at the club. Prior to this visit, however, there will have been opportunities for interaction with members of the Deaf community both in class and at a wide range of social functions.

Fifth, by the time a student enters course V, s/he should have mastered all of the targeted grammatical features of ASL covered in the first four courses. The focus of courses V and VI is on opportunities to use these skills in a wider range of conversational and interactional activities. Thus, by this time, it is assumed that the student has a very strong foundation in the language and now needs guided opportunities for refinement and practice.

Given these general features of the curriculum, it is now possible to examine a few of the specific course objectives and examine the relationship between objectives within a particular course.

ASL I: Included in this course, under the cultural awareness category, there are two objectives which relate to receptive and expressive readiness. These objectives are placed in this category because the modality of the language (gestural-visual) represents a significant cultural difference between the Deaf community and the Hearing community. An awareness of the importance of vision to the Deaf community is crucial for understanding and accepting that community. Thus, the activities in Chapter IV for training the eyes and body attempt not only to build a foundation for acquiring the grammatical and semantic features of ASL, but also serve as an introduction to a significant cultural difference which students need to be aware of from the beginning.

The students' initial exposure to certain grammatical features and lexical items in ASL occurs in the context of commands, questions, and statements. Thus, at this level, it is appropriate to make concentrated use of the techniques and activities discussed in Chapter V. These activities provide very structured contexts for the acquisition of vocabulary and certain grammatical features of ASL. In identifying the target vocabulary, the teacher should draw from these activities those items which are targeted for exposure, those targeted for receptive mastery, and those which are targeted for expressive mastery.

The students are expected, at this level, to be able to initiate, conduct, and terminate a short conversation. It is appropriate that students be held accountable for conversation regulating and facilitating behaviors which will be needed and helpful during short conversations. Exposure to short dialogues will help the students determine the appropriate meaning and use of such behaviors.

Finally, exposure to short narratives, stories, etc., will help students to continue developing their visual awareness skills. While new vocabulary and grammatical features may occur in these stories, narratives, etc., the students are not held accountable for them. Rather, the students are placed in a situation where there is a certain amount of 'give-and-take' with regard to how much they can readily understand and how much they must rely on contextual clues to aid comprehension. Of course, the teacher can control this 'give-and-take' situation by arranging the stories and narratives so that they contain vocabulary items and grammatical features already familiar to the students.

In summary, at this level—ASL I—the students are not expected to possess any in-depth theoretical knowledge of the grammatical features of ASL. Instead, the students are given ample opportunities for experiencing successful and satisfactory communication directly in ASL.

ASL II, III, IV: In these courses, the students' exposure to the culture and community of Deaf individuals is increased by receiving specific information about significant influences on that culture and community—e.g. the NAD, the *Deaf American,* educational programs, etc. In a very real sense, students in this course begin the serious study of ASL as a language because in this course they begin learning the complexities of specific grammatical features of ASL.

Although the students receive written explanations about certain grammatical features, this in and of itself does not mean that the students will acquire mastery of those features. Consequently, in these courses, specially prepared dialogues are used as the vehicle for providing the students with contextual exposure and practice of targeted grammatical features. The basic principle of the spiraling curriculum is that the students are accountable for mastery of specific features across a wide range of linguistic behaviors, and, then in subsequent courses, they are accountable for mastery of increasingly more complex features across the same range of linguistic behaviors. In courses II, III, and IV, the student receives increasingly complex written information and acquisition opportunities relating to pluralization, temporal aspect, classifiers, pronominalization, etc. Dialogues have been chosen as the major vehicle in these courses for presenting structural information in context. Chapter VI presents a detailed discussion of the rationale for using dialogues.

Although there are texts which contain specially developed dialogues, the teacher must realize that no single dialogue will contain examples of *all* types of a single grammatical feature targeted for a given course. Thus, the teacher must examine all of the dialogues which will be used in a given course to determine if there is adequate coverage of the targeted grammatical features. It may be that a particular way of expressing plurality in ASL does not occur in a dialogue which specifically focuses on pluralization, but does occur in another dialogue used later in the course. The teacher may elect to delay spending time on that particular way of expressing plurality until it appears in the later dialogue, or s/he may decide to introduce that way of expressing plurality immediately by means of a story or narrative or some supplemental activity.

In any event, the teacher should not feel that everything about a particular feature must be taught in a single class or a single course. Rather, the teacher should be knowledgable about the range of grammatical features of ASL[1], and determine which aspects of a particular grammatical feature will be covered in each course. Dialogues should then be developed or selected which focus on these grammatical features and which emphasize those aspects targeted for each course.[2]

---

[1]A major aid to the teacher in this area is *American Sign Language: a teacher's resource text on grammar and culture* the companion text by Baker and Cokely, Silver Spring, Md.: T.J. Publishers, Inc. 1980.

[2]The texts, *American Sign Language: student text Units 1-9, Units 10-18, Units 19-27,* provide the teacher and student with twenty-seven dialogues (nine per text) which have been specially developed for courses II, III, and IV.

Vocabulary targeted for these three courses is drawn from the dialogues and reinforced through the use of drills, stories, narratives and other activities. Of course, additional vocabulary is also drawn from stories, narratives, and other class activities. If a specific number of targeted vocabulary items must be stated in the course description or objectives, this number can be estimated by simply counting the targeted vocabulary in the dialogues and activities. (For example, in the dialogues for ASL II, there may be an estimated 450-500 targeted vocabulary items).

Additionally, beginning with ASL II, the student is expected to demonstrate appropriate receptive and expressive mastery of variations of the targeted vocabulary. This also expands the student's vocabulary base. However, the teacher must decide whether the student is accountable for receptive mastery or receptive and expressive mastery of targeted variations. Obviously there will be some variants which the students need only understand but not necessarily use, and others which students should be able to understand and use. The teacher's own variants as well as variants used by the Deaf adults who assist during the course can be introduced to the students by substituting these variants in the dialogues and other activities. The students should receive some information concerning the type of variant (e.g. related to age, geography, ethnicity, formality) and its distribution and use.

Finally, during courses II, III, and IV, the students develop the skills to participate in both teacher-directed and self-directed group discussions. For these objectives, the activities described in Chapter VII provide appropriate sub-objectives for the teacher. It is also in these courses that the students develop skills in understanding and expressing stories and narratives of varying lengths. These conversational skills — group discussions and stories, narratives, etc. — provide another important resource for introducing and practicing grammatical features not covered in the dialogues.

ASL V: By the time a student enters this course, s/he should have mastered all of the targeted grammatical features, possess a reasonably well-developed and extensive vocabulary base, be familiar with a variety of cultural aspects of the Deaf community, and have engaged in a variety of successful interactions with members of the Deaf community. In this course, the focus is on increased opportunities to practice the communicative skills that the student already possesses and to use those skills to develop additional skills. Consequently, approximately 25% of the course is devoted to interactions with members of the Deaf community in both directed and non-directed activities. This increased, regular contact with the Deaf community will provide students with a wide range of opportunities to acquire additional cultural information and attitudes as well as opportunities to use their ASL skills to gain increased competence in the language.

Additionally, the student is exposed to a set of cultural values and attitudes through reading and discussing the play *Sign Me Alice*. This play, based on Shaw's *Pygmalion,* is the reaction of a Deaf man to the various artificial codes for representing English. It offers an in-depth view of the feelings and attitudes of some members of the Deaf community toward these codes. It is a valuable resource for helping students gain more insight into and appreciation for the Deaf community.

ASL VI: By the time a student enters this course, s/he should feel quite comfortable with the language and with the immediate community of users. As such, this course (and to some extent course V) is equivalent to a literature course in a spoken language. However, since the folklore and the 'literature' of the Deaf community does not exist in written form (because ASL is not a written language), access to the 'literature' and heritage of the Deaf community is generally through increased social contact with members of the community. Thus, approximately 50% of the course is devoted to interaction with members of the community in non-classroom settings, if possible. Discussion, expansion, and explanation of this interaction form the basis for the students to continue developing their knowledge of vocabulary and grammatical features, as needed.

Another objective in this course requires that the students prepare and exchange videotaped 'letters' with students in other programs. There are several advantages to this activity: first, the teacher can use the tapes as one form of evaluation; second, the exchange of such letters may provide samples of different regional and social variation; third, it is possible that some of the tapes could be used with students in courses at other levels. Most importantly, this activity provides another opportunity for students to use their skills to interact and communicate with others.

What has been presented so far is a six-course curriculum and a discussion of how the major objectives within a particular course are related. It is also helpful to examine how the objectives within one course are related to similar objectives in other courses. The curriculum matrix which follows indicates the flow and relation of objectives from one course to another. To display this matrix most clearly, the four major categories—cultural awareness, grammatical features, vocabulary, and conversational skills—are given with an abbreviated listing of the relevant objectives for each course. For the sake of legibility, the matrix for each of the four categories is presented separately. However, the reader must remember that each course includes objectives from all four categories. Additionally, the reader must remember that the matrix includes only the major objectives for each course and that sub-objectives must be developed which are appropriate for a given group of students, particular program constraints, and the teacher's style. Thus, a range of rather complex skills may be required to accomplish a given course objective.

A. Cultural Awareness:

ASL I	ASL II	ASL III	ASL IV	ASL V	ASL VI
1) The student will demonstrate receptive readiness.					
2) The student will demonstrate expressive readiness.					
3) The student will receive written information.	1) The student will receive written information.	1) The student will receive written information.	1) The student will receive written information.		
4) The student will write a 2-page reaction report.	2) The student will write a 5-page report.	2) The student will sign a short report in class.	2) The student will sign a medium-length report in class.		
5) The student will attend at least one social function of the Deaf community.	3) The student will attend at least one social function of the Deaf community.	3) The student will attend at least two social functions of the Deaf community.	3) The student will attend at least two social functions of the Deaf community.	1) The student will attend at least two social functions of the Deaf community.	
			4) The student will make one teacher-arranged visit to a Deaf club.	2) The student will make one teacher-arranged visit to a Deaf club.	1) The student will make one teacher-arranged visit to a Deaf club.
			5) The student will subscribe to the *Deaf American* and any local newsletter of the Deaf community.	3) The student will subscribe to the *Deaf American* and any local newsletter of the Deaf community.	2) The student will subscribe to the *Deaf American* and any local newsletter of the Deaf community.
				4) The student will spend 25% of the course interacting with members of the Deaf community.	3) The student will spend 50% of the course interacting with members of the Deaf community.

B. Grammatical Features:

ASL I	ASL II	ASL III	ASL IV	ASL V	ASL VI
1) Receptive mastery of targeted commands, questions and statements. 2) Expressive mastery of targeted commands, questions and statements. 3) Exposure to short ASL dialogues.	1) Receptive mastery of targeted grammatical features in specially prepared dialogues. 2) Expressive mastery of grammatical features in specially prepared dialogues. 3) Appropriate written information on all targeted grammatical features.	1) Receptive mastery of targeted grammatical features in specially prepared dialogues. 2) Expressive mastery of grammatical features in specially prepared dialogues. 3) Appropriate written information on all targeted grammatical features.	1) Receptive mastery of targeted grammatical features in specially prepared dialogues. 2) Expressive mastery of grammatical features in specially prepared dialogues. 3) Appropriate written information on all targeted grammatical features.	1) Receptive mastery of all grammatical features in course activities. 2) Expressive mastery of all grammatical features in course activities.	1) Receptive mastery of all grammatical features in course activities. 2) Expressive mastery of all grammatical features in course activities.

C. Vocabulary (Lexicon):

ASL I	ASL II	ASL III	ASL IV	ASL V	ASL VI
1) Exposure to targeted vocabulary items from activities.	1) Exposure to targeted vocabulary items from activities.	1) Exposure to targeted vocabulary items from activities.	1) Exposure to targeted vocabulary items from activities.	1) Exposure to targeted vocabulary items from activities.	1) Exposure to targeted vocabulary items from activities.
2) Receptive mastery of targeted vocabulary items from activities.	2) Receptive mastery of targeted vocabulary items from dialogues.	2) Receptive mastery of targeted vocabulary items from dialogues.	2) Receptive mastery of targeted vocabulary items from dialogues.	2) Receptive mastery of targeted vocabulary items from activities.	2) Receptive mastery of targeted vocabulary items from activities.
3) Expressive mastery of targeted vocabulary items from activities.	3) Expressive mastery of targeted vocabulary items from dialogues.	3) Expressive mastery of targeted vocabulary items from dialogues.	3) Expressive mastery of targeted vocabulary items from dialogues.	3) Expressive mastery of targeted vocabulary items from activities.	3) Expressive mastery of targeted vocabulary items from activities.
	4) Receptive and expressive mastery of targeted variants.	4) Receptive and expressive mastery of targeted variants.	4) Receptive and expressive mastery of targeted variants.	4) Receptive and expressive mastery of targeted variants.	4) Receptive and expressive mastery of targeted variants.
		5) Receptive and expressive mastery of the manual alphabet and targeted fingerspelled items.	5) Receptive and expressive mastery of targeted fingerspelled items.	5) Receptive mastery of socially restricted targeted signs.	

D. Conversational Skills:

ASL I	ASL II	ASL III	ASL IV	ASL V	ASL VI
1) Receptive and expressive mastery of targeted conversational facilitating behavior.					
2) Receptive and expressive mastery of targeted conversation regulating behavior.					
3) Exposure to short stories, narratives, etc.					
4) Demonstrate ability to initiate, conduct and terminate short, context-specific conversations in ASL.	1) Demonstrate ability to initiate, conduct and terminate medium-length conversations in ASL.	1) Demonstrate ability to initiate, conduct and terminate rather lengthy conversations in ASL.			
	2) Receptive competence for relatively short stories, narratives, etc. in ASL.	2) Receptive competence for medium-length stories, narratives, etc. in ASL.	1) Receptive competence for lengthy stories, narratives etc. in ASL.		
	3) Expressive competence for relatively short stories, narratives, etc. in ASL.	3) Expressive competence for medium-length stories, narratives, etc. in ASL.	2) Expressive competence for lengthy stories, narratives, etc. in ASL.		
		4) Successful participation in context-specific group discussions.	3) Successful participation in group discussions—non-context specific.	1) Successful participation in group generated discussions about their experiences with the Deaf community.	1) Successful participation in group discussions of student-generated topics.
			4) View and discuss the 1910–1920 NAD films.	2) Read and discuss the play Sign Me Alice.	2) Exchange of ASL videotaped 'letters'.

Any curriculum guide must be flexible enough to allow for certain modifications and adaptations due to teacher style, program needs, new research findings, available materials, etc. It is felt that this curriculum guide, because it is not directly linked to any particular text, gives the teacher a certain amount of freedom and responsibility in selecting materials and texts for each course. This guide gives the teacher a way of analyzing the usefulness of available materials by deciding how and where they can be used to achieve course objectives. Thus, the teacher is free to select any text or combination of texts which will best help students master course objectives. However, the teacher has the responsibility for being able to explain and justify why a particular text is the most appropriate text for a given course.

In addition to flexibility, the curriculum guide provides a ready means of appropriately placing students within a particular program. If a student can demonstrate mastery of all of the objectives for course III, s/he should be placed in course IV whether or not s/he has taken courses II and III. In this way, a program can have a more objective means of placing and grouping its students. This also applies to students moving from one course to another: if a student has not mastered all the objectives for course II, s/he generally should not be allowed to enter course III, but should repeat all or part of course II. This is only fair to the other students in course III and to the teacher who expects that all the students will possess a similar minimum knowledge and skill level.

As a teacher or a particular program works with this curriculum guide over a period of time, each of the course objectives will be supported by a range of specific sub-objectives. These sub-objectives, if appropriately developed, should provide a comprehensive checklist of specific skills which a student must possess to move from course to course or to finish the program. These sub-objectives can and should vary as new materials and information become available. Thus, the actual curriculum is always changing and is always sensitive to advances in the field. There are currently several resources which may be very helpful in identifying and developing sub-objectives.

Deaf Heritage: a Narrative History of Deaf America, J. Gannon, NAD, in press.

Sign and Culture: A Reader for Students of ASL, W. Stokoe, Ed., Linstok Press, 1980.

Sign Language and The Deaf Community: Essays in Honor of William C. Stokoe, C. Baker and R. Battison, Eds., NAD, 1980.

The Signs of Language, E. Klima and U. Bellugi, Harvard University Press, 1979.

American Sign Language: a resource text for teachers on grammar and culture, C. Baker and D. Cokely, T.J. Publishers, Inc., 1980.

Principles and Procedures of Teaching Sign Languages, R. Ingram, British Deaf Association, 1977; available from the NAD.

Past and future proceedings of the National Symposium on Sign Language Research and Teaching (NSSLRT), especially the 1980 Symposium which focuses on teaching ASL as a second/foreign language; available from the NAD.

In addition to these resources, *Sign Language Studies* (Linstok Press, Silver Spring, Md.) and *Signs for Our Times* (Linguistics Research Lab, Gallaudet College) provide an ongoing means of keeping up with new developments related to ASL.

In summary, this curriculum guide presents a series of course objectives in a sequence which, it is felt, will best enable the student to acquire communicative competence in ASL. This curriculum guide is intentionally rather skeletal, since the individual teacher or program co-ordinator is currently in the best position to 'fill out' the curriculum by developing specific sub-objectives. However, the guide does present the teacher with a framework for considering the range and complexity of skills involved if students are to achieve the ultimate goal of communicative competence in ASL.

LANGUAGE TEACHING BIBLIOGRAPHY

This bibliography is hardly an exhaustive listing of useful texts and resources for the Sign Language teacher. However, it is felt that these will provide the Sign Language teacher with a solid foundation in second/foreign language teaching methods, evaluation, and curriculum development. In addition, the organizational resources can be an invaluable means of keeping abreast of current developments in second/foreign language teaching.

A. Theoretical Considerations

Alatis, J. and R. Crymes. (Eds.), *The Human Factors in ESL*. TESOL, Georgetown University, Washington, D.C., 1977.

Chastain, K. *Developing Second Language Skills: Theory to Practice*. (2nd Ed.), Chicago, Ill.: Rand McNally College Publishing Co., 1976.

Gattegno, C. *Teaching Foreign Languages in Schools: The Silent Way*. New York: Educational Solutions 1972.

George, H. *Common Errors in Language Learning: Insights from English*. Rawley, Mass.: Newbury House Publishers. 1972.

Hatch, E. (Ed.), *Second Language Acquisition: A Book of Readings*. Rawley, Mass.: Newbury House Publishers. 1978.

Kinselle, V. (Ed.), *Language Teaching and Linguistic Surveys*. London.: Cambridge University Press. 1978.

Mager, R. *Preparing Instructional Objectives*. Palo Alto, California: Fearon Publishers. 1962.

Mager, R. *Goal Analysis,* Belmont, California: Fearon Publishers. 1972

B. Methods

Allen, E. & R. Valette. *Modern Language Classroom Techniques,* New York: Harcourt, Brace, Jovanovich, Inc. 1972.

Altman, H. *Individualizing the Foreign Language Classroom*. Rawley, Mass.: Newbury House. 1972.

Asher, J. "Learning a Second Language Through Commands." *Modern Language Journal 53,* (1), 3–17, 1969.

Bradford, S. *et al. Foreign Language Games,* Maryland Foreign Language Association, 1974.

Maley, A. & A. Duff. *Drama Techniques in Language Learning*. Cambridge, England: Cambridge University Press. 1978.

Oller, J. & J. Richards. (Eds.), *Focus on the Learner: Pragmatic Perspectives for the Language Teacher*. Rawley, Mass.: Newbury House. 1973.

Paulston, C. & M. Bruder. *Teaching English as a Second Language: Techniques and Procedures*. Cambridge, Mass.: Winthrop Publishers, Inc., 1976.

Savignon, S. *Communicative Competence: an Experiment in Foreign Language Teaching*. Philadelphia, Pa.: Center for Curriculum Development, 1972.

Seelye, H. *Teaching Culture: Strategies for Foreign Language Educators*. Skokie, Ill.: National Textbook Company, 1974.

C. Evaluation

Clark, J. *Foreign Language Testing: Theory and Practice*. Center for Curriculum Development, Philadelphia, Pa.,1972.

Clark, J. (Ed.), *Direct Testing of Speaking Proficiency: Theory and Application*. Educational Testing Service, Princeton, N.J., 1978.

Jones, R. & B. Spolsky. (Eds.), *Testing Language Proficiency*. Center for Applied Linguistics, Washington, D.C., 1975.

Lado, R. *Language Testing*. New York: McGraw Hill. 1964.

Palmer, L. & B. Spolsky. (Eds.), *Papers on Language Testing: 1967–1974*. TESOL, Washington, D.C., 1975.

Spolsky, B. (Ed.), *Advances in Language Testing Series: 1*. Center for Applied Linguistics, Washington, D.C., 1979.

Valette, R., *Modern Language Testing*. (2nd Ed.), New York: Harcourt, Brace, Jovanovich. 1977.

D. Resource Journals

Language Learning: A Journal of Applied Linguistics,
University of Michigan,
Ann Arbor, Michigan 48109.

Language in Education: Theory and Practice,
Center for Applied Linguistics,
Washington, D.C. 20007.

E. Organizational Resources

American Council on the Teaching of Foreign Languages (ACTFL)
2 Park Avenue
New York, New York 10016
(212) 689-8021

Center for Applied Linguistics (CAL)
3520 Prospect St., N.W.
Washington, D.C. 20007
(202) 298-9292

ERIC Clearinghouse on Language (ERIC)
3520 Prospect St., N.W.
Washington, D.C. 20007
(202) 298-9292

Linguistic Society of America (LSA)
3520 Prospect St., N.W.
Washington, D.C. 20007
(202) 298-9292

Modern Language Association of America (MLA)
62 Fifth Avenue
New York, New York 10011
(212) 741-5588

SIGN LANGUAGE BIBLIOGRAPHY

The following bibliography on Sign Language is an adapted and updated version of the one originally prepared and distributed by Lawrence Fleischer at the 1978 National Symposium on Sign Language Research and Teaching. We thank him for permission to adapt and include this bibliography. We have removed from Dr. Fleischer's original bibliography any entry which we felt the reader could not easily locate (e.g. working papers, unpublished manuscripts). Thus, the reader should be able to locate any of the entries in the following bibliography. Inclusion of an entry does not constitute an endorsement of the contents of that entry.

A. History of Sign Language

Akerly, S. "Observations on the Language of Signs." *Journal of Science and Arts, 8,* No. 2, 1824, pp. 348–358.

Cochrane, W. "Methodical Signs Instead of Colloquial." *American Annals of the Deaf, 16,* No. 1, 1871, pp. 11–17.

DuChamp, M. "The National Institution for the Deaf and Dumb at Paris." *American Annals of the Deaf, 22,* No. 1, 1877, pp. 1–10.

Fay, G. "The Sign Language: the Basis of Instruction for Deaf-Mutes." *American Annals of the Deaf, 27,* No. 3, 1882, pp. 208–211.

Frishberg, N. "Arbitrariness and Iconicity: Historical Change in American Sign Language." *Language, 51,* 1975, pp. 696–719.

Gallaudet, E. "Is the Sign Language Used to Excess in Teaching Deaf-Mutes." *American Annals of the Deaf, 16,* No. 1, 1871, pp. 26–33.

Gallaudet, E. "The Value of the Sign Language to the Deaf." *American Annals of the Deaf, 32,* No. 3, 1887, pp. 141–147.

Jacobs, J. "The Relation of Written Words to Signs, the Same as Their Relation to Spoken Words." *American Annals of the Deaf and Dumb, 11,* No. 2, 1859, pp. 65–73.

Keep, J. "Natural Signs—Shall They be Abandoned." *American Annals of the Deaf, 16,* No. 1, 1871, pp. 17–25.

Keep, J. "The Sign-Language." *American Annals of the Deaf, 16,* No. 4, 1871, pp. 221–234.

Lane, H. "Notes for a Psycho-History of American Sign Language." *The Deaf American, 30,* No. 1, 1977, pp. 3–7.

"Letter to Professor John R. Keep." *American Annals of the Deaf, 14,* No. 2, 1869, pp. 89–95.

Markowicz, H. "Some Sociolinguistic Considerations of American Sign Language." *Sign Language Studies, 1,* 1972, pp. 15–41.

Peet, H. "Words not 'Representatives' of Signs, but of Ideas." *American Annals of the Deaf, 11,* 1859, pp. 1–8.

Peet, I. "Initial Signs." *American Annals of the Deaf, 13,* 1861, pp. 171–184.

Siegel, J. "The Enlightenment and the Evolution of a Language of Signs in France and England." *Journal of the History of Ideas, 30,* 1969, pp. 96–115.

Siger, L. "Gestures, The Language of Sign, and Human Communication." *American Annals of the Deaf, 113,* No. 1, 1968, pp. 11–28.

Valentine, E. G. "Shall We Abandon the English Order?" *American Annals of the Deaf, 17,* No. 1, 1872, pp. 33–47.

Woodward, J. "Signs of Change: Historical Variation in American Sign Language." *Sign Language Studies, 10,* 1976, pp. 81–94.

Woodward, J. "Historical Bases of American Sign Language." In P. Siple (Ed.), *Understanding Language Through Sign Language Research.* New York: Academic Press, 1978, pp. 333–348.

Woodward, J. & Erting, C. "Synchronic Variation and Historical Change in American Sign Language." *Language Sciences, 37,* 1975, pp. 9–12.

B. Educational Aspects of Sign Language

Baker, C. & R. Battison (Eds.) *Sign Language and the Deaf Community: Essays in Honor of William C. Stokoe.* Silver Spring, Md.: National Association of the Deaf, 1980.

Bellugi, U. & E. Klima. "The Roots of Language in the Sign Talk of the Deaf." *Psychology Today,* June 1972, pp. 61–64; 76.

Bergman, E. "Autonomous and Unique Features of American Sign Language." *American Annals of the Deaf, 117,* No. 1, 1972, pp. 20–24.

Bonvillian, J. & V. Charrow. *Psycholinguistic Implications of Deafness: A Review.* Technical Report, 188, Institute for Mathematical Studies in The Social Sciences, Stanford, Calif, 1972.

Bonvillian, J., K Nelson, & V. Charrow. "Language & Language-Related Skills in Deaf & Hearing Children." *Sign Language Studies, 12,* 1976, pp. 211–250.

Caccamise, F., C. Bradley, R. Battison, R. Blasdell, K. Warren, & T. Hurwitz. "A Project for Standardization and Development of Technical Signs." *American Annals of the Deaf, 122,* No. 1, 1977, pp. 44–49.

Cicourel, A. & R. Boese. "Sign Language Acquisition and the Teaching of Deaf Children." *American Annals of the Deaf, 117,* No. 1, 1972, pp. 27–33 (part 1); *117,* No. 3, 1972, pp. 403–411 (part 2).

Coats, G. "Characteristics of Communication Methods." *American Annals of the Deaf, 95,* No. 5, 1950, pp. 489–490.

Cokely, D. *Pre-College Programs: Guidelines for Manual Communication,* Gallaudet College, Washington, D.C. 1979.

Cokely, D. "Sign Language: Teaching, Interpreting, and Educational Policy." In C. Baker & R. Battison (Eds.), 1980, pp. 137–158.

Cokely, D. & R. Gawlik. "Options: A Position Paper on the Relationship Between Manual English and Sign." *The Deaf American, 25,* No. 9, May 1973, pp. 7–11.

Cokely, D. & R. Gawlik. "Options II: Childrenese as Pidgin." *The Deaf American, 26,* No. 8, April 1974, pp. 5–6.

Collins-Ahlgren, M. "Teaching English as a Second Language to Young Deaf Children: A Case Study." *Journal of Speech and Hearing Disorders,* 39, No. 4, 1974, pp. 486–495.

Collins-Ahlgren, M. "Language Development of Two Deaf Children." *American Annals of the Deaf, 120,* No. 6, 1975, pp. 524–539.

Conrad, R. *The Deaf Schoolchild.* London: Harper & Row, 1979.

Cross, J. "Sign Language and Second Language Teaching." *Sign Language Studies, 16,* 1977, pp. 269–282.

De L'Epee, A. "The True Method of Educating the Deaf and Dumb: Confirmed by Long Experience." *American Annals of the Deaf, 12,* No. 2, 1860, pp. 61–132.

Ellenberger, R. & M. Steyaert. "A Child's Representation of Action in American Sign Language." In P. Siple (Ed.), 1978, pp. 261–270.

Erting, C. "Sign Language and Communication Between Adults and Children." In C. Baker & R. Battison (Eds.), 1980, pp. 159-176.

Fleischer, L. & M. Cottrell. "Sign Language Interpretation Under Four Interpreting Conditions." In H. Murphy (Ed.), *Selected Readings in the Integration of Post-Secondary Deaf Students at CSUN: Center on Deafness Publication Series (No. 1).* Northridge, California: California State University, Northridge, 1976.

Furth, H. "Linguistic Deficiency and Thinking: Research with Deaf Subjects, 1964–69." *Psycholinguistics Bulletin, 76,* No. 1, 1971, pp. 58–72.

Furth, H. *Deafness and Learning: A Psychosocial Approach.* Belmont, Calif.: Wadsworth Publishing Co., Inc., 1973.

Fusfeld, I. "How the Deaf Communicate—Manual Language." *American Annals of the Deaf, 103,* No. 2, 1953, pp. 264–282.

Gallaudet, T. "On the Natural Language of Signs and It's Value and Uses in the Instruction of the Deaf and Dumb." *American Annals of the Deaf, 1,* No. 1, 1847, pp. 55–60 (part 1); *1,* No. 2, 1848, pp. 79–93 (part 2).

Goldin-Meadow, S. & H. Feldman. "The Creation of a Communication System: A Study of Deaf Children of Hearing Parents." *Sign Language Studies 8,* 1975, pp. 225–234.

Goldin-Meadow, S. "Semantic Relations in a Manual Language Created by Deaf Children of Hearing Parents." Paper presented at the Conference of Sign Language and Neurolinguistics, Rochester, New York, 1976.

Hester, M. "Manual Communication." *Proceedings of the International Congress on Education of the Deaf and of the 41st Meeting of the Convention of American Instructors of the Deaf.* Washington, D.C.: Gallaudet College, 1963, pp. 211–321.

Higgins, E. "An Analysis of the Comprehensibility of Three Communication Methods Used with Hearing Impaired Students." *American Annals of the Deaf, 118,* No. 1, 1973, pp. 46–49.

Hoemann, H. & R. Tweney. "Is the Sign Language of the Deaf an Adequate Communication Channel?" *Proceedings of the 81st Convention American Psychological Association,* 11, 1973, pp. 801–802.

Hoffmeister, R., D. Moores & R. Ellenberger. *The Parameters of Sign Language Defined: Translation and Definition Rules.* Research Report, 83, University of Minnesota, January 1975.

Hoffmeister, R., D. Moores & R. Ellenberger. "Some Procedural Guidelines for the Study of the Acquisition of Sign Language." *Sign Language Studies, 7,* 1975, pp. 121–137.

Howse, J. & J. Fitch. "Effects of Parent Orientation in Sign Language on Communication Skills of Preschool Children." *American Annals of the Deaf, 117,* No. 4, 1972, pp. 459–462.

Klopping, H. "Language Understanding of Deaf Students under Three Auditory-Visual Conditions." *American Annals of the Deaf, 117,* No. 3, 1972, pp. 389–392.

Kohl, H. *Language and Education of the Deaf.* New York: Center for Urban Education, 1966.

Lane, H. *The Wild Boy of Aveyron.* Cambridge, Mass.: Harvard University Press, 1976.

Markowicz, H. "What Language Do Deaf Children Acquire? A Review Article." *Sign Language Studies, 3,* 1973, pp. 72–78.

Marmor, G. & L. Petitto. "Simultaneous Communication in the Classroom: How Well is English Grammar Represented?" *Sign Language Studies, 23,* 1979, pp. 99–136.

Mayberry, R. "Manual Communication." In H. Davis & R. Silverman (Eds.), *Hearing and Deafness,* 4th edition. New York: Holt, Rhinehart & Winston, in press.

Meadow, K. "Early Manual Communication in Relation to the Deaf Child's Intellectual, Social, and Communicative Functioning." *American Annals of the Deaf, 113,* No. 1, 1968, pp. 29–41.

Mills, C. & I. K. Jordan. "Timing Sensitivity and Age as Predictors of Sign Language Learning." *Sign Language Studies, 26,* 1980, pp. 15–28.

Mindel, E. & M. Vernon. *They Grow in Silence.* Silver Spring, Md.: The National Association of the Deaf, 1971.

Moores, D. "Psycholinguistics and Deafness." *American Annals of the Deaf, 115,* No. 1, 1970, pp. 37–48.

Moores, J. "Early Linguistic Environment: Interactions of Deaf Parents with their Infants." *Sign Language Studies, 26,* 1980, pp. 1–13.

Murphy, H. & L. Fleischer. "The Effects of Ameslan Versus Siglish Upon Test Scores." *Journal of Rehabilitation of the Deaf, 11,* No. 2, 1977, pp. 15–18.

Olson, J. "A Case for the Use of Sign Language to Stimulate Language Development During the Critical Period for Learning in a Congenitally Deaf Child." *American Annals of the Deaf, 117,* No. 3, 1972, pp. 397–400.

O'Rourke, T. (Ed.) *Psycholinguistics and Total Communication: The State of the Art.* Silver Spring, Md.: American Annals of the Deaf, 1972.

Ovrid, H. "Studies in Manual Communication with Hearing Impaired Children." *The Volta Review,* 73, No. 7, 1971, pp. 428–438.

Penna, K. & F. Caccamise. "Communication Instruction with Hearing-Impaired College Students Within the Manual/Simultaneous Communication Department, NTID." *American Annals of the Deaf, 123,* No. 5, 1978, pp. 572–579.

Prinz, P. & E. Prinz. "Simultaneous Acquisition of ASL and Spoken English (in a Hearing Child of a Deaf Mother and Hearing Father)." *Sign Language Studies, 25,* 1979, pp. 283–296.

Sallop, M. "Language Acquisition: Pantomime and Gesture to Signed English." *Sign Language Studies, 3,* 1973, pp. 29–38.

Schlesinger, H. & K. Meadow. "Development of Maturity in Deaf Children." *Exceptional Children,* 1972.

Schlesinger, H. "Language Acquisition in Four Deaf Children." *Hearing and Speech News,* December 1972, pp. 4–7; pp. 22–28.

Schlesinger, H. "Meaning and Enjoyment: Language Acquisition of Deaf Children." In T. O'Rourke (Ed.), *Psycholinguistics and Total Communication: The State of the Art.* Silver Spring, Md.: American Annals of the Deaf, 1972, pp. 92–102.

Schlesinger, H. & K. Meadow. *Sound and Sign: Child Deafness and Mental Health.* Berkeley, Calif.: University of California Press, 1972.

Siple, P. (Ed.) *Understanding Language Through Sign Language Research.* New York: Academic Press, 1978.

Stevens, R. "Children's Language Should Be Learned and Not Taught." *Sign Language Studies, 11,* 1976, pp. 97–108.

Stevens, R. "Education in Schools for Deaf Children." In C. Baker & R. Battison (Eds.), 1980, pp. 177-191.

Stokoe, W. "A Classroom Experiment in Two Languages." In T. O'Rourke (Ed.), *Psycholinguistics and Total Communication: The State of the Art.* Silver Spring, Md.: American Annals of the Deaf, 1972, pp. 85–91.

Stokoe, W. "The Use of Sign Language in Teaching English." *American Annals of the Deaf, 120,* No. 4, 1975, pp. 417–421.

Stuckless, E. & J. Birch. "The Influence of Early Manual Communication on the Linguistic Development of Deaf Children." *American Annals of the Deaf, 111,* No. 2, 1966, pp. 452–460 (part 1); *111,* No. 3, 1966, pp. 499–504 (part 2).

Tervoort, B. "Esoteric Symbolism in the Communication Behavior of Young Deaf Children." *American Annals of the Deaf, 106,* No. 5, 1961, pp. 436–480.

Tomlinson-Keasey, C. & R. Kelly. "The Development of Thought Processes in Deaf Children." *American Annals of the Deaf, 119,* No. 6, 1974, pp. 693–700.

Tomlinsen-Keasey, C. & R. Kelly. "The Deaf Child's Symbolic World." *American Annals of the Deaf, 123,* No. 4, 1978, pp. 452–459.

Tweney, R., H. Hoemann & C. Andrews. "Semantic Organization in Deaf and Hearing Subjects." *Journal of Psycholinguistic Research, 4,* No. 1, 1975, pp. 61–73.

Vernon, M. & S. Koh. "Early Manual Communication and Deaf Children's Achievement" *American Annals of the Deaf, 115,* No. 5, 1970, pp. 527–535.

Vernon, M. & S. Koh. "Effects of Oral Preschool Compared to Early Manual Communication on Education and Communication in Deaf Children." *American Annals of the Deaf, 115,* No. 6, 1971, pp. 569–574.

Williams, J. "Bilingual Experiences of a Deaf Child." *Sign Language Studies, 10,* 1976, pp. 37–41.

Woodward, J. "Linguistics and Language Teaching." *Teaching English to the Deaf, 1,* 1973, p. 2.

C. Attitudes Toward Sign Language

Anderson, T. "What of the Sign Language?" *American Annals of the Deaf, 83,* No. 2, 1938, pp. 120–130.

Bellugi, U. "Interview for the Deaf American." *The Deaf American, 27,* No. 9, 1975, pp. 12–14.

Bellugi, U. "Attitudes Toward Sign Language." In A. Crammatte & F. Crammatte (Eds.), *Proceedings of the Seventh World Congress of the World Federation of the Deaf.* Silver Spring, Md.: National Association of the Deaf, 1976.

Bragg, B. "Ameslish: Our National Heritage." *American Annals of the Deaf, 118,* No. 6, 1973, pp. 672–674.

Eastman, G. *Sign Me Alice.* Washington, D.C.: Gallaudet College, 1974.

Erting, C. "Language Policy & Deaf Ethnicity in the United States." *Sign Language Studies, 19,* 1978, pp. 139–152.

Greenberg, J. *In This Sign.* New York: Holt, Rhinehart & Winston, 1970.

Gustason, G. "The Language of Communication." *Journal of Rehabilitation of the Deaf,* Annual Volume III, 1973, pp. 83–93.

James, W. "Thought Before Language: A Deaf-Mute's Recollections." *Philosophical Review, 1,* 1892, pp. 613–624.

Kannapell, B. "Bilingualism: A New Direction in the Education of the Deaf." *The Deaf American, 26,* No. 10, 1974, pp. 9–15.

Kannapell, B. "Personal Awareness and Advocacy in the Deaf Community." In C. Baker & R. Battison (Eds.), 1980, pp. 105-116.

Markowicz, H. *American Sign Language: Fact and Fancy.* Washington, D.C.: Gallaudet College, 1977.

Meadow, K. "Sociolinguistics, Sign Language and the Deaf Sub-Culture." In T. O'Rourke (Ed.),*Psycholinguistics and Total Communication: The State of the Art.* Silver Spring, Md.: American Annals of the Deaf, 1972, pp. 19–33.

Meadow, K. "Name Signs as Identity Symbols in the Deaf Community." *Sign Language Studies, 17,* 1977, pp. 237–246.

Moores, D. "Communication—Some Unanswered Questions and Some Unquestioned Answers." In T. O'Rourke (Ed.),*Psycholinguistics and Total Communication: The State of the Art.* Silver Spring, Md.: American Annals of the Deaf, 1972, pp. 1–10.

Newman, L. "Cherry Blossoms Come to Bloom." *The Deaf American, 24,* No. 11, 1972, pp. 25–27.

Padden, C. "The Deaf Community and the Culture of Deaf People." In C. Baker & R. Battison (Eds.), 1980, pp. 89-103.

Padden, C. & H. Markowicz. "Cultural Conflicts Between Hearing and Deaf Communities." In A. Crammatte & F. Crammatte (Eds.),*Proceedings of the Seventh World Congress of the World Federation of the Deaf.* Silver Spring, Md.: National Association of the Deaf, 1976.

Schein, J. "Sign Language: Coming of Age." *Sign Language Studies, 3,* 1973, pp. 113–115.

Schowe, B. "What is the True Sign Language?" *The Deaf American, 28,* No. 1, 1975, pp. 3–4.

Stevens, R. "Children's Language Should Be Learned and Not Taught." *Sign Language Studies, 11,* 1976, pp. 97–108.

Stokoe, W. "Sign Language Diglossia." *Studies in Linguistics, 21,* 1969–1970, pp. 27–41.

Stokoe, W. & R. Battison. "Sign Language, Mental Health, and Satisfying Interaction." In E. Mindel & L. Stein (Eds.) *Proceedings of the First National Symposium on Mental Health Needs of Deaf Adults and Youth.* New York: Grune, Grune & Stratton, in press.

Trybus, R. "Sign Language, Power, and Mental Health." In C. Baker & R. Battison (Eds.), 1980, pp. 201-217.

Vernon, M. & B. Makowsky. "Deafness and Minority Group Dynamics." *The Deaf American, 21,* No. 11, 1969, pp. 3–6.

Woodward, J. "Implications for Sociolinguistic Research Among the Deaf." *Sign Language Studies, 1,* 1972, pp. 107.

Woodward, J. "Language Continuum, a Different Point of View." *Sign Language Studies, 2,* 1973, pp. 81–83.

Woodward, J. "Deaf Awareness." *Sign Language Studies, 3,* 1973, pp. 57–60.

Woodward, J. "Some Observations on Sociolinguistic Variation and American Sign Language." *Kansas Journal of Sociology, 9,* No. 2, 1973, pp. 191–200.

D. Sign Language Research

Abbott, C. "Encodedness and Sign Language." *Sign Language Studies, 7,* 1975, pp. 109–120.

Baker, C. "Eye-openers in ASL." *Sixth California Linguistics Association Conference: Proceedings,* 1976, pp. 1–13.

Baker, C. "What's Not on the Other Hand in American Sign Language." In S. Hufwene, C. Walker & S. Streeven (Eds.)*Papers from the 12th Regional Meeting of the Chicago Linguistic Society.* Chicago, Illinois, 1976.

Baker, C. "Regulators and Turn-taking in American Sign Language Discourse." In L. Friedman (Ed.), *On the Other Hand: New Perspectives on American Sign Language.* New York: Academic Press, 1977, pp. 215–236.

Baker, C. "Sentences in American Sign Language." In C. Baker & R. Battison (Eds.), 1980, pp. 75-86.

Baker, C. & R. Battison (Eds.), *Sign Language and the Deaf Community: Essays in Honor of William C. Stokoe.* Silver Spring, Md.: National Association of the Deaf, 1980.

Baker, C. & C. Padden. *American Sign Language: A Look at its History, Structure, and Community.* Silver Spring, Md.: T.J. Publishers, Inc., 1978.

Baker, C. & C. Padden. "Focusing on the Nonmanual Components of American Sign Language." In P. Siple (Ed.), 1978, pp. 59–90.

Battison, R. "Phonological Deletion in American Sign Language." *Sign Language Studies, 5,* 1974, pp. 1–19.

Battison, R. *Lexical Borrowing in American Sign Language.* Silver Spring, Md.: Linstok Press, 1978.

Battison, R. "Signs Have Parts: A Simple Idea." In C. Baker & R. Battison (Eds.), 1980, pp. 35-51.

Battison, R., H. Markowicz & J. Woodward. "A Good Rule of Thumb: Variable Phonology in American Sign Language." In R. Shuy & R. Rasold (Eds.), *New Ways of Analyzing Variation in English, 2,* Washington, D.C.: Georgetown University Press, 1976.

Bellugi, U. "Studies in Sign Language." In T. O'Rourke (Ed.), *Psycholinguistics and Total Communication: The State of the Art.* Silver Spring, Md.: American Annals of the Deaf, 1972, pp. 68–83.

Bellugi, U. "How Signs Express Complex Meanings." In C. Baker & R. Battison (Eds.), 1980, pp. 53-74.

Bellugi, U. & S. Fischer. "A Comparison of Sign Language and Spoken Language: Rate and Grammatical Mechanisms." *Cognition: International Journal of Cognitive Psychology, 1,* 1972, pp. 173–200.

Bellugi, U. & E. Klima. "Aspects of Sign Language and its Structure." In J. F. Kavanagh and J. E. Cutting (Eds.), *The Role of Speech in Language.* Cambridge: M.I.T. Press, 1975, pp. 171–203.

Bellugi, U. & E. Klima. "Remembering in Signs." *Cognition: International Journal of Cognitive Psychology, 3,* No. 2, 1975, pp. 93–125.

Bellugi, U. & E. Klima. "Two Faces of Sign: Iconic and Abstract." In S. Harnad (Ed.), *Origins and Evolution of Language and Speech.* New York: New York Academy of Sciences, 1975.

Bellugi, U. & P. Siple. "Remembering With and Without Words." In F. Bresson (Ed.), *Current Problems in Psycholinguistics.* Paris: Centre National de la Recherche Scientifique, 1974, pp. 215–236.

Cicourel, A. "Gestural Sign Language and the Study of Nonverbal Communication." *Sign Language Studies, 4,* 1974, pp. 35–76.

Cicourel, A. "Sociolinguistic Aspects of the Use of Sign Language." In I. M. Schlesinger & L. Namir (Eds.), *Sign Language of the Deaf: Psychological, Linguistic, and Sociological Perspectives.* New York: Academic Press, 1978, pp. 271–313.

Cogen, C. "On Three Aspects of Time Expression in American Sign Language." In L. Friedman (Ed.), *On the Other Hand: New Perspectives on American Sign Language*. New York: Academic Press, 1977, pp. 197–214.

Covington, V. "Juncture in American Sign Language." *Sign Language Studies, 2,* 1973, pp. 29–38.

Covington, V. "Features of Stress in American Sign Language." *Sign Language Studies, 2,* 1973, pp. 39–50.

De Matteo, A. "Visual Imagery and Visual Analogues in American Sign Language." In L. Friedman (Ed.), *On the Other Hand: New Perspectives on American Sign Language*. New York: Academic Press, 1977, pp. 109–136.

Edge, V. & L. Hermann. "Verbs and the Determination of Subject in American Sign Language." In L. Friedman (Ed.), *On the Other Hand: New Perspectives on American Sign Language*. New York: Academic Press, 1977, pp. 137–179.

Ellenberger, R. *The Modal Auxiliary Systems of American Sign Language and English.* Research Report 96, University of Minnesota, August, 1975.

Ellenberger, R., D. Moores & R. Hoffmeister. *Early Stages in the Acquisition of Negation by a Deaf Child of Deaf Parents.* Research Report, 94, University of Minnesota, August 1975.

Fischer, S. "Two Processes of Reduplication in the American Sign Language." *Foundations of Language, 9,* 1973, pp. 469–480.

Fischer, S. "Sign Language and Linguistic Universals." In T. Rohrer & N. Ruwet (Eds.), *Actes de Colloque Franco-Allemand de Grammarie Transformationelle, Band II: Etudes de Semantique et Autres.* Tubingen: Max Neimeyer Verland, 1974, pp. 187–204.

Fischer, S. "Influences on Word Order Change in American Sign Language." In C. N. Li (Ed.), *Word Order and Word Order Change.* Austin, Texas: University Press, 1975.

Fischer, S. "The Ontogenetic Development of Language." In E. Strauss (Ed.), *Language and Language Disturbances: Fifth Lexington Conference on Phenomenology.* Pittsburgh, Penn.: Duquesne University Press, 1975, pp. 22–43.

Fischer, S. "Sign Language and Creoles." In P. Siple (Ed.), 1978, pp. 309–332.

Fischer, S. & B. Gough. "Verbs in American Sign Language." *Sign Language Studies, 18,* 1978, pp. 17–48.

Friedman, L. "Space, Time, and Person Reference in American Sign Language." *Language, 51,* 1975, pp. 940–961.

Friedman, L. "Phonological Processes in the American Sign Language." *Proceedings of the First Annual Meeting of the Berkeley Linguistics Society.* Berkeley, Calif.:University of California, Berkeley, 1975, pp. 147–154.

Friedman, L. "The Manifestation of Subject, Object, and Topic in ASL." In C. N. Li (Ed.), *Subject and Topic.* New York: Academic Press, 1976.

Friedman, L. "Formational Properties of American Sign Language." In L. Friedman (Ed.), *On the Other Hand: New Perspectives on American Sign Language.* New York: Academic Press, 1977, pp. 13–56.

Grosjean, F. "The Production of Sign Language: Psycholinguistic Perspectives." *Sign Language Studies, 25,* 1979, pp. 317–329.

Hoemann, H. "Categorical Coding of Sign and English in Short-term Memory by Deaf and Hearing Subjects." In P. Siple (Ed.), 1978, pp. 289–305.

Hoemann, H. & R. Tweney. "Back Translation: A Method for the Analysis of Manual Languages." *Sign Language Studies, 2,* 1973, pp. 51–80.

Hoemann, H. "The Transparency of Meaning of Sign Language Gestures." *Sign Language Studies, 7,* 1975, pp. 151–161.

Hoemann, H. & V. Florian. "Order Constraints in American Sign Language." *Sign Language Studies, 11,* 1976, pp. 121–132.

Hoffmeister, R. & D. Moores. *The Acquisition of Specific Reference in the Linguistic System of a Deaf Child of Deaf Parents.* Research Report, 65, University of Minnesota, June 1974.

Hoffmeister, R., B. Best & D. Moores. *The Acquisition of Sign Language in Deaf Children of Deaf Parents: Progress Report.* Research Report, 65, University of Minnesota, June 1974.

Julesz, B. & I. Hirsch. "Visual and Auditory Perception: An Essay of Comparison." In E. E. David & P. B. Denes (Eds.), *Human Communication: A Unified View.* New York: McGraw-Hill, 1972, pp. 283–340.

Kegl, J. & H. Chinchor. "A Frame Analysis of American Sign Language." In T. Diller (Ed.), *Proceedings of the 13th Annual Meeting, Association for Computational Linguistics.* St. Paul, Minn.: Sperry-Univac, 1975.

Kegl, J. & R. Wilbur. "When Does Structure Stop and Style Begin? Syntax, Morphology, and Phonology vs. Stylistic Variation in American Sign Language." In S. Hufwene, C. Walker, & S. Streeven (Eds.), *Papers from the 12th Regional Meeting of the Chicago Linguistics Society.* Chicago, Illinois, 1976.

Klima, E. "Sound and Its Absence in the Linguistic Symbol." In J. Kavanagh & J. Cutting (Eds.), *The Role of Speech in Language.* Cambridge, Mass.: M.I.T. Press, 1975, pp. 249–270.

Klima, E. & U. Bellugi. "Language in Another Mode." In E. Lenneberg (Ed.), "Language and the Brain, Developmental Aspects." *Neurosciences Research Program Bulletin, 12,* 1974, pp. 539–550.

Klima, E. & U. Bellugi. "Wit and Poetry in American Sign Language." *Sign Language Studies, 8,* 1975, pp. 203–224.

Klima, E. & U. Bellugi. "Perception and Production in Visually Based Language." In D. Aaronson & R. W. Rieber (Eds.), *Developmental Psycholinguistics and Communication Disorders.* New York: New York Academy of Sciences, 1975, pp. 225–235.

Klima, E. & U. Bellugi. "Poetry and Song in a Language Without Sound." *Cognition: International Journal of Cognitive Psychology, 4,* 1976, pp. 45–97.

Klima, E. & U. Bellugi. *The Signs of Language.* Cambridge, Mass.: Harvard University Press, 1979.

Lane, H., P. Boyes-Braem & U. Bellugi. "Preliminaries to Distinctive Features Analysis of Handshapes in American Sign Language." *Cognitive Psychology, 8,* 1976, pp. 263–289.

Liddell, S. "Nonmanual Signals and Relative Clauses in American Sign Language." In P. Siple (Ed.), *Understanding Language Through Sign Language Research.* New York: Academic Press, 1978.

Mandel, M. "Dimensions of Iconicity in American Sign Language." *Proceedings of the Second Annual Meeting of the Berkeley Linguistics Society,* Berkeley, California, 1976.

Mandel, M. "Natural Constraints in Sign Language Phonology: Data From Anatomy." *Sign Language Studies, 23,* 1979, pp. 215–229.

Marmor, G. & L. Petitto. "Simultaneous Communication in the Classroom: How Well is English Grammar Represented?" *Sign Language Studies, 23,* 1979, pp. 99–136.

Mayberry, R. "French Canadian Sign Language: A Study of Inter-Sign Language Comprehension." In P. Siple (Ed.), 1978, pp. 349–372.

McKeever, W., H. Hoemann, V. Florian & A. Van Deventer. "Evidence of Minimal Cerebral Asymmetries for the Processing of English Words and American Sign Language in the Congenitally Deaf." *Neuropsychologics,* in press.

Newport, E. & U. Bellugi. "Linguistic Expression of Category Levels in a Visual-Gestural Language." In E. Rosch (Ed.), *Cognition and Categorization.* Hillsdale, N.J.: Lawrence Erlbaum Associate, in press.

Poisner, H. & H. Lane. "Discrimination of Location in American Sign Language." In P. Siple (Ed.), 1978, pp. 271–288.

Robinson, J. & P. Griffith. "On the Scientific Status of Iconicity." *Sign Language Studies, 25,* 1979, pp. 297–315.

Siple, P. (Ed.), *Understanding Language Through Sign Language Research.* New York: Academic Press, 1978.

Siple, P. "Visual Constraints for Sign Language Communication." *Sign Language Studies,* 19, 1978, pp. 95–110.

Stokoe, W. "Linguistic Description of Sign Language." In F. P. Dinneen (Ed.), *Monograph Series on Language and Linguistics.* Georgetown University, Wash. D.C., 1966, pp. 243–250.

Stokoe, W. *The Study of Sign Language.* Silver Spring, Md.: The National Association of the Deaf, 1971.

Stokoe, W. "Classification and Description of Sign Language." In T. Sebeok (Ed.), *Current Trends in Linguistics, 12,* The Hague, Netherlands: Mouton, 1972.

Stokoe, W. *Semiotics and Human Sign Languages.* The Hague, Netherlands: Mouton, 1972.

Stokoe, W. "The Study and Use of Sign Language." *Sign Language Studies, 10,* 1976, pp. 1–36.

Stokoe, W. "Sign Language versus Spoken Language." *Sign Language Studies, 18,* 1978, pp. 69–90.

Stokoe, W. *Sign Language Structure* (revised edition of 1960 monograph). Silver Spring, Md.: Linstok Press, 1978.

Stokoe, W. (Ed.), *Sign and Culture: A Reader for Students of ASL.* Silver Spring, Md.: Linstok Press, 1980.

Stokoe, W., H. Bernard & C. Padden. "An Elite Group in Deaf Society." *Sign Language Studies, 12,* 1976, pp. 189–210.

Stokoe, W. & R. Kuschel. *A Field Guide for Sign Language Research.* Silver Spring, Md.: Linstok Press, 1979.

Supalla, T. & E. Newport. "How Many Seats in a Chair? The Derivation of Nouns and Verbs in American Sign Language." In P. Siple (Ed.), 1978, pp. 91–132.

Tweney, R., G. Heiman & H. Hoemann. "Psychological Processing of Sign Language: The Effects of Visual Disruption on Sign Intelligibility." *Journal of Experimental Psychology,* in press.

Wilbur, R. *American Sign Language and Sign Systems.* Baltimore, Md.: University Park Press, 1979.

Woodward, J. "Some Characteristics of Pidgin Sign English." *Sign Language Studies, 3,* 1973, pp. 39–46.

Woodward, J. "Inter-Rule Implication in American Sign Language." *Sign Language Studies, 3,* 1973, pp. 47–56.

Woodward, J. "Implicational Variation in ASL: Negative Incorporation." *Sign Language Studies, 5,* 1974, pp. 20–30.

Woodward, J. "Sociolinguistic Research on American Sign Language: An Historical Perspective." In C. Baker & R. Battison (Eds.), 1980, pp. 117-134.

Woodward, J. "Sex Is Definitely a Problem: Interpreters' Knowledge of Signs for Sexual Behavior." *Sign Language Studies, 14,* 1977, pp. 73–88.

Woodward, J. & S. De Santis. "Two to One It Happens: Dynamic Phonology in Two Sign Languages." *Sign Language Studies, 17,* 1977, pp. 329–346.

Woodward, J., C. Erting & S. Oliver. "Facing and Hand(l)ing Variation in American Sign Language Phonology." *Sign Language Studies, 10,* 1976, pp. 43–51.

GLOSSARY

ATTITUDE—A feeling or emotion toward something or someone which is often seen in one's behaviors toward that thing or person.

ATTITUDINAL DEAFNESS—Refers to the values and behaviors of individuals who identify themselves with the Deaf community and are accepted by other members of that community. Generally, this implies that a person has a positive, accepting attitude toward the Deaf community as a cultural group with its own language and values.

AUDIOLOGICAL (AUDIOMETRIC) DEAFNESS— Refers to the physical condition of having a hearing loss.

COMMUNICATIVE COMPETENCE—The ability to recognize and to produce authentic and appropriate linguistic and social behaviors correctly and fluently. This implies not only the ability to produce and understand a language but also a knowledge of the social meanings of linguistic forms and a knowledge of the social and non-linguistic behaviors that are appropriate within a culture.

COMPREHENSION—The ability to understand messages which are linguistic (writing, speaking, signing) or non-linguistic (e.g. traffic signals, noises, movements).

CONTEXT—In general, the personal and environmental factors present during a particular event (e.g. the participants, the place, the time of day, the purpose of the event) which influence the linguistic and non-linguistic behaviors of the participants in that event. Also, context can refer to the words or signs in a sentence which surround other words or signs and, thus, help to give them their particular meaning in that sentence. Thus, context can be both extra-lingual and intra-lingual.

CONVERSATION REGULATORS—A set of linguistic and non-linguistic behaviors which differ from culture to culture and which members of a culture use in conversations to help them take turns effectively, to provide feedback to the speaker/signer, and to "hold the floor", etc.

CONVERSATIONAL COMPETENCE—The ability to fluently and successfully initiate, carry on, and terminate a conversation in a given language with people who use that language.

CRITERION-REFERENCED TESTING—An approach to testing in which performance is measured and reported in terms of certain objective requirements (criteria) which indicate mastery of a skill or knowledge of certain information.

CULTURE—The beliefs, values, patterns of behavior, language, expectations, and achievements of a group of people which are passed on from generation to generation.

CURRICULUM GUIDE—A sequence of reasonably objective statements which indicate the specific skills and/or information which is taught in a particular course or program.

DEAF COMMUNITY—A cultural group comprised of persons who share similar attitudes toward deafness. The "core Deaf community" is comprised of those individuals who have a hearing loss and who share a common language, values, and experiences and a common way of interacting with each other, with non-core members of the Deaf community, and with the hearing community. The wider Deaf community is comprised of indi-

179

viduals (both deaf and hearing) who have positive, accepting attitudes toward deafness which can be seen in their linguistic, social, and political behaviors.

DIALOGUE—A carefully prepared conversation (usually with only two speakers or signers) designed to highlight certain grammatical and/or lexical features of a language. Often a dialogue will focus on some aspect of the culture as a means of providing this information to students.

DIRECT METHOD—A method of teaching a foreign or second language without the use of the students' native language, without translation to or from the students' native language, and without the study of formal grammar. Basically, this approach encourages students to learn the target language directly, without the intervention of their native language.

DRILL—A technique through which students imitate and manipulate linguistic structures/patterns to the point where they will respond automatically and correctly to a language stimulus. The objective of drills is to help the students develop unconscious and automatic control of targeted features of a language.

EXPRESSIVE SKILLS—The ability to encode or produce messages in a particular language either by speaking, signing, or writing.

FOREIGN LANGUAGE—A language for which the student has no immediate access to a community of users of that language and thus must learn cultural values and norms in the classroom and not through community interaction.

FUNCTIONAL YIELD—A criterion often used to determine which features of a language and which lexical items should be taught and the sequence in which they should be taught. This criterion considers the frequency and importance of a particular item or feature and uses this information in determining whether and

when it should be taught or included in a course. Thus, certain features or lexical items will have high functional yield and should be taught early; others will have low functional yield and can be taught later in a course or program.

GOAL—In a curriculum, a goal is a general statement of the skills and knowledge which students should possess by the end of the course. Since goals are general statements, they are often clarified through a series of objectives which can be measured fairly easily. Thus, if an individual masters the stated objectives for a specific goal, it can be assumed that s/he has met the stated goal.

GLOSS—In reference to ASL, a gloss is an English word or words (generally written in capital letters) which are used to represent a specific sign. One difficulty with glosses is that, because they are English words, they have an established meaning(s) which may or may not be equivalent to the meaning(s) of the sign they represent.

INTERACTIVE METHOD—An approach to language teaching which relies heavily on Direct Method philosophy (use of the target language, not the student's native language) and which encourages the use of specific, teacher-directed activities which are designed to: (a) foster early communication in the Target Language, (b) provide concrete, observable feedback to the students about their own success, (c) provide concrete, observable feedback to the teacher about student progress, and (d) encourage early development of students' receptive skills.

LANGUAGE—A system of relatively arbitrary symbols and grammatical signals that change across time and that members of a community share and use for several purposes: to interact with each other, to communicate their ideas, emotions and intentions and to transmit their culture from generation to generation.

LEXICAL ITEM—A particular word/sign, or vocabulary item, in a language.

LEXICON—The words/signs, or the vocabulary, of a language.

LINEAR APPROACH—In reference to curriculum development, a linear approach is one in which skills or information are taught once in a specific course and are not repeated again in that course or in subsequent courses. The students are expected to have mastered that skill or information and once mastered, it is not focused on again.

MEANINGFUL EXPOSURE—In language teaching, meaningful exposure to the language occurs when students are placed in situations in which the language is used for communication purposes and in which contextual clues assist the student in understanding or beginning to understand certain lexical items and grammatical features.

NATIVE LANGUAGE—Generally the term native language refers to the language that a child or adult first learns. Native language is often called "mother tongue", "first language", "L_1", or "NL".

NORM-REFERENCED TESTING—In testing, norm referencing refers to a procedure used for reporting results on a specific test. A test is developed and then administered to a reasonably large group of people—the norm group. An individual's performance on the test is compared with the performance of the norm group. Results are reported in terms of what percentage of the norm group scored above and below that individual's score.

OBJECTIVE—In a curriculum, an objective is a specific description of what the student should be able to do upon completing a specific set of activities. The behavior which is described, or the consequence of that behavior, is observable and measurable. Objectives serve to specify and precisely describe the component features or skills required to accomplish an educational goal.

PRODUCTION—In general, production of a language or productive skills in a language has the same meaning as expressive skills. In this text (particularly in the Evaluation chapter), production is used to refer to those specific features which are important in making signs and for using signs in conversations—e.g. handshape, movement, location, orientation, non-manual behaviors, pausing/phrasing.

READINESS SKILLS—In this text, readiness skills are those abilities which a student should possess in order to successfully acquire ASL—e.g. visual memory, visual discrimination, body comfort.

RECEPTIVE SKILLS—The ability to decode or understand messages in a particular language either by hearing, seeing, or reading.

RELEVANCE—In testing, relevance is the relationship between what is taught or covered in a class and what is measured on a test. Ideally, there should be a high degree of relevance—i.e. the test should measure what was taught in the classroom.

RELIABILITY—In testing, reliability is the degree to which a test is consistent in measuring what it is supposed to measure each time it is given. Reliability can also refer to the degree to which evaluators agree with each other in scoring or rating a particular test. A test must not only be administered reliably, but it must also be scored reliably.

SECOND LANGUAGE—The language a person acquires after their first language, often referred to as "L_2". In general, a second language is one for which the student has immediate access to a community of users and thus can acquire the cultural values and norms of that community through interaction with members of that community and not just in the classroom.

SELECTION—In this text, selection is used to refer to a student's knowledge of and appropriate use of particular lexical items, grammatical features, and conversational behaviors which express a given idea in a particular context.

SIMULATION—In general, a simulation is a situation created by the teacher to parallel or approximate a real-life situation through which the students may acquire new social values, ideas, and behaviors of the target language community as well as new linguistic behaviors.

SPIRALING APPROACH—In reference to curriculum development, a spiraling approach is one in which material or skills are taught in increasingly greater depth at each succeeding level of instruction. Thus certain information or skills may be introduced at one point in a course or program and then dealt with again later in the course or in another course in the program.

SUB-OBJECTIVE—In a curriculum, sub-objectives are detailed statements of the behaviors and performance levels which are necessary for the student to successfully master a major course objective. Generally several sub-objectives are necessary to specify all of the behaviors

or skills required to meet a major course objective.

TARGET LANGUAGE—This term refers to the language which is being taught in a given course and which the students are trying to learn. Often, target language is referred to as "TL".

TARGET VOCABULARY—This term refers to the specific lexical items which are chosen ("targeted") by the teacher to be taught in a class or in a course.

TOTAL IMMERSION—This is an approach to language teaching which places students in an intensive, instructional setting (up to 10 hours per day) in which the aim is to create an environment similar to what students would face if they moved to another country. All instruction is through the target language. Total immersion programs vary in length from a few days to several weeks.

VISUAL DISCRIMINATION—Visual discrimination in ASL involves the ability to recognize and identify the slight differences in handshapes, movements, locations, palm orientations, and non-manual behaviors which can result in a change in the meaning of a sign.

VISUAL MEMORY—Visual memory in ASL involves the ability to remember *how* a given sign or facial expression is made and the *order* in which a series of signs are made in a given task.

Index

Lightning Source UK Ltd.
Milton Keynes UK
UKHW031935071019
351169UK00005B/231/P